THE FIRST AND LAST FREEDOM

THE FIRST AND LAST FREEDOM

by

J. KRISHNAMURTI

with a foreword by
ALDOUS HUXLEY

HarperOne
An Imprint of HarperCollinsPublishers

HarperOne

HarperCollins books may be purchased for educational, business, or sales promotional use. For information, please e-mail the Special Markets Department at SPsales@harpercollins.com.

HarperCollins Web site: http://www.harpercollins.com

HarperCollins®, ☕®, and HarperOne™ are trademarks of HarperCollins Publishers.

FIRST HARPER & ROW PAPERBACK EDITION
PUBLISHED IN 1975.

ISBN: 978-0-06-064831-2
LIBRARY OF CONGRESS CATALOG CARD NUMBER 74-25687

24 25 26 27 28 LBC 62 61 60 59 58

CONTENTS

CONTENTS (CONTINUED)

QUESTIONS AND ANSWERS

CONTENTS (CONTINUED)

FOREWORD

MAN IS AN amphibian who lives simultaneously in two worlds—the given and the home-made, the world of matter, life and consciousness and the world of symbols. In our thinking we make use of a great variety of symbol-systems—linguistic, mathematical, pictorial, musical, ritualistic. Without such symbol-systems we should have no art, no science, no law, no philosophy, not so much as the rudiments of civilization: in other words, we should be animals.

Symbols, then, are indispensable. But symbols—as the history of our own and every other age makes so abundantly clear—can also be fatal. Consider, for example, the domain of science on the one hand, the domain of politics and religion on the other. Thinking in terms of, and acting in response to, one set of symbols, we have come, in some small measure, to understand and control the elementary forces of nature. Thinking in terms of, and acting in response to, another set of symbols, we use these forces as instruments of mass murder and collective suicide. In the first case the explanatory symbols were well chosen, carefully analysed and progressively adapted to the emergent facts of physical existence. In the second case symbols originally ill-chosen were never subjected to thorough-going analysis and never re-formulated so as to harmonize with the emergent facts of human existence. Worse still, these misleading symbols were everywhere treated with a wholly unwarranted respect, as though, in some mysterious way, they were more real than the realities to which they referred. In the contexts of religion and politics, words are not regarded as standing, rather inadequately, for things and events; on the contrary, things and events are regarded as particular illustrations of words.

Up to the present symbols have been used realistically only in those fields which we do not feel to be supremely important. In every situation involving our deeper impulses we have insisted on using symbols, not merely unrealistically, but idolatrously, even insanely. The result is that we have been able to commit, in cold blood and over long periods of time, acts of which the brutes are capable only for brief moments and at the frantic height of rage, desire or fear. Because they use and worship symbols, men can become idealists; and, being idealists, they can transform the animal's intermittent greed into the grandiose imperialisms of a Rhodes or a J. P. Morgan; the animal's intermittent love of bullying into Stalinism or the Spanish Inquisition; the animal's intermittent attachment to its territory into the calculated frenzies of nationalism. Happily, they can also transform the animal's intermittent kindliness into the life-long charity of an Elizabeth Fry or a Vincent de Paul; the animal's intermittent devotion to its mate and its young into that reasoned and persistent co-operation which, up to the present, has proved strong enough to save the world from the consequences of the other, the disastrous kind of idealism. Will it go on being able to save the world? The question cannot be answered. All we can say is that, with the idealists of nationalism holding the A-bomb, the odds in favour of the idealists of co-operation and charity have sharply declined.

Even the best cookery book is no substitute for even the worst dinner. The fact seems sufficiently obvious. And yet, throughout the ages, the most profound philosophers, the most learned and acute theologians have constantly fallen into the error of identifying their purely verbal constructions with facts, or into the yet more enormous error of imagining that symbols are somehow more real than what they stand for. Their word-worship did not go without protest. "Only the spirit," said St. Paul, "gives life; the letter kills." "And why," asks Eckhart, "why do you prate of God? Whatever you say of God is untrue." At the other end of the world the author of one of the *Mahayana sutras* affirmed that "the truth was never preached by the Buddha, seeing that you have to realize it within yourself". Such utterances were felt to be profoundly subversive, and respectable people ignored them. The strange idolatrous over-estimation of words and emblems continued unchecked. Religions declined; but the old habit of formulating creeds and imposing belief in dogmas persisted even among the atheists.

In recent years logicians and semanticists have carried out a very thorough analysis of the symbols, in terms of which men do their thinking. Linguistics has become a science, and one may even study a subject to which the late Benjamin Whorf gave the name of meta-linguistics. All this is greatly to the good; but it is not enough. Logic and semantics, linguistics and meta-linguistics—these are purely intellectual disciplines. They analyse the various ways, correct and incorrect, meaningful and meaningless, in which words can be related to things, processes and events. But they offer no guidance, in regard to the much more funda-mental problem of the relationship of man in his psycho-physical totality, on the one hand, and his two worlds, of data and of symbols, on the other.

In every region and at every period of history, the problem has been repeatedly solved by individual men and women. Even when they spoke or wrote, these individuals created no systems—for they knew that every system is a standing temptation to take symbols too seriously, to pay more attention to words than to the realities for which the words are supposed to stand. Their aim was never to offer ready-made explanations and panaceas; it was to induce people to diagnose and cure their own ills, to get them to go to the place where man's problem and its solution present them-selves directly to experience.

In this volume of selections from the writings and recorded talks of Krishnamurti, the reader will find a clear contem-porary statement of the fundamental human problem, together with an invitation to solve it in the only way in which it can be solved—for and by himself. The collective solutions, to which so many so desperately pin their faith, are never adequate. "To understand the misery and confusion that exist within ourselves, and so in the world, we must first find clarity within ourselves, and that clarity comes about through right thinking. This clarity is not to be organized, for it cannot be exchanged with another. Organized group thought is merely repetitive. Clarity is not the result of verbal assertion, but of intense self-awareness and right thinking. Right thinking is not the outcome of or mere cultivation of the intellect, nor is it conformity to pattern, however worthy and noble. Right thinking comes with self-knowledge. Without understanding yourself, you have no basis for thought; without self-knowledge, what you think is not true."

This fundamental theme is developed by Krishnamurti in passage after passage. "There is hope in men, not in society, not in systems, organized religious systems, but in you and in me." Organized religions, with their mediators, their sacred books, their dogmas, their hierarchies and rituals, offer only a false solution to the basic problem. "When you quote the *Bhagavad Gita*, or the Bible, or some Chinese Sacred Book, surely you are merely repeating, are you not? And what you are repeating is not the truth. It is a lie; for truth cannot be repeated." A lie can be extended, propounded and repeated, but not truth; and when you repeat truth, it ceases to be truth, and therefore sacred books are unimportant. It is through self-knowledge, not through belief in somebody else's symbols, that a man comes to the eternal reality, in which his being is grounded. Belief in the complete adequacy and superlative value of any given symbol-system leads not to liberation, but to history, to more of the same old disasters. "Belief inevitably separates. If you have a belief, or when you seek security in your particular belief, you become separated from those who seek security in some other form of belief. All organized beliefs are based on separation, though they may preach brotherhood." The man who has successfully solved the problem of his relations with the two worlds of data and symbols, is a man who has no beliefs. With regard to the problems of practical life he entertains a series of working hypotheses, which serve his purposes, but are taken no more seriously than any other kind of tool or instrument. With regard to his fellow beings and to the reality in which they are grounded, he has the direct experiences of love and insight. It is to protect himself from beliefs that Krishnamurti has "not read any sacred literature, neither the *Bhagavad Gita* nor the *Upanishads*". The rest of us do not even read sacred literature; we read our favourite newspapers, magazines and detective stories. This means that we approach the crisis of our times, not with love and insight, but "with formulas, with systems"— and pretty poor formulas and systems at that. But "men of good will should not have formulas"; for formulas lead, inevitably, only to "blind thinking". Addiction to formulas is almost universal. Inevitably so; for "our system of up-bringing is based upon *what* to think, not on *how* to think". We are brought up as believing and practising members of some organization—the Communist or the Christian, the Moslem, the Hindu, the Buddhist, the Freudian. Conse-qently "you respond to the challenge, which is always new, according to an old pattern; and therefore your response has no corresponding validity, newness, freshness. If you respond as a Catholic or a Communist, you are responding— are you not?—according to a patterned thought. Therefore your response has no significance. And has not the Hindu, the Mussulman, the Buddhist, the Christian created this problem? As the new religion is the worship of the State, so the old religion was the worship of an idea." If you respond to a challenge according to the old conditioning, your response will not enable you to understand the new chal-lenge. Therefore what "one has to do, in order to meet the new challenge, is to strip oneself completely, denude oneself entirely of the background and meet the challenge anew".

In other words symbols should never be raised to the rank of dogmas, nor should any system be regarded as more than a provisional convenience. Belief in formulas and action in accordance with these beliefs cannot bring us to a solution of our problem. "It is only through creative understanding of ourselves that there can be a creative world, a happy world, a world in which ideas do not exist." A world in which ideas do not exist would be a happy world, because it would be a world without the powerful conditioning forces which compel men to undertake inappropriate action, a world without the hallowed dogmas in terms of which the worst crimes are justified, the greatest follies elaborately rationalized.

An education that teaches us not how but what to think is an education that calls for a governing class of pastors and masters. But "the very idea of leading somebody is anti-social and anti-spiritual". To the man who exercises it, leadership brings gratification of the craving for power; to those who are led, it brings the gratification of the desire for certainty and security. The *guru* provides a kind of dope. But, it may be asked, "What are *you* doing? Are you not acting as our *guru*?" "Surely," Krishnamurti answers, "I am not acting as your *guru*, because, first of all, I am not giving you any gratification. I am not telling you what you should do from moment to moment, or from day to day, but I am just pointing out something to you; you can take it or leave it, depending on you, not on me. I do not demand a thing from you, neither your worship, nor your flattery, nor your insults, nor your gods. I say, This is a fact; take it or leave it. And most of you will leave it, for the obvious reason that you do not find gratification in it."

What is it precisely that Krishnamurti offers? What is it that we can take if we wish, but in all probability shall prefer to leave? It is not, as we have seen, a system of beliefs, a catalogue of dogmas, a set of ready-made notions and ideals. It is not leadership, not mediation, not spiritual direction, not even example. It is not ritual, not a church, not a code, not uplift or any form of inspirational twaddle.

Is it, perhaps, self-discipline? No; for self-discipline is not, as a matter of brute fact, the way in which our problem can be solved. In order to find the solution, the mind must open itself to reality, must confront the givenness of the outer and inner worlds without preconceptions or restrictions. (God's service is perfect freedom. Conversely, perfect freedom is the service of God.) In becoming disciplined, the mind undergoes no radical change; it is the old self, but "tethered, held in control".

Self-discipline joins the list of things which Krishnamurti does *not* offer. Can it be, then, that what he offers is prayer? Again, the reply is in the negative. "Prayer may bring you the answer you seek; but that answer may come from your unconscious, or from the general reservoir, the store-house of all your demands. The answer is not the still voice of God." Consider, Krishnamurti goes on, "what happens when you pray. By constant repetition of certain phrases, and by controlling your thoughts, the mind becomes quiet, doesn't it? At least, the conscious mind becomes quiet. You kneel as the Christians do, or you sit as the Hindus do, and you repeat and repeat, and through that repetition the mind becomes quiet. In that quietness there is the intimation of something. That intimation of something, for which you have prayed, may be from the unconscious, or it may be the response of your memories. But, surely, it is not the voice of reality; for the voice of reality must come to you; it cannot be appealed to, you cannot pray to it. You cannot entice it into your little cage by doing *puja*, *bhajan* and all the rest of it, by offering it flowers, by placating it, by suppressing yourself or emulating others. Once you have learned the trick of quietening the mind, through the repetition of words, and of receiving hints in that quietness, the danger is—unless you are fully alert as to whence those hints come—that you will be caught, and then prayer becomes a substitute for the search for Truth. That which you ask for you get; but it is not the truth. If you want, and if you petition, you will receive, but you will pay for it in the end."

From prayer we pass to yoga, and yoga, we find, is another of the things which Krishnamurti does not offer. For yoga is concentration, and concentration is exclusion. "You build a wall of resistance by concentration on a thought which you have chosen, and you try to ward off all the others." What is commonly called meditation is merely "the cultivation of resistance, of exclusive concentration on an idea of our choice". But what makes you choose? "What makes you say this is good, true, noble, and the rest is not? Obviously the choice is based on pleasure, reward or achievement; or it is merely a reaction of one's conditioning or tradition. Why do you choose at all? Why not examine every thought? When you are interested in the many, why choose one? Why not examine every interest? Instead of creating resistance, why not go into each interest as it arises, and not merely concentrate on one idea, one interest? After all, you are made up of many interests, you have many masks, consciously and unconsciously. Why choose one and discard all the others, in combating which you spend all your energies, thereby creating resistance, conflict and friction. Whereas if you consider every thought as it arises—*every* thought, not just a few thoughts—then there is no exclusion. But it is an arduous thing to examine every thought. Because, as you are looking at one thought, another slips in. But if you are aware without domination or justification, you will see that, by merely looking at that thought, no other thought intrudes. It is only when you condemn, compare, approximate, that other thoughts enter in."

"Judge not that ye be not judged." The gospel precept applies to our dealings with ourselves no less than to our dealings with others. Where there is judgement, where there is comparison and condemnation, openness of mind is absent; there can be no freedom from the tyranny of symbols and systems, no escape from the past and the environment.

16

Introspection with a predetermined purpose, self-examination within the framework of some traditional code, some set of hallowed postulates—these do not, these cannot help us. There is a transcendent spontaneity of life, a 'creative Reality', as Krishnamurti calls it, which reveals itself as immanent only when the perceiver's mind is in a state of 'alert passivity', of 'choiceless awareness'. Judgement and comparison commit us irrevocably to duality. Only choiceless awareness can lead to non-duality, to the reconciliation of opposites in a total understanding and a total love. *Ama et fac quod vis.* If you love, you may do what you will. But if you start by doing what you will, or by doing what you don't will in obedience to some traditional system or notions, ideals and prohibitions, you will never love. The liberating process must begin with the choiceless awareness of what you will and of your reactions to the symbol-system which tells you that you ought, or ought not, to will it. Through this choiceless awareness, as it penetrates the successive layers of the ego and its associated sub-conscious, will come love and understanding, but of another order than that with which we are ordinarily familiar. This choiceless awareness—at every moment and in all the circumstances of life—is the only effective meditation. All other forms of yoga lead either to the blind thinking which results from self-discipline, or to some kind of self-induced rapture, some form of false *samadhi.* The true liberation is "an inner freedom of creative Reality". This "is not a gift; it is to be discovered and experienced. It is not an acquisition to be gathered to yourself to glorify yourself. It is a state of being, as silence, in which there is no becoming, in which there is completeness. This creativeness may not necessarily seek expression; it is not a talent that demands outward manifestation. You need not be a great artist or have an audience; if you seek these, you will miss the inward Reality. It is neither a gift, nor is it the outcome of talent; it is to be found, this imperishable treasure, where thought frees itself from lust, ill-will and ignorance, where thought frees itself from worldliness and personal craving to be. It is to be experienced through right thinking and meditation." Choiceless self-awareness will bring us to the creative Reality which underlies all our destructive make-believes, to the tranquil wisdom which is always there, in spite of ignorance, in spite of the knowledge which is merely ignorance in another form. Knowledge is an affair of symbols and is, all too often, a hindrance to wisdom, to the uncovering of the self from moment to moment. A mind that has come to the stillness of wisdom "shall know being, shall know what it is to love. Love is neither personal nor impersonal. Love is love, not to be defined or described by the mind as exclusive or inclusive. Love is its own eternity; it is the real, the supreme, the immeasurable."

ALDOUS HUXLEY

CHAPTER I

INTRODUCTION

To communicate with one another, even if we know
each other very well, is extremely difficult. I may use words
that may have to you a significance different from mine.
Understanding comes when we, you and I, meet on the
same level at the same time. That happens only when there
is real affection between people, between husband and wife,
between intimate friends. That is real communion. Instantaneous understanding comes when we meet on the same
level at the same time.

It is very difficult to commune with one another easily,
effectively and with definitive action. I am using words which
are simple, which are not technical, because I do not think
that any technical type of expression is going to help us
solve our difficult problems; so I am not going to use any
technical terms, either of psychology or of science. I have
not read any books on psychology or any religious books,
fortunately. I would like to convey, by the very simple words
which we use in our daily life, a deeper significance; but
that is very difficult if you do not know how to listen.

There is an art of listening. To be able really to listen, one
should abandon or put aside all prejudices, pre-formulations
and daily activities. When you are in a receptive state of
mind, things can be easily understood; you are listening
when your real attention is given to something. But unfortunately most of us listen through a screen of resistance. We
are screened with prejudices, whether religious or spiritual,
psychological or scientific; or with our daily worries, desires
and fears. And with these for a screen, we listen. Therefore,
we listen really to our own noise, to our own sound, not to
what is being said. It is extremely difficult to put aside our

training, our prejudices, our inclination, our resistance, and, reaching beyond the verbal expression, to listen so that we understand instantaneously. That is going to be one of our difficulties.

If, during this discourse, anything is said which is opposed to your way of thinking and belief, just listen; do not resist. You may be right, and I may be wrong; but by listening and considering together we are going to find out what is the truth. Truth cannot be given to you by somebody. You have to discover it; and to discover, there must be a state of mind in which there is direct perception. There is no direct perception when there is a resistance, a safeguard, a protection. Understanding comes through being aware of what *is*. To know exactly what *is*, the real, the actual, without interpreting it, without condemning or justifying it, is, surely, the beginning of wisdom. It is only when we begin to interpret, to translate according to our conditioning, according to our prejudice, that we miss the truth. After all, it is like research. To know what something is, what it is exactly, requires research—you cannot translate it according to your moods. Similarly, if we can look, observe, listen, be aware of what *is*, exactly, then the problem is solved. And that is what we are trying to do in all these discourses. I am going to point out to you what *is*, and not translate it according to my fancy; nor should you translate it or interpret it according to your background or training.

Is it not possible, then, to be aware of everything as it is? Starting from there, surely, there can be an understanding. To acknowledge, to be aware of, to get at that which *is*, puts an end to struggle. If I know that I am a liar, and it is a fact which I recognize, then the struggle is over. To acknowledge, to be aware of what one is, is already the beginning of wisdom, the beginning of understanding, which releases you from time. To bring in the quality of time—time, not in the chronological sense, but as the medium, as the psychological process, the process of the mind—is destructive, and creates confusion.

So, we can have understanding of what *is* when we recognize it without condemnation, without justification, without identification. To know that one is in a certain condition, in a certain state, is already a process of liberation; but a man who is not aware of his condition, of his struggle, tries to be something other than he is, which brings about habit. So, then, let us keep in mind that we want to examine what *is*, to observe and be aware of exactly what is the actual, without giving it any slant, without giving it an interpretation. It needs an extraordinarily astute mind, an extraordinarily pliable heart, to be aware of and to follow what *is*; because what *is* is constantly moving, constantly undergoing a transformation, and if the mind is tethered to belief, to knowledge, it ceases to pursue, it ceases to follow the swift movement of what *is*. What *is* is not static, surely—it is constantly moving, as you will see if you observe it very closely. To follow it, you need a very swift mind and a pliable heart—which are denied when the mind is static, fixed in a belief, in a prejudice, in an identification; and a mind and heart that are dry cannot follow easily, swiftly, that which *is*.

One is aware, I think, without too much discussion, too much verbal expression, that there is individual as well as collective chaos, confusion and misery. It is not only in India, but right throughout the world; in China, America, England, Germany, all over the world, there is confusion, mounting sorrow. It is not only national, it is not particularly here, it is all over the world. There is extraordinarily acute suffering, and it is not individual only but collective. So it is a world catastrophe, and to limit it merely to a geographical area, a coloured section of the map, is absurd; because then we shall not understand the full significance of this worldwide as well as individual suffering. Being aware of this confusion, what is our response to-day? How do we react?

There is suffering, political, social, religious; our whole psychological being is confused, and all the leaders, political and religious, have failed us; all the books have lost their significance. You may go to the *Bhagavad Gita* or the Bible or the latest treatise on politics or psychology, and you will find that they have lost that ring, that quality of truth; they have become mere words. You yourself, who are the repeater of those words, are confused and uncertain, and mere repetition of words conveys nothing. Therefore the words and the books have lost their value; that is, if you quote the Bible, or Marx, or the *Bhagavad Gita*, as you who quote it are yourself uncertain, confused, your repetition becomes a lie; because what is written there becomes mere propaganda, and propaganda is not truth. So when you repeat, you have ceased to understand your own state of being. You are merely covering with words of authority your own confusion. But what we are trying to do is to understand this confusion and not cover it up with quotations; so what is your response to it? How do you respond to this extraordinary chaos, this confusion, this uncertainty of existence? Be aware of it, as I discuss it: follow, not my words, but the thought which is active in you. Most of us are accustomed to be spectators and not to partake in the game. We read books but we never write books. It has become our tradition, our national and universal habit, to be the spectators, to look on at a football game, to watch the public politicians and orators. We are merely the outsiders, looking on, and we have lost the creative capacity. Therefore we want to absorb and partake.

But if you are merely observing, if you are merely spectators, you will lose entirely the significance of this discourse, because this is not a lecture which you are to listen to from force of habit. I am not going to give you information which you can pick up in an encyclopædia. What we are trying to do is to follow each other's thoughts, to pursue as far as we can, as profoundly as we can, the intimations, the responses of our own feelings. So please find out what your response is to this cause, to this suffering; not what somebody else's words are, but how you yourself respond. Your response is one of indifference if you benefit by the suffering, by the chaos, if you derive profit from it, either economic, social, political or psychological. Therefore you do not mind if this chaos continues. Surely, the more trouble there is in the world, the more chaos, the more one seeks security. Haven't you noticed it? When there is confusion in the world, psychologically and in every way, you enclose yourself in some kind of security, either that of a bank account or that of an ideology; or else you turn to prayer, you go to the temple—which is really escaping from what is happening in the world. More and more sects are being formed, more and more 'isms' are springing up all over the world. Because the more confusion there is, the more you want a leader, some-body who will guide you out of this mess, so you turn to the religious books, or to one of the latest teachers; or else you act and respond according to a system which appears to solve the problem, a system either of the left or of the right. That is exactly what is happening.

The moment you are aware of confusion, of exactly what *is*, you try to escape from it. Those sects which offer you a system for the solution of suffering, economic, social or religious, are the worst; because then system becomes important and not man—whether it be a religious system, or a system of the left or of the right. System becomes important, the philosophy, the idea, becomes important, and not man; and for the sake of the idea, of the ideology, you are willing to sacrifice all mankind, which is exactly what is happening in the world. This is not merely my interpretation; if you observe, you will find that is exactly what is happening. The system has become important. Therefore, as the system has become important, men, you and I, lose significance; and the controllers of the system, whether religious or social, whether of the left or of the right, assume authority, assume power, and therefore sacrifice you, the individual. That is exactly what is happening.

Now what is the cause of this confusion, this misery? How did this misery come about, this suffering, not only inwardly but outwardly, this fear and expectation of war, the third world war that is breaking out? What is the cause of it?

23

Surely it indicates the collapse of all moral, spiritual values, and the glorification of all sensual values, of the value of things made by the hand or by the mind. What happens when we have no other values except the value of the things of the senses, the value of the products of the mind, of the hand or of the machine? The more significance we give to the sensual value of things, the greater the confusion, is it not? Again, this is not my theory. You do not have to quote books to find out that your values, your riches, your economic and social existence are based on things made by the hand or by the mind. So we live and function and have our being steeped in sensual values, which means that things, the things of the mind, the things of the hand and of the machine, have become important; and when things become important, belief becomes predominantly significant—which is exactly what is happening in the world, is it not?

Thus, giving more and more significance to the values of the senses brings about confusion; and, being in confusion, we try to escape from it through various forms, whether religious, economic or social, or through ambition, through power, through the search for reality. But the real is near, you do not have to seek it; and a man who seeks truth will never find it. Truth is in what *is*—and that is the beauty of it. But the moment you conceive it, the moment you seek it, you begin to struggle; and a man who struggles cannot understand. That is why we have to be still, observant, passively aware. We see that our living, our action, is always within the field of destruction, within the field of sorrow; like a wave, confusion and chaos always overtake us. There is no interval in the confusion of existence.

Whatever we do at present seems to lead to chaos, seems to lead to sorrow and unhappiness. Look at your own life and you will see that our living is always on the border of sorrow. Our work, our social activity, our politics, the various gatherings of nations to stop war, all produce further war. Destruction follows in the wake of living; whatever we do leads to death. That is what is actually taking place.

24

Can we stop this misery at once, and not go on always being caught by the wave of confusion and sorrow? That is, great teachers, whether the Buddha or the Christ, have come; they have accepted faith, making themselves, perhaps, free from confusion and sorrow. But they have never prevented sorrow, they have never stopped confusion. Confusion goes on, sorrow goes on. If you, seeing this social and economic confusion, this chaos, this misery, withdraw into what is called the religious life and abandon the world, you may feel that you are joining these great teachers; but the world goes on with its chaos, its misery and destruction, the everlasting suffering of its rich and poor. So, our problem, yours and mine, is whether we can step out of this misery instantaneously. If, living in the world, you refuse to be a part of it, you will help others out of this chaos—not in the future, not to-morrow, but now. Surely that is our problem. War is probably coming, more destructive, more appalling in its form. Surely we cannot prevent it, because the issues are much too strong and too close. But you and I can perceive the confusion and misery immediately, can we not? We must perceive them, and then we shall be in a position to awaken the same understanding of truth in another. In other words, can you be instantaneously free?—because that is the only way out of this misery. Perception can take place only in the present; but if you say, "I will do it to-morrow", the wave of confusion overtakes you, and you are then always involved in confusion.

Now is it possible to come to that state when you yourself perceive the truth instantaneously and therefore put an end to confusion? I say that it is, and that it is the only possible way. I say it can be done and must be done, not based on supposition or belief. To bring about this extraordinary revolution—which is not the revolution to get rid of the capitalists and install another group—to bring about this wonderful transformation, which is the only true revolution, is the problem. What is generally called revolution is merely the modification or the continuance of the right according to the ideas of the left. The left, after all, is the continuation of the right in a modified form. If the right is based on sensual values, the left is but a continuance of the same sensual values, different only in degree or expression. Therefore true revolution can take place only when you, the individual, become aware in your relationship to another. Surely what you are in your relationship to another, to your wife, your child, your boss, your neighbour, is society. Society by itself is non-existent. Society is what you and I, in our relationship, have created; it is the outward projection of all our own inward psychological states. So if you and I do not understand ourselves, merely transforming the outer, which is the projection of the inner, has no significance whatsoever; that is there can be no significant alteration or modification in society so long as I do not understand myself in relationship to you. Being confused in my relationship, I create a society which is the replica, the outward expression of what I am. This is an obvious fact, which we can discuss. We can discuss whether society, the outward expression, has produced me, or whether I have produced society.

Is it not, therefore, an obvious fact that what I am in my relationship to another creates society and that, without radically transforming myself, there can be no transformation of the essential function of society? When we look to a system for the transformation of society, we are merely evading the question, because a system cannot transform man; man always transforms the system, which history shows. Until I, in my relationship to you, understand myself, I am the cause of chaos, misery, destruction, fear, brutality. Understanding myself is not a matter of time; I can understand myself at this very moment. If I say, "I shall understand myself to-morrow", I am bringing in chaos and misery, my action is destructive. The moment I say that I "shall" understand, I bring in the time element and so am already caught up in the wave of confusion and destruction. Understanding is now, not to-morrow. To-morrow is for the lazy mind, the sluggish mind, the mind that is not interested.

When you are interested in something, you do it instantaneously, there is immediate understanding, immediate transformation. If you do not change now, you will never change, because the change that takes place to-morrow is merely a modification, it is not transformation. Transformation can only take place immediately; the revolution is now, not to-morrow.

When that happens, you are completely without a problem, for then the self is not worried about itself; then you are beyond the wave of destruction.

CHAPTER II

WHAT ARE WE SEEKING?

WHAT IS IT THAT most of us are seeking? What is it
that each one of us wants? Especially in this restless world,
where everybody is trying to find some kind of peace, some
kind of happiness, a refuge, surely it is important to find out,
isn't it?, what it is that we are trying to seek, what it is that
we are trying to discover. Probably most of us are seeking
some kind of happiness, some kind of peace; in a world that
is ridden with turmoil, wars, contention, strife, we want a
refuge where there can be some peace. I think that is what
most of us want. So we pursue, go from one leader to
another, from one religious organization to another, from
one teacher to another.

Now, is it that we are seeking happiness or is it that we
are seeking gratification of some kind from which we hope to
derive happiness? There is a difference between happiness
and gratification. Can you *seek* happiness? Perhaps you can
find gratification but surely you cannot *find* happiness.
Happiness is derivative; it is a by-product of something else.
So, before we give our minds and hearts to something
which demands a great deal of earnestness, attention,
thought, care, we must find out, must we not?, what it is
that we are seeking; whether it is happiness, or gratification.
I am afraid most of us are seeking gratification. We want to
be gratified, we want to find a sense of fullness at the end of
our search.

After all, if one is seeking peace one can find it very easily.
One can devote oneself blindly to some kind of cause,
to an idea, and take shelter there. Surely that does not solve
the problem. Mere isolation in an enclosing idea is not a

release from conflict. So we must find, must we not?, what it is, inwardly, as well as outwardly, that each one of us wants. If we are clear on that matter, then we don't have to go anywhere, to any teacher, to any church, to any organization. Therefore our difficulty is, to be clear in ourselves regarding our intention, is it not? Can we be clear? And does that clarity come through searching, through trying to find out what others say, from the highest teacher to the ordinary preacher in a church round the corner? Have you got to go to somebody to find out? Yet that is what we are doing, is it not? We read innumerable books, we attend many meetings and discuss, we join various organizations—trying thereby to find a remedy to the conflict, to the miseries in our lives. Or, if we don't do all that, we think we have found; that is we say that a particular organization, a particular teacher, a particular book satisfies us; we have found everything we want in that; and we remain in that, crystallized and enclosed.

Do we not seek, through all this confusion, something permanent, something lasting, something which we call real, God, truth, what you like—the name doesn't matter, the word is not the thing, surely. So don't let us be caught in words. Leave that to the professional lecturers. There is a search for something permanent, is there not?, in most of us —something we can cling to, something which will give us assurance, a hope, a lasting enthusiasm, a lasting certainty, because in ourselves we are so uncertain. We do not know ourselves. We know a lot about facts, what the books have said; but we do not know for ourselves, we do not have a direct experience.

And what is it that we call permanent? What is it that we are seeking, which will, or which we hope will give us permanency? Are we not seeking lasting happiness, lasting gratification, lasting certainty? We want something that will endure everlastingly, which will gratify us. If we strip ourselves of all the words and phrases, and actually look at it. this is what we want. We want permanent pleasure, permanent gratification—which we call truth, God or what you will.

Very well, we want pleasure. Perhaps that may be putting it very crudely, but that is actually what we want—knowledge that will give us pleasure, experience that will give us pleasure, a gratification that will not wither away by to-morrow. And we have experimented with various gratifications, and they have all faded away; and we hope now to find permanent gratification in reality, in God. Surely, that is what we are all seeking—the clever ones and the stupid ones, the theorist and the factual person who is striving after something. And is there permanent gratification? Is there something which will endure?

Now, if you seek permanent gratification, calling it God, or truth, or what you will—the name does not matter—surely you must understand, must you not?, the thing you are seeking. When you say, "I am seeking permanent happiness"—God, or truth, or what you like—must you not also understand the thing that is searching, the searcher, the seeker? Because there may be no such thing as permanent security, permanent happiness. Truth may be something entirely different; and I think it *is* utterly different from what you can see, conceive, formulate. Therefore, before we seek something permanent, is it not obviously necessary to understand the seeker? Is the seeker different from the thing he seeks? When you say, "I am seeking happiness", is the seeker different from the object of his search? Is the thinker different from the thought? Are they not a joint phenomenon, rather than separate processes? Therefore it is essential, is it not?, to understand the seeker, before you try to find out what it is he is seeking.

So we have to come to the point when we ask ourselves, really earnestly and profoundly, if peace, happiness, reality, God, or what you will, can be given to us by someone else. Can this incessant search, this longing, give us that extraordinary sense of reality, that creative being, which comes when we really understand ourselves? Does self-knowledge come through search, through following someone else, through belonging to any particular organization, through reading books, and so on? After all, that is the main issue, is it not?, that so long as I do not understand myself, I have no basis for thought, and all my search will be in vain. I can escape into illusions, I can run away from contention, strife, struggle; I can worship another; I can look for my salvation through somebody else. But so long as I am ignorant of myself, so long as I am unaware of the total process of myself, I have no basis for thought, for affection, for action.

But that is the last thing we want: to know ourselves. Surely that is the only foundation on which we can build. But, before we can build, before we can transform, before we can condemn or destroy, we must know that which we are. To go out seeking, changing teachers, *gurus*, practising *yoga*, breathing, performing rituals, following Masters and all the rest of it, is utterly useless, is it not? It has no meaning, even though the very people whom we follow may say: "Study yourself", because what we are, the world is. If we are petty, jealous, vain, greedy—*that* is what we create about us, *that* is the society in which we live.

It seems to me that before we set out on a journey to find reality, to find God, before we can act, before we can have any relationship with another, which is society, it is essential that we begin to understand ourselves first. I consider the earnest person to be one who is completely concerned with this, *first*, and not with how to arrive at a particular goal, because, if you and I do not understand ourselves, how can we, in action, bring about a transformation in society, in relationship, in anything that we do? And it does not mean, obviously, that self-knowledge is opposed to, or isolated from, relationship. It does not mean, obviously, emphasis on the individual, the me, as opposed to the mass, as opposed to another.

Now without knowing yourself, without knowing your own way of thinking and why you think certain things, without knowing the background of your conditioning and why you have certain beliefs about art and religion, about your country and your neighbour and about yourself, how can you think truly about anything? Without knowing your background, without knowing the substance of your thought and whence it comes—surely your search is utterly futile, your action has no meaning, has it? Whether you are an American or a Hindu or whatever your religion is has no meaning either.

Before we can find out what the end-purpose of life is, what it all means—wars, national antagonisms, conflicts, the whole mess—we must begin with ourselves, must we not? It sounds so simple, but it is *extremely* difficult. To follow oneself, to see how one's thought operates, one has to be extraordinarily alert, so that as one begins to be more and more alert to the intricacies of one's own thinking and responses and feelings, one begins to have a greater awareness, not only of oneself but of another with whom one is in relationship. To know oneself is to study oneself in action, which is relationship. The difficulty is that we are so impatient; we want to get on, we want to reach an end, and so we have neither the time nor the occasion to give ourselves the opportunity to study, to observe. Alternatively we have committed ourselves to various activities—to earning a livelihood, to rearing children—or have taken on certain responsibilities of various organizations; we have so committed ourselves in different ways that we have hardly any time for self-reflection, to observe, to study. So really the responsibility of the reaction depends on oneself, not on another. The pursuit, all the world over, of *gurus* and their systems, reading the latest books on this and that, and so on, seems to me so utterly empty, so utterly futile, for you may wander all over the earth but you have to come back to yourself. And, as most of us are totally unaware of ourselves, it is extremely difficult to begin to see clearly the process of our thinking and feeling and acting.

The more you know yourself, the more clarity there is.

Self-knowledge has no end—you don't come to an achievement, you don't come to a conclusion. It is an endless river. As one studies it, as one goes into it more and more, one finds peace. Only when the mind is tranquil—through self-knowledge and not through imposed self-discipline—only then, in that tranquillity, in that silence, can reality come into being. It is only then that there can be bliss, that there can be creative action. And it seems to me that without this understanding, without this experience, merely to read books, to attend talks, to do propaganda, is so infantile—just an activity without much meaning; whereas if one is able to understand oneself, and thereby bring about that creative happiness, that experiencing of something that is not of the mind, then perhaps there can be a transformation in the immediate relationship about us and so in the world in which we live.

CHAPTER III

INDIVIDUAL AND SOCIETY

THE PROBLEM THAT confronts most of us is whether
the individual is merely the instrument of society or the end
of society. Are you and I as individuals to be used, directed,
educated, controlled, shaped to a certain pattern by society
and government; or does society, the State, exist for the
individual? Is the individual the end of society; or is he
merely a puppet to be taught, exploited, butchered as an
instrument of war? That is the problem that is confronting
most of us. That is the problem of the world; whether the
individual is a mere instrument of society, a plaything of
influences to be moulded; or whether society exists for the
individual.

How are you going to find this out? It is a serious problem,
isn't it? If the individual is merely an instrument of society,
then society is much more important than the individual.
If that is true, then we must give up individuality and work
for society; our whole educational system must be entirely
revolutionized and the individual turned into an instrument
to be used and destroyed, liquidated, got rid of. But if society
exists for the individual, then the function of society is not
to make him conform to any pattern but to give him the
feel, the urge of freedom. So we have to find out which is
false.

How would you inquire into this problem? It is a vital
problem, isn't it? It is not dependent on any ideology, either
of the left or of the right; and if it *is* dependent on an
ideology, then it is merely a matter of opinion. Ideas always
breed enmity, confusion, conflict. If you depend on books of

the left or of the right or on sacred books, then you depend on mere opinion, whether of Buddha, of Christ, of capitalism, communism or what you will. They are ideas, not truth. A fact can never be denied. Opinion *about* fact can be denied. If we can discover what the truth of the matter is, we shall be able to act independently of opinion. Is it not, therefore, necessary to discard what others have said? The opinion of the leftist or other leaders is the outcome of their conditioning, so if you depend for your discovery on what is found in books, you are merely bound by opinion. It is not a matter of knowledge.

How is one to discover the truth of this? On that we will act. To find the truth of this, there must be freedom from all propaganda, which means you are capable of looking at the problem independently of opinion. The whole task of education is to awaken the individual. To see the truth of this, you will have to be very clear, which means you cannot depend on a leader. When you choose a leader you do so out of confusion, and so your leaders are also confused, and that is what is happening in the world. Therefore you cannot look to your leader for guidance or help.

A mind that wishes to understand a problem must not only understand the problem completely, wholly, but must be able to follow it swiftly, because the problem is never static. The problem is always new, whether it is a problem of starvation, a psychological problem, or any problem. Any crisis is always new; therefore, to understand it, a mind must always be fresh, clear, swift in its pursuit. I think most of us realize the urgency of an inward revolution, which alone can bring about a radical transformation of the outer, of society. This is the problem with which I myself and all seriously-intentioned people are occupied. How to bring about a fundamental, a radical transformation in society, is our problem; and this transformation of the outer cannot take place without inner revolution. Since society is always static, any action, any reform which is accomplished without this inward revolution becomes equally static; so there

35

is no hope without this constant inward revolution, because, without it, outer action becomes repetitive, habitual. The action of relationship between you and another, between you and me, is society; and that society becomes static, it has no life-giving quality, so long as there is not this constant inward revolution, a creative, psychological transformation; and it is because there is not this constant inward revolution that society is always becoming static, crystallized, and has therefore constantly to be broken up.

What is the relationship between yourself and the misery, the confusion, in and around you? Surely this confusion, this misery, did not come into being by itself. You and I have created it, not a capitalist nor a communist nor a fascist society, but you and I have created it in our relationship with each other. What you are within has been projected without, on to the world; what you are, what you think and what you feel, what you do in your everyday existence, is projected outwardly, and that constitutes the world. If we are miserable, confused, chaotic within, by projection that becomes the world, that becomes society, because the relationship between yourself and myself, between myself and another is society—society is the product of our relationship —and if our relationship is confused, egocentric, narrow, limited, national, we project that and bring chaos into the world.

What you are, the world is. So your problem is the world's problem. Surely, this is a simple and basic fact, is it not? In our relationship with the one or the many we seem somehow to overlook this point all the time. We want to bring about alteration through a system or through a revolution in ideas or values based on a system, forgetting that it is you and I who create society, who bring about confusion or order by the way in which we live. So we must begin near, that is we must concern ourselves with our daily existence, with our daily thoughts and feelings and actions which are revealed in the manner of earning our livelihood and in our relationship with ideas or beliefs. This is our daily existence, is it not? We are concerned with livelihood, getting jobs, earning money; we are concerned with the relationship with our family or with our neighbours, and we are concerned with ideas and with beliefs. Now, if you examine our occupation, it is fundamentally based on envy, it is not just a means of earning a livelihood. Society is so constructed that it is a process of constant conflict, constant becoming; it is based on greed, on envy, envy of your superior; the clerk wanting to become the manager, which shows that he is not just concerned with earning a livelihood, a means of subsistence, but with acquiring position and prestige. This attitude naturally creates havoc in society, in relationship, but if you and I were only concerned with livelihood we should find out the right means of earning it, a means not based on envy. Envy is one of the most destructive factors in relationship because envy indicates the desire for power, for position, and it ultimately leads to politics; both are closely related. The clerk, when he seeks to become a manager, becomes a factor in the creation of power-politics which produce war; so he is directly responsible for war.

What is our relationship based on? The relationship between yourself and myself, between yourself and another —which is society—what is it based on? Surely not on love, though we talk about it. It is not based on love, because if there were love there would be order, there would be peace, happiness between you and me. But in that relationship between you and me there is a great deal of ill-will which assumes the form of respect. If we were both equal in thought, in feeling, there would be no respect, there would be no ill-will, because we would be two individuals meeting, not as disciple and teacher, nor as the husband dominating the wife, nor as the wife dominating the husband. When there is ill-will there is a desire to dominate which arouses jealousy, anger, passion, all of which in our relationship creates constant conflict from which we try to escape, and this produces further chaos, further misery.

Now as regards ideas which are part of our daily existence,

beliefs and formulations, are they not distorting our minds? For what is stupidity? Stupidity is the giving of wrong values to those things which the mind creates, or to those things which the hands produce. Most of our thoughts spring from the self-protective instinct, do they not? Our ideas, oh, so many of them, do they not receive the wrong significance, one which they have not in themselves? Therefore when we believe in any form, whether religious, economic or social, when we believe in God, in ideas, in a social system which separates man from man, in nationalism and so on, surely we are giving a wrong significance to belief, which indicates stupidity, for belief divides people, doesn't unite people. So we see that by the way we live we can produce order or chaos, peace or conflict, happiness or misery.

So our problem, is it not?, is whether there can be a society which is static, and at the same time an individual in whom this constant revolution is taking place. That is, revolution in society must begin with the inner, psychological transformation of the individual. Most of us want to see a radical transformation in the social structure. That is the whole battle that is going on in the world—to bring about a social revolution through communistic or any other means. Now if there is a social revolution, that is an action with regard to the outer structure of man, however radical that social revolution may be its very nature is static if there is no inward revolution of the individual, no psychological transformation. Therefore to bring about a society that is not repetitive, nor static, not disintegrating, a society that is constantly alive, it is imperative that there should be a revolution in the psychological structure of the individual, for without inward, psychological revolution, mere transformation of the outer has very little significance. That is society is always becoming crystallized, static, and is therefore always disintegrating. However much and however wisely legislation may be promulgated, society is always in the process of decay because revolution must take place within, not merely outwardly.

I think it is important to understand this and not slur over it. Outward action, when accomplished, is over, is static; if the relationship between individuals, which is society, is not the outcome of inward revolution, then the social structure, being static, absorbs the individual and therefore makes him equally static, repetitive. Realizing this, realizing the extraordinary significance of this fact, there can be no question of agreement or disagreement. It is a fact that society is always crystallizing and absorbing the individual and that constant, creative revolution can only be in the individual, not in society, not in the outer. That is creative revolution can take place only in individual relationship, which is society. We see how the structure of the present society in India, in Europe, in America, in every part of the world, is rapidly disintegrating; and we know it within our own lives. We can observe it as we go down the streets. We do not need great historians to tell us the fact that our society is crumbling; and there must be new architects, new builders, to create a new society. The structure must be built on a new foundation, on newly discovered facts and values. Such architects do not yet exist. There are no builders, none who, observing, becoming aware of the fact that the structure is collapsing, are transforming themselves into architects. That is our problem. We see society crumbling, disintegrating; and it is we, you and I, who have to be the architects. You and I have to rediscover the values and build on a more fundamental, lasting foundation; because if we look to the professional architects, the political and religious builders, we shall be precisely in the same position as before.

Because you and I are not creative, we have reduced society to this chaos, so you and I have to be creative because the problem is urgent; you and I must be aware of the causes of the collapse of society and create a new structure based not on mere imitation but on our creative understanding. Now this implies, does it not?, negative thinking. Negative thinking is the highest form of understanding. That is in order to understand what is creative thinking, we must approach the problem negatively, because a positive approach to the problem—which is that you and I must become creative in order to build a new structure of society—will be imitative. To understand that which is crumbling, we must investigate it, examine it negatively—not with a positive system, a positive formula, a positive conclusion.

Why is society crumbling, collapsing, as it surely is? One of the fundamental reasons is that the individual, you, has ceased to be creative. I will explain what I mean. You and I have become imitative, we are copying, outwardly and inwardly. Outwardly, when learning a technique, when communicating with each other on the verbal level, naturally there must be some imitation, copy. I copy words. To become an engineer, I must first learn the technique, then use the technique to build a bridge. There must be a certain amount of imitation, copying, in outward technique, but when there is inward, psychological imitation surely we cease to be creative. Our education, our social structure, our so-called religious life, are all based on imitation; that is I fit into a particular social or religious formula. I have ceased to be a real individual; psychologically, I have become a mere repetitive machine with certain conditioned responses, whether those of the Hindu, the Christian, the Buddhist, the German or the Englishman. Our responses are conditioned according to the pattern of society, whether it is eastern or western, religious or materialistic. So one of the fundamental causes of the disintegration of society is imitation, and one of the disintegrating factors is the leader, whose very essence is imitation.

In order to understand the nature of disintegrating society is it not important to inquire whether you and I, the individual, can be creative? We can see that when there is imitation there must be disintegration; when there is authority there must be copying. And since our whole mental, psychological make-up is based on authority, there must be freedom from authority, to be creative. Have you not noticed that in moments of creativeness, those rather happy moments of vital interest, there is no sense of repetition, no sense of copying? Such moments are always new, fresh, creative, happy. So we see that one of the fundamental causes of the disintegration of society is copying, which is the worship of authority.

CHAPTER IV

SELF-KNOWLEDGE

THE PROBLEMS OF the world are so colossal, so very complex, that to understand and so to resolve them one must approach them in a very simple and direct manner; and simplicity, directness, do not depend on outward circumstances nor on our particular prejudices and moods. As I was pointing out, the solution is not to be found through conferences, blue-prints, or through the substitution of new leaders for old, and so on. The solution obviously lies in the creator of the problem, in the creator of the mischief, of the hate and of the enormous misunderstanding that exists between human beings. The creator of this mischief, the creator of these problems, is the individual, you and I, not the world as we think of it. The world is your relationship with another. The world is not something separate from you and me; the world, society, is the relationship that we establish or seek to establish between each other.

So you and I are the problem, and not the world, because the world is the projection of ourselves and to understand the world we must understand ourselves. The world is not separate from us; we are the world, and our problems are the world's problems. This cannot be repeated too often, because we are so sluggish in our mentality that we think the world's problems are not our business, that they have to be resolved by the United Nations or by substituting new leaders for the old. It is a very dull mentality that thinks like that, because we are responsible for this frightful misery and confusion in the world, this ever-impending war. To transform the world, we must begin with ourselves; and what is important in beginning with ourselves is the intention. The intention must be to understand ourselves and not to leave it to others to transform themselves or to bring about a modified change through revolution, either of the left or of the right. It is important to understand that this is our responsibility, yours and mine; because, however small may be the world we live in, if we can transform ourselves, bring about a radically different point of view in our daily existence, then perhaps we shall affect the world at large, the extended relationship with others.

As I said, we are going to try and find out the process of understanding ourselves, which is not an isolating process. It is not withdrawal from the world, because you cannot live in isolation. To be is to be related, and there is no such thing as living in isolation. It is the lack of right relationship that brings about conflicts, misery and strife; however small our world may be, if we can transform our relationship in that narrow world, it will be like a wave extending outward all the time. I think it is important to see that point, that the world is our relationship, however narrow; and if we can bring a transformation there, not a superficial but a radical transformation, then we shall begin actively to transform the world. Real revolution is not according to any particular pattern, either of the left or of the right, but it is a revolution of values, a revolution from sensate values to the values that are not sensate or created by environmental influences. To find these true values which will bring about a radical revolution, a transformation or a regeneration, it is essential to understand oneself. Self-knowledge is the beginning of wisdom, and therefore the beginning of transformation or regeneration. To understand oneself there must be the intention to understand—and that is where our difficulty comes in. Although most of us are discontented, we desire to bring about a sudden change, our discontent is canalized merely to achieve a certain result; being discontented, we either seek a different job or merely succumb to environment. Discontent, instead of setting us aflame, causing us to question life, the whole process of existence, is canalized, and thereby we become mediocre, losing that drive, that intensity to find out the whole significance of existence. Therefore it is important to discover these things for ourselves, because self-knowledge cannot be given to us by another, it is not to be found through any book. We must discover, and to discover there must be the intention, the search, the inquiry. So long as that intention to find out, to inquire deeply, is weak or does not exist, mere assertion or a casual wish to find out about oneself is of very little significance.

Thus the transformation of the world is brought about by the transformation of oneself, because the self is the product and a part of the total process of human existence. To transform oneself, self-knowledge is essential; without knowing what you are, there is no basis for right thought, and without knowing yourself there cannot be transformation. One must know oneself as one is, not as one wishes to be which is merely an ideal and therefore fictitious, unreal; it is only that which *is* that can be transformed, not that which you wish to be. To know oneself as one is requires an extraordinary alertness of mind, because what *is* is constantly undergoing transformation, change, and to follow it swiftly the mind must not be tethered to any particular dogma or belief, to any particular pattern of action. If you would follow anything it is no good being tethered. To know yourself, there must be the awareness, the alertness of mind in which there is freedom from all beliefs, from all idealization because beliefs and ideals only give you a colour, perverting true perception. If you want to know what you are you cannot imagine or have belief in something which you are not. If I am greedy, envious, violent, merely having an ideal of non-violence, of non-greed, is of little value. But to know that one is greedy or violent, to know and understand it, requires an extraordinary perception, does it not? It demands honesty, clarity of thought, whereas to pursue an ideal away from what *is* is an escape; it prevents you from discovering and acting directly upon what you are.

The understanding of what you are, whatever it be—ugly

or beautiful, wicked or mischievous—the understanding of what you are, without distortion, is the beginning of virtue. Virtue is essential, for it gives freedom. It is only in virtue that you can discover, that you can live—not in the *cultivation* of a virtue, which merely brings about respectability, not understanding and freedom. There is a difference between being virtuous and becoming virtuous. Being virtuous comes through the understanding of what *is*, whereas becoming virtuous is postponement, the covering up of what *is* with what you would like to be. Therefore in becoming virtuous you are avoiding action directly upon what *is*. This process of avoiding what *is* through the cultivation of the ideal is considered virtuous; but if you look at it closely and directly you will see that it is nothing of the kind. It is merely a postponement of coming face to face with what *is*. Virtue is not the becoming of what is not; virtue is the understanding of what *is* and therefore the freedom from what *is*. Virtue is essential in a society that is rapidly disintegrating. In order to create a new world, a new structure away from the old, there must be freedom to discover; and to be free, there must be virtue, for without virtue there is no freedom. Can the immoral man who is striving to become virtuous ever know virtue? The man who is not moral can never be free, and therefore he can never find out what reality is. Reality can be found only in understanding what *is*; and to understand what *is*, there must be freedom, freedom from the fear of what *is*.

To understand that process there must be the intention to know what *is*, to follow every thought, feeling and action; and to understand what *is* is extremely difficult, because what *is* is never still, never static, it is always in movement. The what *is* is what you are, not what you would like to be; it is not the ideal, because the ideal is fictitious, but it is actually what you are doing, thinking and feeling from moment to moment. What *is* is the actual, and to understand the actual requires awareness, a very alert, swift mind. But if we begin to condemn what *is*, if we begin to blame or resist it, then we shall not understand its movement. If I want to understand somebody, I cannot condemn him: I must observe, study him. I must love the very thing I am studying. If you want to understand a child, you must love and not condemn him. You must play with him, watch his movements, his idiosyncrasies, his ways of behaviour; but if you merely condemn, resist or blame him, there is no comprehension of the child. Similarly, to understand what *is*, one must observe what one thinks, feels and does from moment to moment. That is the actual. Any other action, any ideal or ideological action, is not the actual; it is merely a wish, a fictitious desire to be something other than what *is*.

To understand what *is* requires a state of mind in which there is no identification or condemnation, which means a mind that is alert and yet passive. We are in that state when we really desire to understand something; when the intensity of interest is there, that state of mind comes into being. When one is interested in understanding what *is*, the actual state of the mind, one does not need to force, discipline, or control it; on the contrary, there is passive alertness, watchfulness. This state of awareness comes when there is interest, the intention to understand.

The fundamental understanding of oneself does not come through knowledge or through the accumulation of experiences, which is merely the cultivation of memory. The understanding of oneself is from moment to moment; if we merely accumulate knowledge of the self, that very knowledge prevents further understanding, because accumulated knowledge and experience becomes the centre through which thought focuses and has its being. The world is not different from us and our activities because it is what we are which creates the problems of the world; the difficulty with the majority of us is that we do not know ourselves directly, but seek a system, a method, a means of operation by which to solve the many human problems.

Now is there a means, a system, of knowing oneself? Any clever person, any philosopher, can invent a system, a

46

method; but surely the following of a system will merely produce a result created by that system, will it not? If I follow a particular method of knowing myself, then I shall have the result which that system necessitates; but the result will obviously not be the understanding of myself. That is by following a method, a system, a means through which to know myself, I shape my thinking, my activities, according to a pattern; but the following of a pattern is not the understanding of oneself.

Therefore there is no method for self-knowledge. Seeking a method invariably implies the desire to attain some result—and that is what we all want. We follow authority—if not that of a person, then of a system, of an ideology—because we want a result which will be satisfactory, which will give us security. We really do not want to understand ourselves, our impulses and reactions, the whole process of our thinking, the conscious as well as the unconscious; we would rather pursue a system which assures us of a result. But the pursuit of a system is invariably the outcome of our desire for security, for certainty, and the result is obviously not the understanding of oneself. When we follow a method, we must have authorities—the teacher, the *guru*, the saviour, the Master—who will guarantee us what we desire; and surely that is not the way to self-knowledge.

Authority prevents the understanding of oneself, does it not? Under the shelter of an authority, a guide, you may have temporarily a sense of security, a sense of well-being, but that is not the understanding of the total process of oneself. Authority in its very nature prevents the full awareness of oneself and therefore ultimately destroys freedom; in freedom alone can there be creativeness. There can be creativeness only through self-knowledge. Most of us are not creative; we are repetitive machines, mere gramophone records playing over and over again certain songs of experience, certain conclusions and memories, either our own or those of another. Such repetition is not creative being—but it is what we want. Because we want to be inwardly secure, we are constantly seeking methods and means for this security, and thereby we create authority, the worship of another, which destroys comprehension, that spontaneous tranquillity of mind in which alone there can be a state of creativeness.

Surely our difficulty is that most of us have lost this sense of creativeness. To be creative does not mean that we must paint pictures or write poems and become famous. That is not creativeness—it is merely the capacity to express an idea, which the public applauds or disregards. Capacity and creativeness should not be confused. Capacity is not creativeness. Creativeness is quite a different state of being, is it not? It is a state in which the self is absent, in which the mind is no longer a focus of our experiences, our ambitions, our pursuits and our desires. Creativeness is not a continuous state, it is new from moment to moment, it is a movement in which there is not the 'me', the 'mine', in which the thought is not focused on any particular experience, ambition, achievement, purpose and motive. It is only when the self is not that there is creativeness—that state of being in which alone there can be reality, the creator of all things. But that state cannot be conceived or imagined, it cannot be formulated or copied, it cannot be attained through any system, through any philosophy, through any discipline; on the contrary, it comes into being only through understanding the total process of oneself.

The understanding of oneself is not a result, a culmination; it is seeing oneself from moment to moment in the mirror of relationship—one's relationship to property, to things, to people and to ideas. But we find it difficult to be alert, to be aware, and we prefer to dull our minds by following a method, by accepting authorities, superstitions and gratifying theories; so our minds become weary, exhausted and insensitive. Such a mind cannot be in a state of creativeness. That state of creativeness comes only when the self, which is the process of recognition and accumulation, ceases to be; because, after all, consciousness as the 'me' is the centre of

48

recognition, and recognition is merely the process of the accumulation of experience. But we are all afraid to be nothing, because we all want to be something. The little man wants to be a big man, the unvirtuous wants to be virtuous, the weak and obscure crave power, position and authority. This is the incessant activity of the mind. Such a mind cannot be quiet and therefore can never understand the state of creativeness.

In order to transform the world about us, with its misery, wars, unemployment, starvation, class divisions and utter confusion, there must be a transformation in ourselves. The revolution must begin within oneself—but not according to any belief or ideology, because revolution based on an idea, or in conformity to a particular pattern, is obviously no revolution at all. To bring about a fundamental revolution in oneself, one must understand the whole process of one's thought and feeling in relationship. That is the only solution to all our problems—not to have more disciplines, more beliefs, more ideologies and more teachers. If we can understand ourselves as we are from moment to moment without the process of accumulation, then we shall see how there comes a tranquillity that is not a product of the mind, a tranquillity that is neither imagined nor cultivated; and only in that state of tranquillity can there be creativeness.

CHAPTER V

ACTION AND IDEA

I should like to discuss the problem of action. This may be rather abstruse and difficult at the beginning but I hope that by thinking it over we shall be able to see the issue clearly, because our whole existence, our whole life, is a process of action.

Most of us live in a series of actions, of seemingly unrelated, disjointed actions, leading to disintegration, to frustration. It is a problem that concerns each one of us, because we live by action and without action there is no life, there is no experience, there is no thinking. Thought is action; and merely to pursue action at one particular level of consciousness, which is the outer, merely to be caught up in outward action without understanding the whole process of action itself, will inevitably lead us to frustration, to misery.

Our life is a series of actions or a process of action at different levels of consciousness. Consciousness is experiencing, naming and recording. That is consciousness is challenge and response, which is experiencing, then terming or naming, and then recording, which is memory. This process is action, is it not? Consciousness is action; and without challenge, response, without experiencing, naming or terming, without recording, which is memory, there is no action.

Now action creates the actor. That is the actor comes into being when action has a result, an end in view. If there is no result in action, then there is no actor; but if there is an end or a result in view, then action brings about the actor.

Thus actor, action, and end or result, is a unitary process, a single process, which comes into being when action has an end in view. Action towards a result is will; otherwise there is no will, is there? The desire to achieve an end brings about will, which is the actor—I want to achieve, I want to write a book, I want to be a rich man, I want to paint a picture.

We are familiar with these three states: the actor, the action, and the end. That is our daily existence. I am just explaining what *is*; but we will begin to understand how to transform what *is* only when we examine it clearly, so that there is no illusion or prejudice, no bias with regard to it. Now these three states which constitute experience—the actor, the action, and the result—are surely a process of becoming. Otherwise there is no becoming, is there? If there is no actor, and if there is no action towards an end, there is no becoming; but life as we know it, our daily life, is a process of becoming. I am poor and I act with an end in view, which is to become rich. I am ugly and I want to become beautiful. Therefore my life is a process of becoming something. The will to be is the will to become, at different levels of consciousness, in different states, in which there is challenge, response, naming and recording. Now this becoming is strife, this becoming is pain, is it not? It is a constant struggle: I am this, and I want to become that.

Therefore, then, the problem is: Is there not action without this becoming? Is there not action without this pain, without this constant battle? If there is no end, there is no actor, because action with an end in view creates the actor. But can there be action without an end in view, and therefore no actor—that is without the desire for a result? Such action is not a becoming, and therefore not a strife. There is a state of action, a state of experiencing, without the experiencer and the experience. This sounds rather philosophical but it is really quite simple.

In the moment of experiencing, you are not aware of yourself as the experiencer apart from the experience; you are in a state of experiencing. Take a very simple example: you are angry. In that moment of anger there is neither the experiencer nor the experience; there is only experiencing. But the moment you come out of it, a split second after the experiencing, there is the experiencer and the experience, the actor and the action with an end in view—which is to get rid of or to suppress the anger. We are in this state repeatedly, in the state of experiencing; but we always come out of it and give it a term, naming and recording it, and thereby giving continuity to becoming.

If we can understand action in the fundamental sense of the word then that fundamental understanding will affect our superficial activities also; but first we must understand the fundamental nature of action. Now is action brought about by an idea? Do you have an idea first and act afterwards? Or does action come first and then, because action creates conflict, you build around it an idea? Does action create the actor or does the actor come first?

It is very important to discover which comes first. If the idea comes first, then action merely conforms to an idea, and therefore it is no longer action but imitation, compulsion according to an idea. It is very important to realize this; because, as our society is mostly constructed on the intellectual or verbal level, the idea comes first with all of us and action follows. Action is then the handmaid of an idea, and the mere construction of ideas is obviously detrimental to action. Ideas breed further ideas, and when there is merely the breeding of ideas there is antagonism, and society becomes top-heavy with the intellectual process of ideation. Our social structure is very intellectual; we are cultivating the intellect at the expense of every other factor of our being and therefore we are suffocated with ideas.

Can ideas ever produce action, or do ideas merely mould thought and therefore limit action? When action is compelled by an idea, action can never liberate man. It is extraordinarily important for us to understand this point. If an idea shapes action, then action can never bring about the

52

solution to our miseries because, before it can be put into action, we have first to discover how the idea comes into being. The investigation of ideation, of the building up of ideas, whether of the socialists, the capitalists, the communists, or of the various religions, is of the utmost importance, especially when our society is at the edge of a precipice, inviting another catastrophe, another excision. Those who are really serious in their intention to discover the human solution to our many problems must first understand this process of ideation.

What do we mean by an idea? How does an idea come into being? And can idea and action be brought together? Suppose I have an idea and I wish to carry it out. I seek a method of carrying out that idea, and we speculate, waste our time and energies in quarrelling over how the idea should be carried out. So, it is really very important to find out how ideas come into being; and after discovering the truth of that we can discuss the question of action. Without discussing ideas, merely to find out how to act has no meaning.

Now how do you get an idea—a very simple idea, it need not be philosophical, religious or economic? Obviously it is a process of thought, is it not? Idea is the outcome of a thought process. Without a thought process, there can be no idea. So I have to understand the thought process itself before I can understand its product, the idea. What do we mean by thought? When do you think? Obviously thought is the result of a response, neurological or psychological, is it not? It is the immediate response of the senses to a sensation, or it is psychological, the response of stored-up memory. There is the immediate response of the nerves to a sensation, and there is the psychological response of stored-up memory, the influence of race, group, *guru*, family, tradition, and so on—all of which you call thought. So the thought process is the response of memory, is it not? You would have no thoughts if you had no memory; and the response of memory to a certain experience brings the thought process into action.

53

Say, for example, I have the stored-up memories of nationalism, calling myself a Hindu. That reservoir of memories of
past responses, actions, implications, traditions, customs,
responds to the challenge of a Mussulman, a Buddhist or a
Christian, and the response of memory to the challenge
inevitably brings about a thought process. Watch the thought
process operating in yourself and you can test the truth of
this directly. You have been insulted by someone, and that
remains in your memory; it forms part of the background.
When you meet the person, which is the challenge, the
response is the memory of that insult. So the response of
memory, which is the thought process, creates an idea;
therefore the idea is always conditioned—and this is important to understand. That is to say the idea is the result of
the thought process, the thought process is the response of
memory, and memory is always conditioned. Memory is
always in the past, and that memory is given life in the
present by a challenge. Memory has no life in itself; it
comes to life in the present when confronted by a challenge.
And all memory, whether dormant or active, is conditioned,
is it not?

Therefore there has to be quite a different approach.
You have to find out for yourself, inwardly, whether you
are acting on an idea, and if there can be action without
ideation. Let us find out what that is: action which is not
based on an idea.

When do you act without ideation? When is there an
action which is not the result of experience? An action
based on experience is, as we said, limiting, and therefore a
hindrance. Action which is not the outcome of an idea is
spontaneous when the thought process, which is based on
experience, is not controlling action; which means that there
is action independent of experience when the mind is not
controlling action. That is the only state in which there is
understanding: when the mind, based on experience, is not
guiding action: when thought, based on experience, is not
shaping action. What is action, when there is no thought

process? Can there be action without thought process? That is I want to build a bridge, a house. I know the technique, and the technique tells me how to build it. We call that action. There is the action of writing a poem, of painting, of governmental responsibilities, of social, environmental responses. All are based on an idea or previous experience, shaping action. But is there an action when there is no ideation?

Surely there is such action when the idea ceases; and the idea ceases only when there is love. Love is not memory. Love is not experience. Love is not the thinking about the person that one loves, for then it is merely thought. You cannot *think* of love. You can think of the person you love or are devoted to—your *guru*, your image, your wife, your husband; but the thought, the symbol, is not the real which is love. Therefore love is not an experience.

When there is love there is action, is there not?, and is that action not liberating? It is not the result of mentation, and there is no gap between love and action, as there is between idea and action. Idea is always old, casting its shadow on the present and we are ever trying to build a bridge between action and idea. When there is love—which is not mentation, which is not ideation, which is not memory, which is not the outcome of an experience, of a practised discipline—then that very love is action. That is the only thing that frees. So long as there is mentation, so long as there is the shaping of action by an idea which is experience, there can be no release; and so long as that process continues, all action is limited. When the truth of this is seen, the quality of love, which is not mentation, which you cannot think about, comes into being.

One has to be aware of this total process, of how ideas come into being, how action springs from ideas, and how ideas control action and therefore limit action, depending on sensation. It doesn't matter *whose* ideas they are, whether from the left or from the extreme right. So long as we cling to ideas, we are in a state in which there can be no experiencing at all. Then we are merely living in the field of time—in the past, which gives further sensation, or in the future, which is another form of sensation. It is only when the mind is free from idea that there can be experiencing.

Ideas are not truth; and truth is something that must be experienced directly, from moment to moment. It is not an experience which you *want*—which is then merely sensation. Only when one can go beyond the bundle of ideas—which is the 'me', which is the mind, which has a partial or complete continuity—only when one can go beyond that, when thought is completely silent, is there a state of experiencing. Then one shall know what truth is.

CHAPTER VI

BELIEF

BELIEF AND KNOWLEDGE are very intimately related to desire; and perhaps, if we can understand these two issues, we can see how desire works and understand its complexities.

One of the things, it seems to me, that most of us eagerly accept and take for granted is the question of beliefs. I am not attacking beliefs. What we are trying to do is to find out why we accept beliefs; and if we can understand the motives, the causation of acceptance, then perhaps we may be able not only to understand why we do it, but also be free of it. One can see how political and religious beliefs, national and various other types of beliefs, do separate people, do create conflict, confusion, and antagonism—which is an obvious fact; and yet we are unwilling to give them up. There is the Hindu belief, the Christian belief, the Buddhist—innumerable sectarian and national beliefs, various political ideologies, all contending with each other, trying to convert each other. One can see, obviously, that belief is separating people, creating intolerance; is it possible to live without belief? One can find that out only if one can study oneself in relationship to a belief. Is it possible to live in this world without a belief—not change beliefs, not substitute one belief for another, but be entirely free from *all* beliefs, so that one meets life anew each minute? This, after all, is the truth: to have the capacity of meeting everything anew, from moment to moment, without the conditioning reaction of the past, so that there is not the cumulative effect which acts as a barrier between oneself and that which *is*.

If you consider, you will see that one of the reasons for

the desire to accept a belief is fear. If we had no belief, what would happen to us? Shouldn't we be very frightened of what might happen? If we had no pattern of action, based on a belief—either in God, or in communism, or in socialism, or in imperialism, or in some kind of religious formula, some dogma in which we are conditioned—we should feel utterly lost, shouldn't we? And is not this acceptance of a belief the covering up of that fear—the fear of being really nothing, of being empty? After all, a cup is useful only when it is empty; and a mind that is filled with beliefs, with dogmas, with assertions, with quotations, is really an uncreative mind; it is merely a repetitive mind. To escape from that fear—that fear of emptiness, that fear of loneliness, that fear of stagnation, of not arriving, not succeeding, not achieving, not being something, not becoming something—is surely one of the reasons, is it not?, why we accept beliefs so eagerly and greedily. And, through acceptance of belief, do we understand ourselves? On the contrary. A belief, religious or political, obviously hinders the understanding of ourselves. It acts as a screen through which we are looking at ourselves. And can we look at ourselves without beliefs? If we remove those beliefs, the many beliefs that one has, is there anything left to look at? If we have no beliefs with which the mind has identified itself, then the mind, without identification, is capable of looking at itself as it is—and then, surely, there is the beginning of the understanding of oneself.

It is really a very interesting problem, this question of belief and knowledge. What an extraordinary part it plays in our life! How many beliefs we have! Surely the more intellectual, the more cultured, the more spiritual, if I can use that word, a person is, the less is his capacity to understand. The savages have innumerable superstitions, even in the modern world. The more thoughtful, the more awake, the more alert are perhaps the less believing. That is because belief binds, belief isolates; and we see that is so throughout the world, the economic and the political world, and also in

58

the so-called spiritual world. You believe there is God, and perhaps I believe that there is no God; or you believe in the complete state control of everything and of every individual, and I believe in private enterprise and all the rest of it; you believe that there is only one Saviour and through him you can achieve your goal, and I don't believe so. Thus you with your belief and I with mine are asserting ourselves. Yet we both talk of love, of peace, of unity of mankind, of one life—which means absolutely nothing; because actually the very belief is a process of isolation. You are a Brahmin, I a non-Brahmin; you are a Christian, I a Mussulman, and so on. You talk of brotherhood and I also talk of the same brotherhood, love and peace; but in actuality we are separated, we are dividing ourselves. A man who wants peace and who wants to create a new world, a happy world, surely cannot isolate himself through any form of belief. Is that clear? It may be verbally, but, if you see the significance and validity and the truth of it, it will begin to act.

We see that where there is a process of desire at work there must be the process of isolation through belief, because obviously you believe in order to be secure economically, spiritually, and also inwardly. I am not talking of those people who believe for economic reasons, because they are brought up to depend on their jobs and therefore will be Catholics, Hindus—it does not matter what—as long as there is a job for them. We are also not discussing those people who cling to a belief for the sake of convenience. Perhaps with most of us it is equally so. For convenience, we believe in certain things. Brushing aside these economic reasons, we must go more deeply into it. Take the people who believe strongly in anything, economic, social or spiritual; the process behind it is the psychological desire to be secure, is it not? And then there is the desire to continue. We are not discussing here whether there is or there is not continuity; we are only discussing the urge, the constant impulse to believe. A man of peace, a man who would really understand the whole process of human existence, cannot be bound by a

59

belief, can he? He sees his desire at work as a means to being secure. Please do not go to the other side and say that I am preaching non-religion. That is not my point at all. My point is that as long as we do not understand the process of desire in the form of belief, there must be contention, there must be conflict, there must be sorrow, and man will be against man—which is seen every day. So if I perceive, if I am aware, that this process takes the form of belief, which is an expression of the craving for inward security, then my problem is not that I should believe this or that but that I should free myself from the desire to be secure. Can the mind be free from the desire for security? That is the problem— not what to believe and how much to believe. These are merely expressions of the inward craving to be secure psychologically, to be certain about something, when every- thing is so uncertain in the world.

Can a mind, can a conscious mind, can a personality be free from this desire to be secure? We want to be secure and therefore need the aid of our estates, our property and our family. We want to be secure inwardly and also spiritually by erecting walls of belief, which are an indication of this craving to be certain. Can you as an individual be free from this urge, this craving to be secure, which expresses itself in the desire to believe in something? If we are not free of all that, we are a source of contention; we are not peace- making; we have no love in our hearts. Belief destroys; and this is seen in our everyday life. Can I see myself when I am caught in this process of desire, which expresses itself in clinging to a belief? Can the mind free itself from belief— not find a substitute for it but be entirely free from it? You cannot verbally answer "yes" or "no" to this; but you can definitely give an answer if your intention is to become free from belief. You then inevitably come to the point at which you are seeking the means to free yourself from the urge to be secure. Obviously there is no security inwardly which, as you like to believe, will continue. You like to believe there is a God who is carefully looking after your petty little things, telling you whom you should see, what you should do and how you should do it. This is childish and immature thinking. You think the Great Father is watching every one of us. That is a mere projection of your own personal liking. It is obviously not true. Truth must be something entirely different.

Our next problem is that of knowledge. Is knowledge necessary to the understanding of truth? When I say "I know", the implication is that there is knowledge. Can such a mind be capable of investigating and searching out what is reality? And besides, what is it we know, of which we are so proud? Actually what is it we know? We know information; we are full of information and experience based on our conditioning, our memory and our capacities. When you say "I know", what do you mean? Either the acknowledgement that you know is the recognition of a fact, of certain information, or it is an experience that you have had. The constant accumulation of information, the acquisition of various forms of knowledge, all constitutes the assertion "I know"; and you start translating what you have read, according to your background, your desire, your experience. Your knowledge is a thing in which a process similar to the process of desire is at work. Instead of belief we substitute knowledge. "I know, I have had experience, it cannot be refuted; my experience is that, on that I completely rely"; these are indications of that knowledge. But when you go behind it, analyse it, look at it more intelligently and carefully, you will find that the very assertion "I know" is another wall separating you and me. Behind that wall you take refuge, seeking comfort, security. Therefore the more knowledge a mind is burdened with, the less capable it is of understanding.

I do not know if you have ever thought of this problem of acquiring knowledge—whether knowledge does ultimately help us to love, to be free from those qualities which produce conflict in ourselves and with our neighbours; whether knowledge ever frees the mind of ambition. Because ambition is, after all, one of the qualities that destroy relationship, that put man against man. If we would live at peace with each other, surely ambition must completely come to an end—not only political, economic, social ambition, but also the more subtle and pernicious ambition, the spiritual ambition —to *be* something. Is it ever possible for the mind to be free from this accumulating process of knowledge, this desire to know?

It is a very interesting thing to watch how in our life these two, knowledge and belief, play an extraordinarily powerful part. Look how we worship those who have immense knowledge and erudition! Can you understand the meaning of it? If you would find something new, experience something which is not a projection of your imagination, your mind must be free, must it not? It must be capable of seeing something new. Unfortunately, every time you see something new you bring in all the information known to you already, all your knowledge, all your past memories; and obviously you become incapable of looking, incapable of receiving anything that is new, that is not of the old. Please don't immediately translate this into detail. If I do not know how to get back to my house, I shall be lost; if I do not know how to run a machine, I shall be of little use. That is quite a different thing. We are not discussing that here. We are discussing knowledge that is used as a means to security, the psychological and inward desire to be something. What do you get through knowledge? The authority of knowledge, the weight of knowledge, the sense of importance, dignity, the sense of vitality and what-not? A man who says "I know", "There is" or "There is not" surely has stopped thinking, stopped pursuing this whole process of desire.

Our problem then, as I see it, is that we are bound, weighed down by belief, by knowledge; and is it possible for a mind to be free from yesterday and from the beliefs that have been acquired through the process of yesterday? Do you understand the question? Is it possible for me as an individual and you as an individual to live in this society and yet be free from the beliefs in which we have been brought up? Is it possible for the mind to be free of all that knowledge, all that authority? We read the various scriptures, religious books. There they have very carefully described what to do, what not to do, how to attain the goal, what the goal is and what God is. You all know that by heart and you have pursued that. That is your knowledge, that is what you have acquired, that is what you have learnt; along that path you pursue. Obviously what you pursue and seek, you will find. But is it reality? Is it not the projection of your own knowledge? It is not reality. Is it possible to realize that *now*—not to-morrow, but now—and say "I see the truth of it", and let it go, so that your mind is not crippled by this process of imagination, of projection?

Is the mind capable of freedom from belief? You can only be free from it when you understand the inward nature of the causes that make you hold on to it, not only the conscious but the unconscious motives as well, that make you believe. After all, we are not merely a superficial entity functioning on the conscious level. We can find out the deeper conscious and unconscious activities if we give the unconscious mind a chance, because it is much quicker in response than the conscious mind. While your conscious mind is quietly thinking, listening and watching, the unconscious mind is much more active, much more alert and much more receptive; it can, therefore, have an answer. Can the mind which has been subjugated, intimidated, forced, compelled to believe, can such a mind be free to think? Can it look anew and remove the process of isolation between you and another? Please do not say that belief brings people together. It does not. That is obvious. No organized religion has ever done that. Look at yourselves in your own country. You are all believers, but are you all together? Are you all united? You yourselves know you are not. You are divided into so many petty little parties, castes; you know the innumerable divisions. The process is the same right through the world—whether in the east or in the west—Christians destroying Christians, murdering each other for petty little things, driving people into camps and so on, the whole horror of war. Therefore belief does not unite people. That is so clear. If that is clear and that is true, and if you see it, then it must be followed. But the difficulty is that most of us do not see, because we are not capable of facing that inward insecurity, that inward sense of being alone. We want something to lean on, whether it is the State, whether it is the caste, whether it is nationalism, whether it is a Master or a Saviour or anything else. And when we see the falseness of all this, the mind then is capable—it may be temporarily for a second—of seeing the truth of it; even though when it is too much for it, it goes back. But to see temporarily is sufficient; if you can see it for a fleeting second, it is enough; because you will then see an extraordinary thing taking place. The unconscious is at work, though the conscious may reject. It is not a progressive second; but that second is the only thing, and it will have its own results, even in spite of the conscious mind struggling against it.

So our question is: "Is it possible for the mind to be free from knowledge and belief?" Is not the mind made up of knowledge and belief? Is not the structure of the mind belief and knowledge? Belief and knowledge are the processes of recognition, the centre of the mind. The process is enclosing, the process is conscious as well as unconscious. Can the mind be free of its own structure? Can the mind cease to be? That is the problem. Mind, as we know it, has belief behind it, has desire, the urge to be secure, knowledge, and accumulation of strength. If, with all its power and superiority, one cannot think for oneself, there can be no peace in the world. You may talk about peace, you may organize political parties, you may shout from the housetops; but you cannot have peace; because in the mind is the very basis which creates contradiction, which isolates and separates. A man of peace, a man of earnestness, cannot isolate himself and yet talk of brotherhood and peace. It is just a game, political or religious, a sense of achievement and ambition. A man who is really earnest about this, who wants to discover, has to face the problem of knowledge and belief; he has to go behind it, to discover the whole process of desire at work, the desire to be secure, the desire to be certain.

A mind that would be in a state in which the new can take place—whether it be the truth, whether it be God, or what you will—must surely cease to acquire, to gather; it must put aside all knowledge. A mind burdened with knowledge cannot possibly understand, surely, that which is real, which is not measurable.

CHAPTER VII

EFFORT

FOR MOST OF US, our whole life is based on effort, some kind of volition. We cannot conceive of an action without volition, without effort; our life is based on it. Our social, economic and so-called spiritual life is a series of efforts, always culminating in a certain result. And we think effort is essential, necessary.

Why do we make effort? Is it not, put simply, in order to achieve a result, to become something, to reach a goal? If we do not make an effort, we think we shall stagnate. We have an idea about the goal towards which we are constantly striving; and this striving has become part of our life. If we want to alter ourselves, if we want to bring about a radical change in ourselves, we make a tremendous effort to eliminate the old habits, to resist the habitual environmental influences and so on. So we are used to this series of efforts in order to find or achieve something, in order to live at all.

Is not all such effort the activity of the self? Is not effort self-centred activity? If we make an effort from the centre of the self, it must inevitably produce more conflict, more confusion, more misery. Yet we keep on making effort after effort. Very few of us realize that the self-centred activity of effort does not clear up any of our problems. On the contrary, it increases our confusion and our misery and our sorrow. We know this; and yet we continue hoping somehow to break through this self-centred activity of effort, the action of the will.

I think we shall understand the significance of life, if we

understand what it means to make an effort. Does happiness come through effort? Have you ever tried to be happy? It is impossible, is it not? You struggle to be happy and there is no happiness, is there? Joy does not come through suppression, through control or indulgence. You may indulge but there is bitterness at the end. You may suppress or control, but there is always strife in the hidden. Therefore happiness does not come through effort, nor joy through control and suppression; and still all our life is a series of suppressions, a series of controls, a series of regretful indulgences. Also there is a constant overcoming, a constant struggle with our passions, our greed and our stupidity. So do we not strive, struggle, make effort, in the hope of finding happiness, finding something which will give us a feeling of peace, a sense of love? Yet does love or understanding come by strife? I think it is very important to understand what we mean by struggle, strife or effort.

Does not effort mean a struggle to change what *is* into what is not, or into what it should be or should become? That is we are constantly struggling to avoid facing what *is*, or we are trying to get away from it or to transform or modify what *is*. A man who is truly content is the man who understands what *is*, gives the right significance to what *is*. That is true contentment; it is not concerned with having few or many possessions but with the understanding of the whole significance of what *is*; and that can only come when you recognize what *is*, when you are aware of it, not when you are trying to modify it or change it.

So we see that effort is a strife or a struggle to transform that which *is* into something which you wish it to be. I am only talking about psychological struggle, not the struggle with a physical problem, like engineering or some discovery or transformation which is purely technical. I am only talking of that struggle which is psychological and which always overcomes the technical. You may build with great care a marvellous society, using the infinite knowledge science has given us. But so long as the psychological strife and struggle and battle are not understood and the psychologica. overtones and currents are not overcome, the structure of society, however marvellously built, is bound to crash, as has happened over and over again.

Effort is a distraction from what *is*. The moment I accept what *is* there is no struggle. Any form of struggle or strife is an indication of distraction; and distraction, which is effort, must exist so long as psychologically I wish to transform what *is* into something it is not.

First we must be free to see that joy and happiness do not come through effort. Is creation through effort, or is there creation only with the cessation of effort? When do you write, paint or sing? When do you create? Surely when there is no effort, when you are completely open, when on all levels you are in complete communication, completely integrated. Then there is joy and then you begin to sing or write a poem or paint or fashion something. The moment of creation is not born of struggle.

Perhaps in understanding the question of creativeness we shall be able to understand what we mean by effort. Is creativeness the outcome of effort, and are we aware in those moments when we are creative? Or is creativeness a sense of total self-forgetfulness, that sense when there is no turmoil, when one is wholly unaware of the movement of thought, when there is only a complete, full, rich being? Is that state the result of travail, of struggle, of conflict, of effort? I do not know if you have ever noticed that when you do something easily, swiftly, there is no effort, there is complete absence of struggle; but as our lives are mostly a series of battles, conflicts and struggles, we cannot imagine a life, a state of being, in which strife has fully ceased.

To understand the state of being without strife, that state of creative existence, surely one must inquire into the whole problem of effort. We mean by effort the striving to fulfil oneself, to become something, don't we? I am this, and I want to become that; I am not that, and I must become that. In becoming 'that', there is strife, there is battle, conflict, struggle. In this struggle we are concerned inevitably with fulfilment through the gaining of an end; we seek self-fulfilment in an object, in a person, in an idea, and that demands constant battle, struggle, the effort to become, to fulfil. So we have taken this effort as inevitable; and I wonder if it *is* inevitable—this struggle to become something? Why is there this struggle? Where there is the desire for fulfilment, in whatever degree and at whatever level, there must be struggle. Fulfilment is the motive, the drive behind the effort; whether it is in the big executive, the housewife, or a poor man, there is this battle to become, to fulfil, going on.

Now why is there the desire to fulfil oneself? Obviously, the desire to fulfil, to become something, arises when there is awareness of being nothing. Because I am nothing, because I am insufficient, empty, inwardly poor, I struggle to become something; outwardly or inwardly I struggle to fulfil myself in a person, in a thing, in an idea. To fill that void is the whole process of our existence. Being aware that we are empty, inwardly poor, we struggle either to collect things outwardly, or to cultivate inward riches. There is effort only when there is an escape from that inward void through action, through contemplation, through acquisition, through achievement, through power, and so on. That is our daily existence. I am aware of my insufficiency, my inward poverty, and I struggle to run away from it or to fill it. This running away, avoiding, or trying to cover up the void, entails struggle, strife, effort.

Now if one does not make an effort to run away, what happens? One lives with that loneliness, that emptiness; and in accepting that emptiness one will find that there comes a creative state which has nothing to do with strife, with effort. Effort exists only so long as we are trying to avoid that inward loneliness, emptiness, but when we look at it, observe it, when we accept what *is* without avoidance, we will find there comes a state of being in which all strife ceases. That state of being is creativeness and it is not the result of strife.

But when there is understanding of what *is*, which is emptiness, inward insufficiency, when one lives with that insufficiency and understands it fully, there comes creative reality, creative intelligence, which alone brings happiness.

Therefore action as we know it is really reaction, it is a ceaseless becoming, which is the denial, the avoidance of what *is*; but when there is awareness of emptiness without choice, without condemnation or justification, then in that understanding of what *is* there is action, and this action is creative being. You will understand this if you are aware of yourself in action. Observe yourself as you are acting, not only outwardly but see also the movement of your thought and feeling. When you are aware of this movement you will see that the thought process, which is also feeling and action, is based on an idea of becoming. The idea of becoming arises only when there is a sense of insecurity, and that sense of insecurity comes when one is aware of the inward void. If you are aware of that process of thought and feeling, you will see that there is a constant battle going on, an effort to change, to modify, to alter what *is*. This is the effort to become, and becoming is a direct avoidance of what *is*. Through self-knowledge, through constant awareness, you will find that strife, battle, the conflict of becoming, leads to pain, to sorrow and ignorance. It is only if you are aware of inward insufficiency and live with it without escape, accepting it wholly, that you will discover an extraordinary tranquillity, a tranquillity which is not put together, made up, but a tranquillity which comes with understanding of what *is*. Only in that state of tranquillity is there creative being.

CHAPTER VIII

CONTRADICTION

WE SEE CONTRADICTION in us and about us; because we are in contradiction, there is lack of peace in us and therefore outside us. There is in us a constant state of denial and assertion—what we *want* to be and what we are. The state of contradiction creates conflict and this conflict does not bring about peace—which is a simple, obvious fact. This inward contradiction should not be translated into some kind of philosophical dualism, because that is a very easy escape. That is by saying that contradiction is a state of dualism we think we have solved it—which is obviously a mere convention, a contributory escape from actuality.

Now what do we mean by conflict, by contradiction? Why is there a contradiction in me?—this constant struggle to be something apart from what I am. I am this, and I want to be that. This contradiction in us is a fact, not a metaphysical dualism. Metaphysics has no significance in understanding what *is*. We may discuss, say, dualism, what it is, if it exists, and so on; but of what value is it if we don't know that there is contradiction in us, opposing desires, opposing interests, opposing pursuits? I want to be good and I am not able to be. This contradiction, this opposition in us, must be understood because it creates conflict; and in conflict, in struggle, we cannot create individually. Let us be clear on the state we are in. There is contradiction, so there must be struggle; and struggle is destruction, waste. In that state we can produce nothing but antagonism, strife, more bitterness and sorrow. If we can understand this fully and hence be free of contradiction, then there can be inward peace, which will bring understanding of each other.

71

The problem is this. Seeing that conflict is destructive, wasteful, why is it that in each of us there is contradiction? To understand that, we must go a little further. Why is there the sense of opposing desires? I do not know if we are aware of it in ourselves—this contradiction, this sense of wanting and not wanting, remembering something and trying to forget it in order to find something new. Just watch it. It is very simple and very normal. It is not something extraordinary. The fact is, there is contradiction. Then why does this contradiction arise?

What do we mean by contradiction? Does it not imply an impermanent state which is being opposed by another impermanent state? I think I have a permanent desire, I posit in myself a permanent desire and another desire arises which contradicts it; this contradiction brings about conflict, which is waste. That is to say there is a constant denial of one desire by another desire, one pursuit overcoming another pursuit. Now, is there such a thing as a permanent desire? Surely, *all* desire is impermanent—not metaphysically, but actually. I want a job. That is I look to a certain job as a means of happiness; and when I get it, I am dissatisfied. I want to become the manager, then the owner, and so on and on, not only in this world, but in the so-called spiritual world—the teacher becoming the principal, the priest becoming the bishop, the pupil becoming the master.

This constant becoming, arriving at one state after another, brings about contradiction, does it not? Therefore, why not look at life not as one permanent desire but as a series of fleeting desires always in opposition to each other? Hence the mind need not be in a state of contradiction. If I regard life not as a permanent desire but as a series of temporary desires which are constantly changing, then there is no contradiction.

Contradiction arises only when the mind has a fixed point of desire; that is when the mind does not regard *all* desire as moving, transient, but seizes upon one desire and makes that into a permanency—only then, when other desires arise, is there contradiction. But all desires are in constant movement, there is no fixation of desire. There is no fixed point in desire; but the mind establishes a fixed point because it treats everything as a means to arrive, to gain; and there must be contradiction, conflict, as long as one is arriving. You want to arrive, you want to succeed, you want to find an ultimate God or truth which will be your permanent satisfaction. Therefore you are not seeking truth, you are not seeking God. You are seeking lasting gratification, and that gratification you clothe with an idea, a respectable-sounding word such as God, truth; but actually we are all seeking gratification, and we place that gratification, that satisfaction, at the highest point, calling it God, and the lowest point is drink. So long as the mind is seeking gratification, there is not much difference between God and drink. Socially, drink may be bad; but the inward desire for gratification, for gain, is even more harmful, is it not? If you really want to find truth, you must be extremely honest, not merely at the verbal level but altogether; you must be extraordinarily clear, and you cannot be clear if you are unwilling to face facts.

Now what brings about contradiction in each one of us? Surely it is the desire to become something, is it not? We all want to become something: to become successful in the world and, inwardly, to achieve a result. So long as we think in terms of time, in terms of achievement, in terms of position, there must be contradiction. After all, the mind is the product of time. Thought is based on yesterday, on the past; and so long as thought is functioning within the field of time, thinking in terms of the future, of becoming, gaining, achieving, there must be contradiction, because then we are incapable of facing exactly what *is*. Only in realizing, in understanding, in being choicelessly aware of what *is*, is there a possibility of freedom from that disintegrating factor which is contradiction.

Therefore it is essential, is it not?, to understand the whole process of our thinking, for it is there that we find contradiction. Thought itself has become a contradiction because we have not understood the total process of ourselves; and that understanding is possible only when we are fully aware of our thought, not as an observer operating upon his thought, but integrally and without choice—which is extremely arduous. Then only is there the dissolution of that contradiction which is so detrimental, so painful.

So long as we are trying to achieve a psychological result, so long as we want inward security, there must be a contradiction in our life. I do not think that most of us are aware of this contradiction; or, if we are, we do not see its real significance. On the contrary, contradiction gives us an impetus to live; the very element of friction makes us feel that we are alive. The effort, the struggle of contradiction, gives us a sense of vitality. That is why we love wars, that is why we enjoy the battle of frustrations. So long as there is the desire to achieve a result, which is the desire to be psychologically secure, there must be a contradiction; and where there is contradiction, there cannot be a quiet mind. Quietness of mind is essential to understand the whole significance of life. Thought can never be tranquil; thought, which is the product of time, can never find that which is timeless, can never know that which is beyond time. The very nature of our thinking is a contradiction, because we are always thinking in terms of the past or of the future; therefore we are never fully cognizant, fully aware of the present.

To be fully aware of the present is an extraordinarily difficult task because the mind is incapable of facing a fact directly without deception. Thought is the product of the past and therefore it can only think in terms of the past or of the future; it cannot be completely aware of a fact in the present. So long as thought, which is the product of the past, tries to eliminate contradiction and all the problems that it creates, it is merely pursuing a result, trying to achieve an end, and such thinking only creates more contradiction and hence conflict, misery and confusion in us and, therefore, about us.

To be free of contradiction, one must be aware of the present without choice. How can there be choice when you are confronted with a fact? Surely the understanding of the fact is made impossible so long as thought is trying to operate upon the fact in terms of becoming, changing, altering. Therefore self-knowledge is the beginning of understanding; without self-knowledge, contradiction and conflict will continue. To know the whole process, the totality of oneself, does not require any expert, any authority. The pursuit of authority only breeds fear. No expert, no specialist, can show us how to understand the process of the self. One has to study it for oneself. You and I can help each other by talking about it, but none can unfold it for us, no specialist, no teacher, can explore it for us. We can be aware of it only in our relationship—in our relationship to things, to property, to people and to ideas. In relationship we shall discover that contradiction arises when action is approximating itself to an idea. The idea is merely the crystallization of thought as a symbol, and the effort to live up to the symbol brings about a contradiction.

Thus, so long as there is a pattern of thought, contradiction will continue; to put an end to the pattern, and so to contradiction, there must be self-knowledge. This understanding of the self is not a process reserved for the few. The self is to be understood in our everyday speech, in the way we think and feel, in the way we look at another. If we can be aware of every thought, of every feeling, from moment to moment, then we shall see that in relationship the ways of the self are understood. Then only is there a possibility of that tranquillity of mind in which alone the ultimate reality can come into being.

CHAPTER IX

WHAT IS THE SELF?

Do WE KNOW WHAT we mean by the self? By that, I mean the idea, the memory, the conclusion, the experience, the various forms of nameable and unnameable intentions, the conscious endeavour to be or not to be, the accumulated memory of the unconscious, the racial, the group, the individual, the clan, and the whole of it all, whether it is projected outwardly in action or projected spiritually as virtue; the striving after all this is the self. In it is included the competition, the desire to be. The whole process of that is the self; and we know actually when we are faced with it that it is an evil thing. I am using the word 'evil' intentionally, because the self is dividing: the self is self-enclosing: its activities, however noble, are separative and isolating. We know all this. We also know those extraordinary moments when the self is not there, in which there is no sense of endeavour, of effort, and which happens when there is love.

It seems to me that it is important to understand how experience strengthens the self. If we are earnest, we should understand this problem of experience. Now what do we mean by experience? We have experience all the time, impressions; and we translate those impressions, and we react or act according to them; we are calculating, cunning, and so on. There is the constant interplay between what is seen objectively and our reaction to it, and interplay between the conscious and the memories of the unconscious.

According to my memories, I react to whatever I see, to whatever I feel. In this process of reacting to what I see, what I feel, what I know, what I believe, experience is taking place, is it not? Reaction, response to something seen, is experience. When I see you, I react; the naming of that reaction is experience. If I do not name that reaction it is not an experience. Watch your own responses and what is taking place about you. There is no experience unless there is a naming process going on at the same time. If I do not recognize you, how can I have the experience of meeting you? It sounds simple and right. Is it not a fact? That is if I do not react according to my memories, according to my conditioning, according to my prejudices, how can I know that I have had an experience?

Then there is the projection of various desires. I desire to be protected, to have security inwardly; or I desire to have a Master, a *guru*, a teacher, a God; and I experience that which I have projected; that is I have projected a desire which has taken a form, to which I have given a name; to that I react. It is my projection. It is my naming. That desire which gives me an experience makes me say: "I have experience", "I have met the Master", or "I have not met the Master". You know the whole process of naming an experience. Desire is what you call experience, is it not?

When I desire silence of the mind, what is taking place? What happens? I see the importance of having a silent mind, a quiet mind, for various reasons; because the *Upanishads* have said so, religious scriptures have said so, saints have said it, and also occasionally I myself feel how good it is to be quiet, because my mind is so very chatty all the day. At times I feel how nice, how pleasurable it is to have a peaceful mind, a silent mind. The desire is to experience silence. I want to have a silent mind, and so I ask "How can I get it?" I know what this or that book says about meditation, and the various forms of discipline. So through discipline I seek to experience silence. The self, the 'me', has therefore established itself in the experience of silence.

I want to understand what is truth; that is my desire, my longing; then there follows my projection of what I consider to be the truth, because I have read lots about it; I have

77

heard many people talk about it; religious scriptures have described it. I want all that. What happens? The very want, the very desire is projected, and I experience because I recognize that projected state. If I did not recognize that state, I would not call it truth. I recognize it and I experience it; and that experience gives strength to the self, to the 'me', does it not? So the self becomes entrenched in the experience. Then you say "I know", "the Master exists", "there is God" or "there is no God"; you say that a particular political system is right and all others are not.

So experience is always strengthening the 'me'. The more you are entrenched in your experience, the more does the self get strengthened. As a result of this, you have a certain strength of character, strength of knowledge, of belief, which you display to other people because you know they are not as clever as you are, and because you have the gift of the pen or of speech and you are cunning. Because the self is still acting, so your beliefs, your Masters, your castes, your economic system are all a process of isolation, and they therefore bring contention. You must, if you are at all serious or earnest in this, dissolve this centre completely and not justify it. That is why we must understand the process of experience.

Is it possible for the mind, for the self, not to project, not to desire, not to experience? We see that all experiences of the self are a negation, a destruction, and yet we call them positive action, don't we? That is what we call the positive way of life. To undo this whole process is, to you, negation. Are you right in that? Can we, you and I, as individuals, go to the root of it and understand the process of the self? Now what brings about dissolution of the self? Religious and other groups have offered identification, have they not? "Identify yourself with a larger, and the self disappears", is what they say. But surely identification is still the process of the self; the larger is simply the projection of the 'me', which I experience and which therefore strengthens the 'me'.

All the various forms of discipline, belief and knowledge

surely only strengthen the self. Can we find an element which will dissolve the self? Or is that a wrong question? That is what we want basically. We want to find something which will dissolve the 'me', do we not? We think there are various means, namely, identification, belief, etc.; but all of them are at the same level; one is not superior to the other, because all of them are equally powerful in strengthening the self, the 'me'. So can I see the 'me' wherever it functions, and see its destructive forces and energy? Whatever name I may give to it, it is an isolating force, it is a destructive force, and I want to find a way of dissolving it. You must have asked this yourself—"I see the 'I' functioning all the time and always bringing anxiety, fear, frustration, despair, misery, not only to myself but to all around me. Is it possible for that self to be dissolved, not partially but completely?" Can we go to the root of it and destroy it? That is the only way of truly functioning, is it not? I do not want to be partially intelligent but intelligent in an integrated manner. Most of us are intelligent in layers, you probably in one way and I in some other way. Some of you are intelligent in your business work, some others in your office work, and so on; people are intelligent in different ways; but we are not integrally intelligent. *To be integrally intelligent means to be without the self.* Is it possible?

Is it possible for the self to be completely absent now? You know it is possible. What are the necessary ingredients, requirements? What is the element that brings it about? Can I find it? When I put that question "Can I find it?" surely I am convinced that it is possible; so I have already created an experience in which the self is going to be strengthened, is it not? Understanding of the self requires a great deal of intelligence, a great deal of watchfulness, alertness, watching ceaselessly, so that it does not slip away. I, who am very earnest, want to dissolve the self. When I say that, I know it is possible to dissolve the self. The moment I say "I want to dissolve this", in that there is still the experiencing of the self; and so the self is strengthened.

So how is it possible for the self not to experience? One can see that the state of creation is not at all the experience of the self. Creation is when the self is not there, because creation is not intellectual, is not of the mind, is not self-projected, is something beyond all experiencing. So is it possible for the mind to be quite still, in a state of non-recognition, or non-experiencing, to be in a state in which creation can take place, which means when the self is not there, when the self is absent? The problem is this, is it not? Any movement of the mind, positive or negative, is an experience which actually strengthens the 'me'. Is it possible for the mind not to recognize? That can only take place when there is complete silence, but not the silence which is an experience of the self and which therefore strengthens the self.

Is there an entity apart from the self, which looks at the self and dissolves the self? Is there a spiritual entity which supersedes the self and destroys it, which puts it aside? We think there is, don't we? Most religious people think there is such an element. The materialist says, "It is impossible for the self to be destroyed; it can only be conditioned and restrained—politically, economically and socially; we can hold it firmly within a certain pattern and we can break it; and therefore it can be made to lead a high life, a moral life, and not to interfere with anything but to follow the social pattern, and to function merely as a machine". That we know. There are other people, the so-called religious ones —they are not really religious, though we call them so— who say, "Fundamentally, there is such an element. If we can get into touch with it, it will dissolve the self".

Is there such an element to dissolve the self? Please see what we are doing. We are forcing the self into a corner. If you allow yourself to be forced into the corner, you will see what will happen. We should like there to be an element which is timeless, which is not of the self, which, we hope, will come and intercede and destroy the self—and which we call God. Now is there such a thing which the mind can conceive? There may be or there may not be; that is not the point.

But when the mind seeks a timeless spiritual state which will go into action in order to destroy the self, is that not another form of experience which is strengthening the 'me'? When you believe, is that not what is actually taking place? When you believe that there is truth, God, the timeless state, immortality, is that not the process of strengthening the self? The self has projected that thing which you feel and believe will come and destroy the self. So, having projected this idea of continuance in a timeless state as a spiritual entity, you have an experience; and such experience only strengthens the self; and therefore what have you done? You have not really destroyed the self but only given it a different name, a different quality; the self is still there, because you have experienced it. Thus our action from the beginning to the end is the same action, only we think it is evolving, growing, becoming more and more beautiful; but, if you observe inwardly, it is the same action going on, the same 'me' functioning at different levels with different labels, different names.

When you see the whole process, the cunning, extraordinary inventions, the intelligence of the self, how it covers itself up through identification, through virtue, through experience, through belief, through knowledge; when you see that the mind is moving in a circle, in a cage of its own making, what happens? When you are aware of it, fully cognizant of it, then are you not extraordinarily quiet— not through compulsion, not through any reward, not through any fear? When you recognize that every movement of the mind is merely a form of strengthening the self, when you observe it, see it, when you are completely aware of it in action, when you come to that point—not ideologically, verbally, not through projected experiencing, but when you are actually in that state—then you will see that the mind, being utterly still, has no power of creating. Whatever the mind creates is in a circle, within the field of the self. When the mind is non-creating there is creation, which is not a recognizable process.

Reality, truth, is not to be recognized. For truth to come, belief, knowledge, experiencing, the pursuit of virtue—all this must go. The virtuous person who is conscious of pursuing virtue can never find reality. He may be a very decent person; but that is entirely different from being a man of truth, a man who understands. To the man of truth, truth has come into being. A virtuous man is a righteous man, and a righteous man can never understand what is truth because virtue to him is the covering of the self, the strengthening of the self, because he is pursuing virtue. When he says "I must be without greed", the state of non-greed which he experiences only strengthens the self. That is why it is so important to be poor, not only in the things of the world but also in belief and in knowledge. A man with worldly riches or a man rich in knowledge and belief will never know anything but darkness, and will be the centre of all mischief and misery. But if you and I, as individuals, can see this whole working of the self, then we shall know what love is. I assure you that is the only reformation which can possibly change the world. Love is not of the self. Self cannot recognize love. You say "I love"; but then, in the very saying of it, in the very experiencing of it, love is not. But, when you know love, self is not. When there is love, self is not.

CHAPTER X

FEAR

WHAT IS FEAR? Fear can exist only in relation to something, not in isolation. How can I be afraid of death, how can I be afraid of something I do not know? I can be afraid only of what I know. When I say I am afraid of death, am I really afraid of the unknown, which is death, or am I afraid of losing what I have known? My fear is not of death but of losing my association with things belonging to me. My fear is always in relation to the known, not to the unknown.

My inquiry now is how to be free from the fear of the known, which is the fear of losing my family, my reputation, my character, my bank account, my appetites and so on. You may say that fear arises from conscience; but your conscience is formed by your conditioning, so conscience is still the result of the known. What do I know? Knowledge is having ideas, having opinions about things, having a sense of continuity as in relation to the known, and no more. Ideas are memories, the result of experience, which is response to challenge. I am afraid of the known, which means I am afraid of losing people, things or ideas, I am afraid of discovering what I am, afraid of being at a loss, afraid of the pain which might come into being when I have lost or have not gained or have no more pleasure.

There is fear of pain. Physical pain is a nervous response, but psychological pain arises when I hold on to things that give me satisfaction, for then I am afraid of anyone or anything that may take them away from me. The psychological accumulations prevent psychological pain as long as they are undisturbed; that is I am a bundle of accumulations, experiences, which prevent any serious form of disturbance —and I do not want to be disturbed. Therefore I am afraid of anyone who disturbs them. Thus my fear is of the known, I am afraid of the accumulations, physical or psychological, that I have gathered as a means of warding off pain or preventing sorrow. But sorrow is in the very process of accumulating to ward off psychological pain. Knowledge also helps to prevent pain. As medical knowledge helps to prevent physical pain, so beliefs help to prevent psychological pain, and that is why I am afraid of losing my beliefs, though I have no perfect knowledge or concrete proof of the reality of such beliefs. I may reject some of the traditional beliefs that have been foisted on me because my own experience gives me strength, confidence, understanding; but such beliefs and the knowledge which I have acquired are basically the same—a means of warding off pain.

Fear exists so long as there is accumulation of the known, which creates the fear of losing. Therefore fear of the unknown is really fear of losing the accumulated known. Accumulation invariably means fear, which in turn means pain; and the moment I say "I must not lose" there is fear. Though my intention in accumulating is to ward off pain, pain is inherent in the process of accumulation. The very things which I have create fear, which is pain.

The seed of defence brings offence. I want physical security; thus I create a sovereign government, which necessitates armed forces, which means war, which destroys security. Wherever there is a desire for self-protection, there is fear. When I see the fallacy of demanding security I do not accumulate any more. If you say that you see it but you cannot help accumulating, it is because you do not really see that, inherently, in accumulation there is pain.

Fear exists in the process of accumulation and belief in something is part of the accumulative process. My son dies, and I believe in reincarnation to prevent me psychologically from having more pain; but, in the very process of believing, there is doubt. Outwardly I accumulate things, and bring

84

war; inwardly I accumulate beliefs, and bring pain. So long as I want to be secure, to have bank accounts, pleasures and so on, so long as I want to become something, physiologically or psychologically, there must be pain. The very things I am doing to ward off pain bring me fear, pain.

Fear comes into being when I desire to be in a particular pattern. To live without fear means to live without a particular pattern. When I demand a particular way of living that in itself is a source of fear. My difficulty is my desire to live in a certain frame. Can I not break the frame? I can do so only when I see the truth: that the frame is causing fear and that this fear is strengthening the frame. If I say I must break the frame because I want to be free of fear, then I am merely following another pattern which will cause further fear. Any action on my part based on the desire to break the frame will only create another pattern, and therefore fear. How am I to break the frame without causing fear, that is without any conscious or unconscious action on my part with regard to it? This means that I must not act, I must make no movement to break the frame. What happens to me when I am simply looking at the frame without doing anything about it? I see that the mind itself is the frame, the pattern; it lives in the habitual pattern which it has created for itself. Therefore, the mind itself is fear. Whatever the mind does goes towards strengthening an old pattern or furthering a new one. This means that whatever the mind does to get rid of fear causes fear.

Fear finds various escapes. The common variety is identification, is it not?—identification with the country, with the society, with an idea. Haven't you noticed how you respond when you see a procession, a military procession or a religious procession, or when the country is in danger of being invaded? You then identify yourself with the country, with a being, with an ideology. There are other times when you identify yourself with your child, with your wife, with a particular form of action, or inaction. Identification is a process of self-forgetfulness. So long as I am conscious of the

85

'me' I know there is pain, there is struggle, there is constant fear. But if I can identify myself with something greater, with something worth while, with beauty, with life, with truth, with belief, with knowledge, at least temporarily, there is an escape from the 'me', is there not? If I talk about "my country" I forget myself temporarily, do I not? If I can say something about God, I forget myself. If I can identify myself with my family, with a group, with a particular party, with a certain ideology, then there is a temporary escape.

Identification therefore is a form of escape from the self, even as virtue is a form of escape from the self. The man who pursues virtue is escaping from the self and he has a narrow mind. That is not a virtuous mind, for virtue is something which cannot be pursued. The more you try to become virtuous, the more strength you give to the self, to the 'me'. Fear, which is common to most of us in different forms, must always find a substitute and must therefore increase our struggle. The more you are identified with a substitute, the greater the strength to hold on to that for which you are prepared to struggle, to die, because fear is at the back.

Do we now know what fear is? Is it not the non-acceptance of what is? We must understand the word 'acceptance'. I am not using that word as meaning the effort made to accept. There is no question of accepting when I perceive what is. When I do not see clearly what is, then I bring in the process of acceptance. Therefore fear is the non-acceptance of what is. How can I, who am a bundle of all these reactions, responses, memories, hopes, depressions, frustrations, who am the result of the movement of consciousness blocked, go beyond? Can the mind, without this blocking and hindrance, be conscious? We know, when there is no hindrance, what extraordinary joy there is. Don't you know when the body is perfectly healthy there is a certain joy, well-being; and don't you know when the mind is completely free, without any block, when the centre of recognition as the 'me' is not there, you experience a certain joy? Haven't you experienced this state when the self is absent? Surely we all have.

There is understanding and freedom from the self only when I can look at it completely and integrally as a whole; and I can do that only when I understand the whole process of all activity born of desire which is the very expression of thought—for thought is not different from desire—without justifying it, without condemning it, without suppressing it; if I can understand that, then I shall know if there is the possibility of going beyond the restrictions of the self.

CHAPTER XI

SIMPLICITY

I WOULD LIKE TO discuss what is simplicity, and perhaps from that arrive at the discovery of sensitivity. We seem to think that simplicity is merely an outward expression, a withdrawal: having few possessions, wearing a loin-cloth, having no home, putting on few clothes, having a small bank account. Surely that is not simplicity. That is merely an outward show. It seems to me that simplicity is essential; but simplicity can come into being only when we begin to understand the significance of self-knowledge.

Simplicity is not merely adjustment to a pattern. It requires a great deal of intelligence to be simple and not merely conform to a particular pattern, however worthy outwardly. Unfortunately most of us begin by being simple externally, in outward things. It is comparatively easy to have few things and to be satisfied with few things; to be content with little and perhaps to share that little with others. But a mere outward expression of simplicity in things, in possessions, surely does not imply the simplicity of inward being. Because, as the world is at present, more and more things are being urged upon us, outwardly, externally. Life is becoming more and more complex. In order to escape from that, we try to renounce or be detached from things— from cars, from houses, from organizations, from cinemas, and from the innumerable circumstances outwardly thrust upon us. We think we shall be simple by withdrawing. A great many saints, a great many teachers, have renounced the world; and it seems to me that such a renunciation on the part of any of us does not solve the problem. Simplicity which is fundamental, real, can only come into being inwardly; and from that there is an outward expression. How to be simple, then, is the problem; because that simplicity makes one more and more sensitive. A sensitive mind, a sensitive heart, is essential, for then it is capable of quick perception, quick reception.

One can be inwardly simple, surely, only by understanding the innumerable impediments, attachments, fears, in which one is held. But most of us *like* to be held—by people, by possessions, by ideas. We like to be prisoners. Inwardly we *are* prisoners, though outwardly we seem to be very simple. Inwardly we are prisoners to our desires, to our wants, to our ideals, to innumerable motivations. Simplicity cannot be found unless one is free inwardly. Therefore it must begin inwardly, not outwardly.

There is an extraordinary freedom when one understands the whole process of belief, why the mind is attached to a belief. When there is freedom from beliefs, there is simplicity. But that simplicity requires intelligence, and to be intelligent one must be aware of one's own impediments. To be aware, one must be constantly on the watch, not established in any particular groove, in any particular pattern of thought or action. After all, what one is inwardly does affect the outer. Society, or any form of action, is the projection of ourselves, and without transforming inwardly mere legislation has very little significance outwardly; it may bring about certain reforms, certain adjustments, but what one is inwardly always overcomes the outer. If one is inwardly greedy, ambitious, pursuing certain ideals, that inward complexity does eventually upset, overthrow outward society, however carefully planned it may be.

Therefore one must begin within—not exclusively, not rejecting the outer. You come to the inner, surely, by understanding the outer, by finding out how the conflict, the struggle, the pain, exists outwardly; as one investigates it more and more, naturally one comes into the psychological states which produce the outward conflicts and miseries.

The outward expression is only an indication of our inward state, but to understand the inward state one must approach through the outer. Most of us do that. In understanding the inner—not exclusively, not by rejecting the outer, but by understanding the outer and so coming upon the inner —we will find that, as we proceed to investigate the inward complexities of our being, we become more and more sensitive, free. It is this inward simplicity that is so essential, because that simplicity creates sensitivity. A mind that is not sensitive, not alert, not aware, is incapable of any receptivity, any creative action. Conformity as a means of making ourselves simple really makes the mind and heart dull, insensitive. Any form of authoritarian compulsion, imposed by the government, by oneself, by the ideal of achievement, and so on—any form of conformity must make for insensitivity, for not being simple inwardly. Outwardly you may conform and give the appearance of simplicity, as so many religious people do. They practise various disciplines, join various organizations, meditate in a particular fashion, and so on—all giving an appearance of simplicity, but such conformity does not make for simplicity. Compulsion of any kind can never lead to simplicity. On the contrary, the more you suppress, the more you substitute, the more you sublimate, the less there is simplicity, but the more you understand the process of sublimation, suppression, substitution, the greater the possibility of being simple.

Our problems—social, environmental, political, religious —are so complex that we can solve them only by being simple, not by becoming extraordinarily erudite and clever. A simple person sees much more directly, has a more direct experience, than the complex person. Our minds are so crowded with an infinite knowledge of facts, of what others have said, that we have become incapable of being simple and having direct experience ourselves. These problems demand a new approach; and they can be so approached only when we are simple, inwardly really simple. That simplicity comes only through self-knowledge, through understanding ourselves; the ways of our thinking and feeling; the movements of our thoughts; our responses; how we conform, through fear, to public opinion, to what others say, what the Buddha, the Christ, the great saints have said—all of which indicates our nature to conform, to be safe, to be secure. When one is seeking security, one is obviously in a state of fear and therefore there is no simplicity.

Without being simple, one cannot be sensitive—to the trees, to the birds, to the mountains, to the wind, to all the things which are going on about us in the world; if one is not simple one cannot be sensitive to the inward intimation of things. Most of us live so superficially, on the upper level of our consciousness; there we try to be thoughtful or intelligent, which is synonymous with being religious; there we try to make our minds simple, through compulsion, through discipline. But that is not simplicity. When we force the upper mind to be simple, such compulsion only hardens the mind, does not make the mind supple, clear, quick. To be simple in the whole, total process of our consciousness is extremely arduous; because there must be no inward reservation, there must be an eagerness to find out, to inquire into the process of our being, which means to be awake to every intimation, to every hint; to be aware of our fears, of our hopes, and to investigate and to be free of them more and more and more. Only then, when the mind and the heart are really simple, not encrusted, are we able to solve the many problems that confront us.

Knowledge is not going to solve our problems. You may know, for example, that there is reincarnation, that there is a continuity after death. You *may* know, I don't say you do; or you may be convinced of it. But that does not solve the problem. Death cannot be shelved by your theory, or by information, or by conviction. It is much more mysterious, much deeper, much more creative than that.

One must have the capacity to investigate all these things anew; because it is only through *direct experience* that our problems are solved, and to have direct experience there must be simplicity, which means there must be sensitivity. A mind is made dull by the weight of knowledge. A mind is made dull by the past, by the future. Only a mind that is capable of adjusting itself to the present, continually, from moment to moment, can meet the powerful influences and pressures constantly put upon us by our environment.

Thus a religious man is not really one who puts on a robe or a loin-cloth, or lives on one meal a day, or has taken innumerable vows to be this and not to be that, but is he who is inwardly simple, who is not *becoming* anything. Such a mind is capable of extraordinary receptivity, because there is no barrier, there is no fear, there is no going towards something; therefore it is capable of receiving grace, God, truth, or what you will. But a mind that is *pursuing* reality is not a simple mind. A mind that is seeking out, searching, groping, agitated, is not a simple mind. A mind that conforms to any pattern of authority, inward or outward, cannot be sensitive. And it is only when a mind is really sensitive, alert, aware of all its own happenings, responses, thoughts, when it is no longer becoming, is no longer shaping itself to *be* something—only then is it capable of receiving that which is truth. It is only then that there can be happiness, for happiness is not an end—it is the result of reality. When the mind and the heart have become simple and therefore sensitive—not through any form of compulsion, direction, or imposition—then we shall see that our problems can be tackled very simply. However complex our problems, we shall be able to approach them freshly and see them differently. That is what is wanted at the present time: people who are capable of meeting this outward confusion, turmoil, antagonism anew, creatively, simply—not with theories nor formulas, either of the left or of the right. You *cannot* meet it anew if you are not simple.

A problem can be solved only when we approach it thus. We cannot approach it anew if we are thinking in terms of certain patterns of thought, religious, political or otherwise.

So we must be free of all these things, to be simple. That is why it is so important to be aware, to have the capacity to understand the process of our own thinking, to be cognizant of ourselves totally; from that there comes a simplicity, there comes a humility which is not a virtue or a practice. Humility that is gained ceases to be humility. A mind that makes itself humble is no longer a humble mind. It is only when one has humility, not a cultivated humility, that one is able to meet the things of life that are so pressing, because then one is not important, one doesn't look through one's own pressures and sense of importance; one looks at the problem for itself and then one is able to solve it.

CHAPTER XII

AWARENESS

To KNOW OURSELVES means to know our relationship with the world—not only with the world of ideas and people, but also with nature, with the things we possess. That is our life—life being relationship to the whole. Does the understanding of that relationship demand specialization? Obviously not. What it demands is awareness to meet life as a whole. How is one to be aware? That is our problem. How is one to have that awareness—if I may use this word without making it mean specialization? How is one to be capable of meeting life as a whole?—which means not only personal relationship with your neighbour but also with nature, with the things that you possess, with ideas, and with the things that the mind manufactures as illusion, desire and so on. How is one to be aware of this whole process of relationship? Surely that is our life, is it not? There is no life without relationship; and to understand this relationship does not mean isolation. On the contrary, it demands a full recognition or awareness of the total process of relationship.

How is one to be aware? How are we aware of anything? How are you aware of your relationship with a person? How are you aware of the trees, the call of a bird? How are you aware of your reactions when you read a newspaper? Are we aware of the superficial responses of the mind, as well as the inner responses? How are we aware of anything? First we are aware, are we not?, of a response to a stimulus, which is an obvious fact; I see the trees, and there is a response, then sensation, contact, identification and desire. That is the ordinary process, isn't it? We can observe what actually takes place, without studying any books.

So through identification you have pleasure and pain. And our 'capacity' is this concern with pleasure and the avoidance of pain, is it not? If you are interested in something, if it gives you pleasure, there is 'capacity' immediately; there is an awareness of that fact immediately; and if it is painful the 'capacity' is developed to avoid it. So long as we are looking to 'capacity' to understand ourselves, I think we shall fail; because the understanding of ourselves does not depend on capacity. It is not a technique that you develop, cultivate and increase through time, through constantly sharpening. This awareness of oneself can be tested, surely, in the action of relationship; it can be tested in the way we talk, the way we behave. Watch yourself without any identification, without any comparison, without any condemnation; just watch, and you will see an extraordinary thing taking place. You not only put an end to an activity which is unconscious—because most of our activities are unconscious—you not only bring that to an end, but, further, you are aware of the motives of that action, without inquiry, without digging into it.

When you are aware, you see the whole process of your thinking and action; but it can happen only when there is no condemnation. When I condemn something, I do not understand it, and it is one way of avoiding any kind of understanding. I think most of us do that purposely; we condemn immediately and we think we have understood. If we do not condemn but regard it, are aware of it, then the content, the significance of that action begins to open up. Experiment with this and you will see for yourself. Just be aware—without any sense of justification—which may appear rather negative but is not negative. On the contrary, it has the quality of passivity which is direct action; and you will discover this, if you experiment with it.

After all, if you want to understand something, you have to be in a passive mood, do you not? You cannot keep on thinking about it, speculating about it or questioning it. You have to be sensitive enough to receive the content of it.

It is like being a sensitive photographic plate. If I want to understand you, I have to be passively aware; then you begin to tell me all your story. Surely that is not a question of capacity or specialization. In that process we begin to understand ourselves—not only the superficial layers of our consciousness, but the deeper, which is much more important; because *there* are all our motives or intentions, our hidden, confused demands, anxieties, fears, appetites. Outwardly we may have them all under control but inwardly they are boiling. Until those have been completely understood through awareness, obviously there cannot be freedom, there cannot be happiness, there is no intelligence.

Is intelligence a matter of specialization?—intelligence being the total awareness of our process. And is that intelligence to be cultivated through any form of specialization? Because that is what is happening, is it not? The priest, the doctor, the engineer, the industrialist, the business man, the professor—we have the mentality of all that specialization.

To realize the highest form of intelligence—which is truth, which is God, which cannot be described—to realize that, we think we have to make ourselves specialists. We study, we grope, we search out; and, with the mentality of the specialist or looking to the specialist, we study ourselves in order to develop a capacity which will help to unravel our conflicts, our miseries.

Our problem is, if we are at all aware, whether the conflicts and the miseries and the sorrows of our daily existence can be solved by another; and if they cannot, how is it possible for us to tackle them? To understand a problem obviously requires a certain intelligence, and that intelligence cannot be derived from or cultivated through specialization. It comes into being only when we are passively aware of the whole process of our consciousness, which is to be aware of ourselves without choice, without choosing what is right and what is wrong. When you are passively aware, you will see that out of that passivity—which is not idleness,

96

which is not sleep, but extreme alertness—the problem has quite a different significance; which means there is no longer identification with the problem and therefore there is no judgement and hence the problem begins to reveal its content. If you are able to do that constantly, continuously, then every problem can be solved fundamentally, not superficially. That is the difficulty, because most of us are incapable of being passively aware, letting the problem tell the story without our interpreting it. We do not know how to look at a problem dispassionately. We are not capable of it, unfortunately, because we want a result from the problem, we want an answer, we are looking to an end; or we try to translate the problem according to our pleasure or pain; or we have an answer already on how to deal with the problem. Therefore we approach a problem, which is always new, with the old pattern. The challenge is always the new, but our response is always the old; and our difficulty is to meet the challenge adequately, that is fully. The problem is always a problem of relationship—with things, with people or with ideas; there is no other problem; and to meet the problem of relationship, with its constantly varying demands—to meet it rightly, to meet it adequately—one has to be aware passively. This passivity is not a question of determination, of will, of discipline; to be aware that we are *not* passive is the beginning. To be aware that we want a particular answer to a particular problem—surely that is the beginning: to know ourselves in relationship to the problem and how we deal with the problem. Then as we begin to know ourselves in relationship to the problem—how we respond, what are our various prejudices, demands, pursuits, in meeting that problem—this awareness will reveal the process of our own thinking, of our own inward nature; and in that there is a release.

What is important, surely, is to be aware without choice, because choice brings about conflict. The chooser is in confusion, therefore he chooses; if he is not in confusion, there is no choice. Only the person who is confused chooses what he shall do or shall not do. The man who is clear and simple does not choose; what is, is. Action based on an idea is obviously the action of choice and such action is not liberating; on the contrary, it only creates further resistance, further conflict, according to that conditioned thinking.

The important thing, therefore, is to be aware from moment to moment without accumulating the experience which awareness brings; because, the moment you accumulate, you are aware only according to that accumulation, according to that pattern, according to that experience. That is your awareness is conditioned by your accumulation and therefore there is no longer observation but merely translation. Where there is translation, there is choice, and choice creates conflict; in conflict there can be no understanding.

Life is a matter of relationship; and to understand that relationship, which is not static, there must be an awareness which is pliable, an awareness which is alertly passive, not aggressively active. As I said, this passive awareness does not come through any form of discipline, through any practice. It is to be just aware, from moment to moment, of our thinking and feeling, not only when we are awake; for we shall see, as we go into it more deeply, that we begin to dream, that we begin to throw up all kinds of symbols which we translate as dreams. Thus we open the door into the hidden, which becomes the known; but to find the unknown, we must go beyond the door—surely, that is our difficulty. Reality is not a thing which is knowable by the mind, because the mind is the result of the known, of the past; therefore the mind must understand itself and its functioning, its truth, and only then is it possible for the unknown to *be*.

CHAPTER XIII

DESIRE

FOR MOST OF US, desire is quite a problem: the desire for property, for position, for power, for comfort, for immortality, for continuity, the desire to be loved, to have something permanent, satisfying, lasting, something which is beyond time. Now, what *is* desire? What is this thing that is urging, compelling us? I am not suggesting that we should be satisfied with what we have or with what we are, which is merely the opposite of what we want. We are trying to see what desire is, and if we can go into it tentatively, hesitantly, I think we shall bring about a transformation which is not a mere substitution of one object of desire for another object of desire. This is generally what we mean by 'change', is it not? Being dissatisfied with one particular object of desire, we find a substitute for it. We are everlastingly moving from one object of desire to another which we consider to be higher, nobler, more refined; but, however refined, desire is still desire, and in this movement of desire there is endless struggle, the conflict of the opposites.

Is it not, therefore, important to find out what is desire and whether it can be transformed? What is desire? Is it not the symbol and its sensation? Desire is sensation with the object of its attainment. Is there desire without a symbol and its sensation? Obviously not. The symbol may be a picture, a person, a word, a name, an image, an idea which gives me a sensation, which makes me feel that I like or dislike it; if the sensation is pleasurable, I want to attain, to possess, to hold on to its symbol and continue in that pleasure. From time to time, according to my inclinations and intensities, I change the picture, the image, the object.

99

With one form of pleasure I am fed up, tired, bored, so I seek a new sensation, a new idea, a new symbol. I reject the old sensation and take on a new one, with new words, new significances, new experiences. I resist the old and yield to the new which I consider to be higher, nobler, more satisfying. Thus in desire there is a resistance and a yielding, which involves temptation; and of course in yielding to a particular symbol of desire there is always the fear of frustration.

If I observe the whole process of desire in myself I see that there is always an object towards which my mind is directed for further sensation, and that in this process there is involved resistance, temptation and discipline. There is perception, sensation, contact and desire, and the mind becomes the mechanical instrument of this process, in which symbols, words, objects are the centre round which all desire, all pursuits, all ambitions are built; that centre is the 'me'. Can I dissolve that centre of desire—not one particular desire, one particular appetite or craving, but the whole structure of desire, of longing, hoping, in which there is always the fear of frustration? The more I am frustrated, the more strength I give to the 'me'. So long as there is hoping, longing, there is always the background of fear, which again strengthens that centre. And revolution is possible only at that centre, not on the surface, which is merely a process of distraction, a superficial change leading to mischievous action.

When I am aware of this whole structure of desire, I see how my mind has become a dead centre, a mechanical process of memory. Having tired of one desire, I automatically want to fulfil myself in another. My mind is always experiencing in terms of sensation, it is the instrument of sensation. Being bored with a particular sensation, I seek a new sensation, which may be what I call the realization of God; but it is still sensation. I have had enough of this world and its travail and I want peace, the peace that is everlasting; so I meditate, control, I shape my mind in order to experience that peace. The experiencing of that peace is still sensation. So my mind is the mechanical instrument of sensation, of memory, a dead centre from which I act, think. The objects I pursue are the projections of the mind as symbols from which it derives sensations. The word 'God', the word 'love', the word 'communism', the word 'democracy', the word 'nationalism'—these are all symbols which give sensations to the mind, and therefore the mind clings to them. As you and I know, every sensation comes to an end, and so we proceed from one sensation to another; and every sensation strengthens the habit of seeking further sensation. Thus the mind becomes merely an instrument of sensation and memory, and in that process we are caught. So long as the mind is seeking further experience it can only think in terms of sensation; and any experience that may be spontaneous, creative, vital, strikingly new, it immediately reduces to sensation and pursues that sensation, which then becomes a memory. Therefore the experience is dead and the mind becomes merely a stagnant pool of the past.

If we have gone into it at all deeply we are familiar with this process; and we seem to be incapable of going beyond. We *want* to go beyond, because we are tired of this endless routine, this mechanical pursuit of sensation; so the mind projects the idea of truth, of God; it dreams of a vital change and of playing a principal part in that change, and so on and on and on. Hence there is never a creative state. In myself I see this process of desire going on, which is mechanical, repetitive, which holds the mind in a process of routine and makes of it a dead centre of the past in which there is no creative spontaneity. Also there are sudden moments of creation, of that which is not of the mind, which is not of memory, which is not of sensation or of desire.

Our problem, therefore, is to understand desire—not how far it should go or where it should come to an end, but to understand the whole process of desire, the cravings, the longings, the burning appetites. Most of us think that possessing very little indicates freedom from desire—and how we worship those who have but few things! A loin-cloth, a robe, symbolizes our desire to be free from desire; but that again is a very superficial reaction. Why begin at the superficial level of giving up outward possessions when your mind is crippled with innumerable wants, innumerable desires, beliefs, struggles? Surely it is *there* that the revolution must take place, not in how much you possess or what clothes you wear or how many meals you eat. But we are impressed by these things because our minds are very superficial.

Your problem and my problem is to see whether the mind can ever be free from desire, from sensation. Surely creation has nothing to do with sensation; reality, God, or what you will, is not a state which can be experienced as sensation. When you have an experience, what happens? It has given you a certain sensation, a feeling of elation or depression. Naturally, you try to avoid, put aside, the state of depression; but if it is a joy, a feeling of elation, you pursue it. Your experience has produced a pleasurable sensation and you want more of it; and the 'more' strengthens the dead centre of the mind, which is ever craving further experience. Hence the mind cannot experience anything new, it is *incapable* of experiencing anything new, because its approach is always through memory, through recognition; and that which is recognized through memory is not truth, creation, reality. Such a mind cannot experience reality; it can only experience sensation, and creation is not sensation, it is something that is everlastingly new from moment to moment.

Now I realize the state of my own mind; I see that it is the instrument of sensation and desire, or rather that it *is* sensation and desire, and that it is mechanically caught up in routine. Such a mind is incapable of ever receiving or feeling out the new; for the new must obviously be something beyond sensation, which is always the old. So, this mechanical process with its sensations has to come to an end, has it not? The wanting more, the pursuit of symbols, words, images, with their sensation—all that has to come to an end. Only then is it possible for the mind to be in that state of creativeness in which the new can always come into being. If you will understand without being mesmerized by words, by habits, by ideas, and see how important it is to have the new constantly impinging on the mind, then, perhaps, you will understand the process of desire, the routine, the boredom, the constant craving for experience. Then I think you will begin to see that desire has very little significance in life for a man who is really seeking. Obviously there are certain physical needs: food, clothing, shelter, and all the rest of it. But they never become psychological appetites, things on which the mind builds itself as a centre of desire. Beyond the physical needs, *any* form of desire—for greatness, for truth, for virtue—becomes a psychological process by which the mind builds the idea of the 'me' and strengthens itself at the centre.

When you see this process, when you are really aware of it without opposition, without a sense of temptation, without resistance, without justifying or judging it, then you will discover that the mind is capable of receiving the new and that the new is never a sensation; therefore it can never be recognized, re-experienced. It is a state of being in which creativeness comes without invitation, without memory; and that is reality.

CHAPTER XIV

RELATIONSHIP AND ISOLATION

LIFE IS EXPERIENCE, experience in relationship. One cannot live in isolation; so life is relationship and relationship is action. And how can one have that capacity for understanding relationship which is life? Does not relationship mean not only communion with people but intimacy with things and ideas? Life is relationship, which is expressed through contact with things, with people and with ideas. In understanding relationship we shall have capacity to meet life fully, adequately. So our problem is not capacity—for capacity is not independent of relationship—but rather the understanding of relationship, which will naturally produce the capacity for quick pliability, for quick adjustment, for quick response.

Relationship, surely, is the mirror in which you discover yourself. Without relationship you are not; to be is to be related; to be related is existence. You exist only in relationship; otherwise you do not exist, existence has no meaning. It is not because you *think* you are that you come into existence. You exist because you are related; and it is the lack of understanding of relationship that causes conflict.

Now there is no understanding of relationship, because we use relationship merely as a means of furthering achievement, furthering transformation, furthering becoming. But relationship is a means of self-discovery, because relationship is *to be*; it is existence. Without relationship, I am not. To understand myself, I must understand relationship. Relationship is a mirror in which I can see myself. That mirror can either be distorted, or it can be 'as is', reflecting that which *is*. But most of us see in relationship, in that mirror, things we would *rather* see; we do not see what *is*. We would rather idealize, escape, we would rather live in the future than understand that relationship in the immediate present.

Now if we examine our life, our relationship with another, we shall see that it is a process of isolation. We are really not concerned with another; though we talk a great deal about it, actually we are not concerned. We are related to someone only so long as that relationship gratifies us, so long as it gives us a refuge, so long as it satisfies us. But the moment there is a disturbance in the relationship which produces discomfort in ourselves, we discard that relationship. In other words, there is relationship only so long as we are gratified. This may sound harsh, but if you really examine your life very closely you will see it is a fact; and to avoid a fact is to live in ignorance, which can never produce right relationship. If we look into our lives and observe relationship, we see it is a process of building resistance against another, a wall over which we look and observe the other; but we always retain the wall and remain behind it, whether it be a psychological wall, a material wall, an economic wall or a national wall. So long as we live in isolation, behind a wall, there is no relationship with another; and we live enclosed because it is much more gratifying, we think it is much more secure. The world is so disruptive, there is so much sorrow, so much pain, war, destruction, misery, that we want to escape and live within the walls of security of our own psychological being. So, relationship with most of us is actually a process of isolation, and obviously such relationship builds a society which is also isolating. That is exactly what is happening throughout the world: you remain in your isolation and stretch your hand over the wall, calling it nationalism, brotherhood or what you will, but actually sovereign governments, armies, continue. Still clinging to your own limitations, you think you can create world unity, world peace—which is impossible. So long as you have a frontier, whether national, economic, religious or social, it is

105

an obvious fact that there cannot be peace in the world.

The process of isolation is a process of the search for power; whether one is seeking power individually or for a racial or national group there must be isolation, because the very desire for power, for position, is separatism. After all, that is what each one wants, is it not? He wants a powerful position in which he can dominate, whether at home, in the office, or in a bureaucratic régime. Each one is seeking power, and in seeking power he will establish a society which is based on power, military, industrial, economic, and so on—which again is obvious. Is not the desire for power in its very nature isolating? I think it is very important to understand this, because the man who wants a peaceful world, a world in which there are no wars, no appalling destruction, no catastrophic misery on an immeasurable scale, must understand this fundamental question, must he not? A man who is affectionate, who is kindly, has no sense of power, and therefore such a man is not bound to any nationality, to any flag. He has no flag.

There is no such thing as living in isolation—no country, no people, no individual, can live in isolation; yet, because you are seeking power in so many different ways, you breed isolation. The nationalist is a curse because through his very nationalistic, patriotic spirit, he is creating a wall of isolation. He is so identified with his country that he builds a wall against another. What happens when you build a wall against something? That something is constantly beating against your wall. When you resist something, the very resistance indicates that you are in conflict with the other. So nationalism, which is a process of isolation, which is the outcome of the search for power, cannot bring about peace in the world. The man who is a nationalist and talks of brotherhood is telling a lie; he is living in a state of contradiction.

Can one live in the world without the desire for power, for position, for authority? Obviously one can. One does it when one does not identify oneself with something greater.

This identification with something greater—the party, the country, the race, the religion, God—is the search for power. Because you in yourself are empty, dull, weak, you like to identify yourself with something greater. That desire to identify yourself with something greater is the desire for power.

Relationship is a process of self-revelation, and, without knowing oneself, the ways of one's own mind and heart, merely to establish an outward order, a system, a cunning formula, has very little meaning. What is important is to understand oneself in relationship with another. Then relationship becomes not a process of isolation but a movement in which you discover your own motives, your own thoughts, your own pursuits; and that very discovery is the beginning of liberation, the beginning of transformation.

CHAPTER XV

THE THINKER AND THE THOUGHT

IN ALL OUR experiences, there is always the experiencer, the observer, who is gathering to himself more and more or denying himself. Is that not a wrong process and is that not a pursuit which does not bring about the creative state? If it is a wrong process, can we wipe it out completely and put it aside? That can come about only when I experience, not as a thinker experiences, but when I am aware of the false process and see that there is only a state in which the thinker is the thought.

So long as I am experiencing, so long as I am becoming, there must be this dualistic action; there must be the thinker and the thought, two separate processes at work; there is no integration, there is always a centre which is operating through the will of action to be or not to be—collectively, individually, nationally and so on. Universally, this is the process. So long as effort is divided into the experiencer and the experience, there must be deterioration. Integration is only possible when the thinker is no longer the observer. That is, we know at present there are the thinker and the thought, the observer and the observed, the experiencer and the experienced; there are two different states. Our effort is to bridge the two.

The will of action is always dualistic. Is it possible to go beyond this will which is separative and discover a state in which this dualistic action is not? That can only be found when we directly experience the state in which the thinker is the thought. We now think the thought is separate from the thinker; but is that so? We would like to think it is, because then the thinker can explain matters through his thought. The effort of the thinker is to become more or become less; and therefore, in that struggle, in that action of the will, in 'becoming', there is always the deteriorating factor; we are pursuing a false process and not a true process.

Is there a division between the thinker and the thought? So long as they are separate, divided, our effort is wasted; we are pursuing a false process which is destructive and which is the deteriorating factor. We think the thinker is separate from his thought. When I find that I am greedy, possessive, brutal, I think I should not be all this. The thinker then tries to alter his thoughts and therefore effort is made to 'become'; in that process of effort he pursues the false illusion that there are two separate processes, whereas there is only one process. I think therein lies the fundamental factor of deterioration.

Is it possible to experience that state when there is only one entity and not two separate processes, the experiencer and the experience? Then perhaps we shall find out what it is to be creative, and what the state is in which there is no deterioration at any time, in whatever relationship man may be.

I am greedy. I and greed are not two different states; there is only one thing and that is greed. If I am aware that I am greedy, what happens? I make an effort not to be greedy, either for sociological reasons or for religious reasons; that effort will always be in a small limited circle; I may extend the circle but it is always limited. Therefore the deteriorating factor is there. But when I look a little more deeply and closely, I see that the maker of effort is the cause of greed and he is greed itself; and I also see that there is no 'me' and greed, existing separately, but that there is only greed. If I realize that I am greedy, that there is not the observer who is greedy but I am myself greed, then our whole question is entirely different; our response to it is entirely different; then our effort is not destructive.

What will you do when your whole being is greed, when

whatever action you do is greed? Unfortunately, we don't think along those lines. There is the 'me', the superior entity, the soldier who is controlling, dominating. To me that process is destructive. It is an illusion and we know why we do it. I divide myself into the high and the low in order to continue. If there is only greed, completely, not 'I' operating greed, but I am entirely greed, then what happens? Surely then there is a different process at work altogether, a different problem comes into being. It is that problem which is creative, in which there is no sense of 'I' dominating, becoming, positively or negatively. We must come to that state if we would be creative. In that state, there is no maker of effort. It is not a matter of verbalizing or of trying to find out what that state is; if you set about it in that way you will lose and you will never find. What is important is to see that the maker of effort and the object towards which he is making effort are the same. That requires enormously great understanding, watchfulness, to see how the mind divides itself into the high and the low— the high being the security, the permanent entity—but still remaining a process of thought and therefore of time. If we can understand this as direct experience, then you will see that quite a different factor comes into being.

CHAPTER XVI

CAN THINKING SOLVE OUR PROBLEMS?

THOUGHT HAS NOT solved our problems and I don't think it ever will. We have relied on the intellect to show us the way out of our complexity. The more cunning, the more hideous, the more subtle the intellect is, the greater the variety of systems, of theories, of ideas. And ideas do not solve any of our human problems; they never have and they never will. The mind is not the solution; the way of thought is obviously not the way out of our difficulty. It seems to me that we should first understand this process of thinking, and perhaps be able to go beyond—for when thought ceases, perhaps we shall be able to find a way which will help us to solve our problems, not only the individual but also the collective.

Thinking has not solved our problems. The clever ones, the philosophers, the scholars, the political leaders, have not really solved any of our human problems—which are the relationship between you and another, between you and myself. So far we have used the mind, the intellect, to help us investigate the problem and thereby are hoping to find a solution. Can thought ever dissolve our problems? Is not thought, unless it is in the laboratory or on the drawing-board, always self-protecting, self-perpetuating, conditioned? Is not its activity self-centred? And can such thought ever resolve any of the problems which thought itself has created? Can the mind, which has created the problems, resolve those things that it has itself brought forth?

Surely thinking is a reaction. If I ask you a question, you respond to it—you respond according to your memory, to your prejudices, to your upbringing, to the climate, to the whole background of your conditioning; you reply accordingly, you think accordingly. The centre of this background is the 'me' in the process of action. So long as that background is not understood, so long as that thought process, that self which creates the problem, is not understood and put an end to, we are bound to have conflict, within and without, in thought, in emotion, in action. No solution of any kind, however clever, however well thought out, can ever put an end to the conflict between man and man, between you and me. Realizing this, being aware of how thought springs up and from what source, then we ask, "Can thought ever come to an end?"

That is one of the problems, is it not? Can thought resolve our problems? By thinking over the problem, have you resolved it? Any kind of problem—economic, social, religious—has it ever been really solved by thinking? In your daily life, the more you think about a problem, the more complex, the more irresolute, the more uncertain it becomes. Is that not so?—in our actual, daily life? You may, in thinking out certain facets of the problem, see more clearly another person's point of view, but thought cannot see the completeness and fullness of the problem—it can only see partially and a partial answer is not a complete answer, therefore it is not a solution.

The more we think over a problem, the more we investigate, analyse and discuss it, the more complex it becomes. So is it possible to look at the problem comprehensively, wholly? How is this possible? Because that, it seems to me, is our major difficulty. Our problems are being multiplied—there is imminent danger of war, there is every kind of disturbance in our relationships—and how can we understand all that comprehensively, as a whole? Obviously it can be solved only when we can look at it as a whole—not in compartments, not divided. When is that possible? Surely it is only possible when the process of thinking—which has its source in the 'me', the self, in the background of tradition, of conditioning, of prejudice, of hope, of despair—has come to an end. Can we understand this self, not by analysing, but by seeing the thing as it is, being aware of it as a fact and not as a theory?—not seeking to dissolve the self in order to achieve a result but seeing the activity of the self, the 'me', constantly in action? Can we *look* at it, without any movement to destroy or to encourage? That is the problem, is it not? If, in each one of us, the centre of the 'me' is non-existent, with its desire for power, position, authority, continuance, self-preservation, surely our problems will come to an end!

The self is a problem that thought cannot resolve. There must be an awareness which is not of thought. To be aware, without condemnation or justification, of the activities of the self—just to be aware—is sufficient. If you are aware in order to find out *how* to resolve the problem, in order to transform it, in order to produce a result, then it is still within the field of the self, of the 'me'. So long as we are seeking a result, whether through analysis, through awareness, through constant examination of every thought, we are still within the field of thought, which is within the field of the 'me', of the 'I', of the ego, or what you will.

As long as the activity of the mind exists, surely there can be no love. When there is love, we shall have no social problems. But love is not something to be acquired. The mind can seek to acquire it, like a new thought, a new gadget, a new way of thinking; but the mind cannot be in a state of love so long as thought is acquiring love. So long as the mind is seeking to be in a state of non-greed, surely it is still greedy, is it not? Similarly, so long as the mind wishes, desires, and practises in order to be in a state in which there is love, surely it denies that state, does it not?

Seeing this problem, this complex problem of living, and being aware of the process of our own thinking and realizing that it actually leads nowhere—when we deeply realize that, then surely there is a state of intelligence which is not individual or collective. Then the problem of the relationship of the individual to society, of the individual to the community, of the individual to reality, ceases; because then there is only intelligence, which is neither personal nor impersonal. It is this intelligence alone, I feel, that can solve our immense problems. That cannot be a result; it comes into being only when we understand this whole total process of thinking, not only at the conscious level but also at the deeper, hidden levels of consciousness.

To understand any of these problems we have to have a very quiet mind, a very still mind, so that the mind can look at the problem without interposing ideas or theories, without any distraction. That is one of our difficulties—because thought has become a distraction. When I want to understand, look at something, I don',t have to think about it—I *look* at it. The moment I begin to think, to have ideas, opinions about it, I am already in a state of distraction, looking away from the thing which I must understand. So thought, when you have a problem, becomes a distraction —thought being an idea, opinion, judgement, comparison —which prevents us from looking and thereby understanding and resolving the problem. Unfortunately for most of us thought has become so important. You say, "How can I exist, be, without thinking? How can I have a blank mind?" To have a blank mind is to be in a state of stupor, idiocy or what you will, and your instinctive reaction is to reject it. But surely a mind that is very quiet, a mind that is not distracted by its own thought, a mind that is open, can look at the problem very directly and very simply. And it is this capacity to look without any distraction at our problems that is the only solution. For that there must be a quiet, tranquil mind.

Such a mind is not a result, is not an end-product of a practice, of meditation, of control. It comes into being through no form of discipline or compulsion or sublimation, without any effort of the 'me', of thought; it comes into being when I understand the whole process of thinking— when I can see a fact without any distraction. In that state of tranquillity of a mind that is really still there is love. And it is love alone that can solve all our human problems.

CHAPTER XVII

THE FUNCTION OF THE MIND

WHEN YOU OBSERVE your own mind you are observing not only the so-called upper levels of the mind but also watching the unconscious; you are seeing what the mind actually does, are you not? That is the only way you can investigate. Do not superimpose what it *should* do, how it *should* think or act and so on; that would amount to making mere statements. That is if you say the mind should be this or should not be that, then you stop all investigation and all thinking; or, if you quote some high authority, then you equally stop thinking, don't you? If you quote Buddha, Christ or XYZ, there is an end to all pursuit, to all thinking and all investigation. So one has to guard against that. You must put aside all these subtleties of the mind if you would investigate this problem of the self together with me.

What is the function of the mind? To find that out, you must know what the mind is actually doing. What does your mind do? It is all a process of thinking, is it not? Otherwise, the mind is not there. So long as the mind is not thinking, consciously or unconsciously, there is no consciousness. We have to find out what the mind that we use in our everyday life, and also the mind of which most of us are unconscious, does in relation to our problems. We must look at the mind as it is and not as it should be.

Now what is mind as it is functioning? It is actually a process of isolation, is it not? Fundamentally that is what the process of thought is. It is thinking in an isolated form, yet remaining collective. When you observe your own thinking, you will see it is an isolated, fragmentary process. You are thinking according to your reactions, the reactions of your memory, of your experience, of your knowledge, of your belief. You are reacting to all that, aren't you? If I say that there must be a fundamental revolution, you immediately react. You will object to that word 'revolution' if you have got good investments, spiritual or otherwise. So your reaction is dependent on your knowledge, on your belief, on your experience. That is an obvious fact. There are various forms of reaction. You say "I must be brotherly", "I must co-operate", "I must be friendly", "I must be kind", and so on. What are these? These are all reactions; but the funda-mental reaction of thinking is a process of isolation. You are watching the process of your own mind, each one of you, which means watching your own action, belief, knowledge, experience. All these give security, do they not? They give security, give strength to the process of thinking. That process only strengthens the 'me', the mind, the self—whether you call that self high or low. All our religions, all our social sanctions, all our laws are for the support of the individual, the individual self, the separative action; and in opposition to that there is the totalitarian state. If you go deeper into the unconscious, there too it is the same process that is at work. There, we are the collective influenced by the environment, by the climate, by the society, by the father, the mother, the grandfather. There again is the desire to assert, to dominate as an individual, as the 'me'.

Is not the function of the mind, as we know it and as we function daily, a process of isolation? Aren't you seeking individual salvation? You are going to be somebody in the future; or in this very life you are going to be a great man, a great writer. Our whole tendency is to be separated. Can the mind do anything else but that? Is it possible for the mind not to think separatively, in a self-enclosed manner, fragmentarily? That is impossible. So we worship the mind; the mind is extraordinarily important. Don't you know, the moment you are a little bit cunning, a little bit alert, and have a little accumulated information and knowledge, how important you become in society? You know how you worship those who are intellectually superior, the lawyers, the professors, the orators, the great writers, the explainers and the expounders! You have cultivated the intellect and the mind.

The function of the mind is to be separated; otherwise your mind is not there. Having cultivated this process for centuries we find we cannot co-operate; we can only be urged, compelled, driven by authority, fear, either economic or religious. If that is the actual state, not only consciously but also at the deeper levels, in our motives, our intentions, our pursuits, how can there be co-operation? How can there be intelligent coming together to do something? As that is almost impossible, religions and organized social parties force the individual to certain forms of discipline. Discipline then becomes imperative if we want to come together, to do things together.

Until we understand how to transcend this separative thinking, this process of giving emphasis to the 'me' and the 'mine', whether in the collective form or in individual form, we shall not have peace; we shall have constant conflict and wars. Our problem is how to bring an end to the separative process of thought. Can thought ever destroy the self, thought being the process of verbalization and of reaction? Thought is nothing else but reaction; thought is not creative. Can such thought put an end to itself? That is what we are trying to find out. When I think along these lines: "I must discipline", "I must think more properly", "I must be this or that", thought is compelling itself, urging itself, disciplining itself to be something or not to be something. Is that not a process of isolation? It is therefore not that integrated intelligence which functions as a whole, from which alone there can be co-operation.

How are you to come to the end of thought? Or rather how is thought, which is isolated, fragmentary and partial, to come to an end? How do you set about it? Will your so-called discipline destroy it? Obviously, you have not succeeded all these long years, otherwise you would not be here. Please examine the disciplining process, which is solely a thought process, in which there is subjection, repression, control, domination—all affecting the unconscious, which asserts itself later as you grow older. Having tried for such a long time to no purpose, you must have found that discipline is obviously not the process to destroy the self. The self cannot be destroyed through discipline, because discipline is a process of strengthening the self. Yet all your religions support it; all your meditations, your assertions are based on this. Will knowledge destroy the self? Will belief destroy it? In other words, will anything that we are at present doing, any of the activities in which we are at present engaged in order to get at the root of the self, will any of that succeed? Is not all this a fundamental waste in a thought process which is a process of isolation, of reaction? What do you do when you realize fundamentally or deeply that thought cannot end itself? What happens? Watch yourself. When you are fully aware of this fact, what happens? You understand that any reaction is conditioned and that, through conditioning, there can be no freedom either at the beginning or at the end—and freedom is always at the beginning and not at the end.

When you realize that any reaction is a form of conditioning and therefore gives continuity to the self in different ways, what actually takes place? You must be very clear in this matter. Belief, knowledge, discipline, experience, the whole process of achieving a result or an end, ambition, becoming something in this life or in a future life—all these are a process of isolation, a process which brings destruction, misery, wars, from which there is no escape through collective action, however much you may be threatened with concentration camps and all the rest of it. Are you aware of that fact? What is the state of the mind which says "It is so", "That is my problem", "That is exactly where I am", "I see what knowledge and discipline can do, what ambition does"? Surely, if you see all that, there is already a different process at work.

We see the ways of the intellect but we do not see the way of love. The way of love is not to be found through the intellect. The intellect, with all its ramifications, with all its desires, ambitions, pursuits, must come to an end for love to come into existence. Don't you know that when you love, you co-operate, you are not thinking of yourself? That is the highest form of intelligence—not when you love as a superior entity or when you are in a good position, which is nothing but fear. When your vested interests are there, there can be no love; there is only the process of exploitation, born of fear. So love can come into being only when the mind is not there. Therefore you must understand the whole process of the mind, the function of the mind.

It is only when we know how to love each other that there can be co-operation, that there can be intelligent functioning, a coming together over any question. Only then is it possible to find out what God is, what truth is. Now, we are trying to find truth through intellect, through imitation— which is idolatry. Only when you discard completely, through understanding, the whole structure of the self, can that which is eternal, timeless, immeasurable, come into being. You cannot go to it; it comes to you.

CHAPTER XVIII

SELF-DECEPTION

I WOULD LIKE TO discuss or consider the question of self-deception, the delusions that the mind indulges in and imposes upon itself and upon others. That is a very serious matter, especially in a crisis of the kind which the world is facing. But in order to understand this whole problem of self-deception we must follow it not merely at the verbal level but intrinsically, fundamentally, deeply. We are too easily satisfied with words and counter-words; we are worldly-wise; and, being worldly-wise, all that we can do is to hope that something will happen. We see that the explanation of war does not stop war; there are innumerable historians, theologians and religious people explaining war and how it comes into being but wars still go on, perhaps more destructive than ever. Those of us who are really earnest must go beyond the word, must seek this fundamental revolution within ourselves. That is the only remedy which can bring about a lasting, fundamental redemption of mankind.

Similarly, when we are discussing this kind of self-deception, I think we should guard against any superficial explanations and rejoinders; we should, if I may suggest it, not merely listen to a speaker but follow the problem as we know it in our daily life; that is we should watch ourselves in thinking and in action, watch how we affect others and how we proceed to act from ourselves.

What is the reason, the basis, for self-deception? How many of us are actually aware that we are deceiving ourselves? Before we can answer the question "What is self-deception and how does it arise?", must we not be aware that we are deceiving ourselves? Do we know that we are deceiving ourselves? What do we mean by this deception? I think it is very important, because the more we deceive ourselves the greater is the strength in the deception; for it gives us a certain vitality, a certain energy, a certain capacity which entails the imposing of our deception on others. So gradually we are not only imposing deception on ourselves but on others. It is an interacting process of self-deception. Are we aware of this process? We think we are capable of thinking very clearly, purposefully and directly; and are we aware that, in this process of thinking, there is self-deception?

Is not thought itself a process of search, a seeking of justification, of security, of self-protection, a desire to be well thought of, a desire to have position, prestige and power? Is not this desire to be, politically, or religio-sociologically, the very cause of self-deception? The moment I want something other than the purely materialistic necessities, do I not produce, do I not bring about, a state which easily accepts? Take, for example, this: many of us are interested to know what happens after death; the older we are, the more interested we are. We want to know the truth of it. How shall we find it? Certainly not by reading nor through the different explanations.

How will you find it out? First, you must purge your mind completely of every factor that is in the way—every hope, every desire to continue, every desire to find out what is on that other side. Because the mind is constantly seeking security, it has the desire to continue and hopes for a means of fulfilment, for a future existence. Such a mind, though it is seeking the truth of life after death, reincarnation or whatever it is, is incapable of discovering that truth, is it not? What is important is not whether reincarnation is true or not but how the mind seeks justification, through self-deception, of a fact which may or may not be. What is important is the approach to the problem, with what motivation, with what urge, with what desire you come to it.

The seeker is always imposing this deception upon himself; no one can impose it upon him; he himself does it. We create deception and then we become slaves to it. The fundamental factor of self-deception is this constant desire to be something in this world and in the world hereafter. We know the result of wanting to be something in this world; it is utter confusion, where each is competing with the other, each is destroying the other in the name of peace; you know the whole game we play with each other, which is an extraordinary form of self-deception. Similarly, we want security in the other world, a position.

So we begin to deceive ourselves the moment there is this urge to be, to become or to achieve. That is a very difficult thing for the mind to be free from. That is one of the basic problems of our life. Is it possible to live in this world and be nothing? Then only is there freedom from all deception, because then only is the mind not seeking a result, the mind is not seeking a satisfactory answer, the mind is not seeking any form of justification, the mind is not seeking security in any form, in any relationship. That takes place only when the mind realizes the possibilities and subtleties of deception and therefore, with understanding, abandons every form of justification, security—which means the mind is capable, then, of being completely nothing. Is that possible?

So long as we deceive ourselves in any form, there can be no love. So long as the mind is capable of creating and imposing upon itself a delusion, it obviously separates itself from collective or integrated understanding. That is one of our difficulties; we do not know how to co-operate. All that we know is that we try to work together towards an end which both of us bring into being. There can be co-operation only when you and I have no common aim created by thought. What is important to realize is that co-operation is only possible when you and I do not desire to be anything. When you and I desire to be something, then belief and all the rest of it become necessary, a self-projected Utopia is necessary. But if you and I are anonymously creating, without any self-deception, without any barriers of belief and knowledge, without a desire to be secure, then there is true co-operation.

Is it possible for us to co-operate, for us to be together without an end in view? Can you and I work together without seeking a result? Surely that is true co-operation, is it not? If you and I think out, work out, plan out a result and we are working together towards that result, then what is the process involved? Our thoughts, our intellectual minds, are of course meeting; but emotionally, the whole being may be resisting it, which brings about deception, which brings about conflict between you and me. It is an obvious and observable fact in our everyday life. You and I agree to do a certain piece of work intellectually but unconsciously, deeply, you and I are at battle with each other. I want a result to my satisfaction; I want to dominate; I want my name to be ahead of yours, though I am said to be working with you. So we both, who are creators of that plan, are really opposing each other, even though outwardly you and I agree as to the plan.

Is it not important to find out whether you and I can co-operate, commune, live together in a world where you and I are as nothing; whether we are able really and truly to co-operate not at the superficial level but fundamentally? That is one of our greatest problems, perhaps the greatest. I identify myself with an object and you identify yourself with the same object; both of us are interested in it; both of us are intending to bring it about. Surely this process of thinking is very superficial, because through identification we bring about separation—which is so obvious in our everyday life. You are a Hindu and I a Catholic; we both preach brotherhood, and we are at each other's throats. Why? That is one of our problems, is it not? Unconsciously and deeply, you have your beliefs and I have mine. By talking about brotherhood, we have not solved the whole problem of beliefs but have only theoretically and intellectually agreed that this should be so; inwardly and deeply, we are against each other.

Until we dissolve those barriers which are a self-deception, which give us a certain vitality, there can be no co-operation between you and me. Through identification with a group, with a particular idea, with a particular country, we can never bring about co-operation.

Belief does not bring about co-operation; on the contrary, it divides. We see how one political party is against another, each believing in a certain way of dealing with economic problems, and so they are all at war with one another. They are not resolved in solving, for instance, the problem of starvation. They are concerned with the theories which are going to solve that problem. They are not actually concerned with the problem itself but with the method by which the problem will be solved. Therefore there must be contention between the two, because they are concerned with the idea and not with the problem. Similarly, religious people are against each other, though verbally they say they have all one life, one God; you know all that. Inwardly their beliefs, their opinions, their experiences are destroying them and are keeping them separate.

Experience becomes a dividing factor in our human relationship; experience is a way of deception. If I have experienced something, I cling to it, I do not go into the whole problem of the process of experiencing but, because I have experienced, that is sufficient and I cling to it; thereby I impose, through that experience, self-deception.

Our difficulty is that each of us is so identified with a particular belief, with a particular form or method of bringing about happiness, economic adjustment, that our mind is captured by that and we are incapable of going deeper into the problem; therefore we desire to remain aloof individually in our particular ways, beliefs and experiences. Until we dissolve them, through understanding—not only at the superficial level, but at the deeper level also—there can be no peace in the world. That is why it is important for those who are really serious, to understand this whole problem—the desire to become, to achieve, to gain—not only at the superficial level but fundamentally and deeply; otherwise there can be no peace in the world.

Truth is not something to be gained. Love cannot come to those who have a desire to hold on to it, or who like to become identified with it. Surely such things come when the mind does not seek, when the mind is completely quiet, no longer creating movements and beliefs upon which it can depend, or from which it derives a certain strength, which is an indication of self-deception. It is only when the mind understands this whole process of desire that it can be still. Only then is the mind not in movement to be or not to be; then only is there the possibility of a state in which there is no deception of any kind.

CHAPTER XIX

SELF-CENTRED ACTIVITY

Most of us, I think, are aware that every form of persuasion, every kind of inducement, has been offered us to resist self-centred activities. Religions, through promises, through fear of hell, through every form of condemnation, have tried in different ways to dissuade man from this constant activity that is born from the centre of the 'me'. These having failed, political organizations have taken over. There again, persuasion; there again the ultimate utopian hope. Every form of legislation from the very limited to the extreme, including concentration camps, has been used and enforced against any form of resistance. Yet we go on in our self-centred activity, which is the only kind of action we seem to know. If we think about it at all, we try to modify; if we are aware of it, we try to change the course of it; but fundamentally, deeply, there is no transformation, there is no radical cessation of that activity. The thoughtful are aware of this; they are also aware that when that activity from the centre ceases, only then can there be happiness. Most of us take it for granted that self-centred activity is natural and that the consequential action, which is inevitable, can only be modified, shaped and controlled. Now those who are a little more serious, more earnest, not sincere—because sincerity is the way of self-deception—must find out whether, being aware of this extraordinary total process of self-centred activity, one can go beyond.

To understand what this self-centred activity is, one must obviously examine it, look at it, be aware of the entire process. If one can be aware of it, then there is the possibility of its dissolution; but to be aware of it requires a certain understanding, a certain intention to face the thing as it is and not to interpret, not to modify, not to condemn it. We have to be aware of what we are doing, of all the activity which springs from that self-centred state; we must be conscious of it. One of our primary difficulties is that the moment we are conscious of that activity, we want to shape it, we want to control it, we want to condemn it or we want to modify it, so we are seldom able to look at it directly. When we do, very few of us are capable of knowing what to do.

We realize that self-centred activities are detrimental, are destructive, and that every form of identification—such as with a country, with a particular group, with a particular desire, the search for a result here or hereafter, the glorification of an idea, the pursuit of an example, the pursuit of virtue and so on—is essentially the activity of a self-centred person. All our relationships, with nature, with people, with ideas, are the outcome of that activity. Knowing all this, what is one to do? All such activity must voluntarily come to an end—not self-imposed, not influenced, not guided.

Most of us are aware that this self-centred activity creates mischief and chaos but we are only aware of it in certain directions. Either we observe it in others and are ignorant of our own activities or being aware, in relationship with others, of our own self-centred activity we want to transform, we want to find a substitute, we want to go beyond. Before we can deal with it we must know how this process comes into being, must we not? In order to understand something, we must be capable of looking at it; and to look at it we must know its various activities at different levels, conscious as well as unconscious—the conscious directives, and also the self-centred movements of our unconscious motives and intentions.

I am only conscious of this activity of the 'me' when I am opposing, when consciousness is thwarted, when the 'me' is desirous of achieving a result, am I not? Or I am conscious of that centre when pleasure comes to an end and I want to have more of it; then there is resistance and a purposive shaping of the mind to a particular end which will give me a delight, a satisfaction; I am aware of myself and my activities when I am pursuing virtue consciously. Surely a man who pursues virtue consciously is unvirtuous. Humility cannot be pursued, and that is the beauty of humility.

This self-centred process is the result of time, is it not? So long as this centre of activity exists in any direction, conscious or unconscious, there is the movement of time and I am conscious of the past and the present in conjunction with the future. The self-centred activity of the 'me' is a time process. It is memory that gives continuity to the activity of the centre, which is the 'me'. If you watch yourself and are aware of this centre of activity, you will see that it is only the process of time, of memory, of experiencing and translating every experience according to a memory; you will also see that self-activity is recognition, which is also the process of the mind.

Can the mind be free from all this? It may be possible at rare moments; it may happen to most of us when we do an unconscious, unintentional, unpurposive act; but is it possible for the mind ever to be completely free from self-centred activity? That is a very important question to put to ourselves, because in the very putting of it, you will find the answer. If you are aware of the total process of this self-centred activity, fully cognizant of its activities at different levels of your consciousness, then surely you have to ask yourselves if it is possible for that activity to come to an end. Is it possible not to think in terms of time, not to think in terms of what I shall be, what I have been, what I am? For from such thought the whole process of self-centred activity begins; there, also, begins the determination to become, the determination to choose and to avoid, which are all a process of time. We see in that process infinite mischief, misery, confusion, distortion, deterioration.

Surely the process of time is not revolutionary. In the process of time there is no transformation; there is only a continuity and no ending, there is nothing but recognition. It is only when you have complete cessation of the time process, of the activity of the self, that there is a revolution, a transformation, the coming into being of the new.

Being aware of this whole total process of the 'me' in its activity, what is the mind to do? It is only with renewal, it is only with revolution—*not through evolution*, not through the 'me' becoming, but through the 'me' completely coming to an end—that there is the new. The time process cannot bring the new; time is not the way of creation.

I do not know if any of you have had a moment of creativity. I am not talking of putting some vision into action; I mean that moment of creation when there is no recognition. At that moment, there is that extraordinary state in which the 'me', as an activity through recognition, has ceased. If we are aware, we shall see that in that state there is no experiencer who remembers, translates, recognizes and then identifies; there is no thought process, which is of time. In that state of creation, of creativity of the new, which is timeless, there is no action of the 'me' at all.

Our question surely is: Is it possible for the mind to be in that state, not momentarily, not at rare moments, but—I would rather not use the words 'everlasting' or 'for ever', because that would imply time—but to be in that state without regard to time? Surely that is an important discovery to be made by each one of us, because that is the door to love; all other doors are activities of the self. Where there is action of the self, there is no love. Love is not of time. You cannot practise love. If you do, then it is a self-conscious activity of the 'me' which hopes through loving to gain a result.

Love is not of time; you cannot come upon it through any conscious effort, through any discipline, through identification, which is all of the process of time. The mind, knowing only the process of time, cannot recognize love. Love is the only thing that is eternally new. Since most of us have cultivated the mind, which is the result of time, we do not know what love is. We talk about love; we say we love people, that we love our children, our wife, our neighbour, that we love nature; but the moment we are conscious that we love, self-activity has come into being; therefore it ceases to be love.

This total process of the mind is to be understood only through relationship—relationship with nature, with people, with our own projections, with everything about us. Life is nothing but relationship. Though we may attempt to isolate ourselves from relationship, we cannot exist without it. Though relationship is painful we cannot run away, by means of isolation, by becoming a hermit and so on. All these methods are indications of the activity of the self. Seeing this whole picture, being aware of the whole process of time as consciousness, without any choice, without any determined, purposive intention, without the desire for any result, you will see that this process of time comes to an end voluntarily—not induced, not as a result of desire. It is only when that process comes to an end that love is, which is eternally new.

We do not have to seek truth. Truth is not something far away. It is the truth about the mind, truth about its activities from moment to moment. If we are aware of this moment-to-moment truth, of this whole process of time, that awareness releases consciousness or the energy which is intelligence, love. So long as the mind uses consciousness as self-activity, time comes into being with all its miseries, with all its conflicts, with all its mischief, its purposive deceptions; and it is only when the mind, understanding this total process, ceases, that love can be.

CHAPTER XX

TIME AND TRANSFORMATION

I WOULD LIKE TO TALK a little about what is time, because I think the enrichment, the beauty and significance of that which is timeless, of that which is true, can be experienced only when we understand the whole process of time. After all, we are seeking, each in his own way, a sense of happiness, of enrichment. Surely a life that has significance, the riches of true happiness, is not of time. Like love, such a life is timeless; and to understand that which is timeless, we must not approach it through time but rather understand time. We must not utilize time as a means of attaining, realizing, apprehending the timeless. That is what we are doing most of our lives: spending time in trying to grasp that which is timeless, so it is important to understand what we mean by time, because I think it is possible to be free of time. It is very important to understand time as a whole and not partially.

It is interesting to realize that our lives are mostly spent in time—time, not in the sense of chronological sequence, of minutes, hours, days and years, but in the sense of psychological memory. We live by time, we are the result of time. Our minds are the product of many yesterdays and the present is merely the passage of the past to the future. Our minds, our activities, our being, are founded on time; without time we cannot think, because thought is the result of time, thought is the product of many yesterdays and there is no thought without memory. Memory is time; for there are two kinds of time, the chronological and the psychological. There is time as yesterday by the watch and as yesterday by memory. You cannot reject chronological time; it would be absurd—you would miss your train. But is there really any time at all apart from chronological time? Obviously there is time as yesterday but is there time as the mind thinks of it? Is there time apart from the mind? Surely time, psychological time, is the product of the mind. Without the foundation of thought there is no time—time merely being memory as yesterday in conjunction with to-day, which moulds to-morrow. That is, memory of yesterday's experience in response to the present is creating the future—which is still the process of thought, a path of the mind. The thought process brings about psychological progress in time but is it real, as real as chronological time? And can we use that time which is of the mind as a means of understanding the eternal, the timeless? As I said, happiness is not of yesterday, happiness is not the product of time, happiness is always in the present, a timeless state. I do not know if you have noticed that when you have ecstasy, a creative joy, a series of bright clouds surrounded by dark clouds, in that moment there is no time: there is only the immediate present. The mind, coming in after the experiencing in the present, remembers and wishes to continue it, gathering more and more of itself, thereby creating time. So time is created by the 'more'; time is acquisition and time is also detachment, which is still an acquisition of the mind. Therefore merely disciplining the mind in time, conditioning thought within the framework of time, which is memory, surely does not reveal that which is timeless.

Is transformation a matter of time? Most of us are accustomed to think that time is necessary for transformation: I am something, and to change what I am into what I should be requires time. I am greedy, with greed's results of confusion, antagonism, conflict, and misery; to bring about the transformation, which is non-greed, we think time is necessary. That is to say time is considered as a means of evolving something greater, of becoming something. The problem is this: One is violent, greedy, envious, angry, vicious or passionate. To transform what *is*, is time necessary? First of all, why do we want to change what *is*, or bring about a transformation? Why? Because what we are dissatisfies us; it creates conflict, disturbance, and, disliking that state, we want something better, something nobler, more idealistic. Therefore we desire transformation because there is pain, discomfort, conflict. Is conflict overcome by time? If you say it will be overcome by time, you are still in conflict. You may say it will take twenty days or twenty years to get rid of conflict, to change what you are, but during that time you are still in conflict and therefore time does not bring about transformation. When we use time as a means of acquiring a quality, a virtue or a state of being, we are merely postponing or avoiding what *is*; and I think it is important to understand this point. Greed or violence causes pain, disturbance in the world of our relationship with another, which is society; and being conscious of this state of disturbance, which we term greed or violence, we say to ourselves, "I will get out of it in time. I will practise non-violence, I will practise non-envy, I will practise peace." Now, you want to practise non-violence because violence is a state of disturbance, conflict, and you think that in time you will gain non-violence and overcome the conflict. What is actually happening? Being in a state of conflict you want to achieve a state in which there is no conflict. Now is that state of no conflict the result of time, of a duration? Obviously not; because, while you are achieving a state of non-violence, you are still being violent and are therefore still in conflict.

Our problem is, can a conflict, a disturbance, be overcome in a period of time, whether it be days, years or lives? What happens when you say, "I am going to practise non-violence during a certain period of time"? The very practice indicates that you are in conflict, does it not? You would not practise if you were not resisting conflict; you say the resistance to conflict is necessary in order to overcome conflict and for that resistance you must have time. But the very resistance to conflict is itself a form of conflict. You are spending your energy in resisting conflict in the form of what you call greed, envy or violence but your mind is still in conflict, so it is important to see the falseness of the process of depending on time as a means of overcoming violence and thereby be free of that process. Then you are able to be what you are: a psychological disturbance which is violence itself.

To understand anything, any human or scientific problem, what is important, what is essential? A quiet mind, is it not?, a mind that is intent on understanding. It is not a mind that is exclusive, that is trying to concentrate—which again is an effort of resistance. If I really want to understand something, there is immediately a quiet state of mind. When you want to listen to music or look at a picture which you love, which you have a feeling for, what is the state of your mind? Immediately there is a quietness, is there not? When you are listening to music, your mind does not wander all over the place; you are listening. Similarly, when you want to understand conflict, you are no longer depending on time at all; you are simply confronted with what *is*, which is conflict. Then immediately there comes a quietness, a stillness of mind. When you no longer depend on time as a means of transforming what *is* because you see the falseness of that process, then you are confronted with what *is*, and as you are interested to understand what *is*, naturally you have a quiet mind. In that alert yet passive state of mind there is understanding. So long as the mind is in conflict, blaming, resisting, condemning, there can be no understanding. If I want to understand you, I must not condemn you, obviously. It is that quiet mind, that still mind, which brings about transformation. When the mind is no longer resisting, no longer avoiding, no longer discarding or blaming what *is* but is simply passively aware, then in that passivity of the mind you will find, if you really go into the problem, that there comes a transformation.

Revolution is only possible now, not in the future;

regeneration is to-day, not to-morrow. If you will experiment with what I have been saying, you will find that there is immediate regeneration, a newness, a quality of freshness; because the mind is always still when it is interested, when it desires or has the intention to understand. The difficulty with most of us is that we have not the intention to understand, because we are afraid that, if we understood, it might bring about a revolutionary action in our life and therefore we resist. It is the defence mechanism that is at work when we use time or an ideal as a means of gradual transformation.

Thus regeneration is only possible in the present, not in the future, not to-morrow. A man who relies on time as a means through which he can gain happiness or realize truth or God is merely deceiving himself; he is living in ignorance and therefore in conflict. A man who sees that time is not the way out of our difficulty and who is therefore free from the false, such a man naturally has the intention to understand; therefore his mind is quiet spontaneously, without compulsion, without practice. When the mind is still, tranquil, not seeking any answer or any solution, neither resisting nor avoiding—it is only then that there can be a regeneration, because then the mind is capable of perceiving what is true; and it is truth that liberates, not your effort to be free.

CHAPTER XXI

POWER AND REALIZATION

WE SEE THAT A radical change is necessary in society, in ourselves, in our individual and group relationships; how is it to be brought about? If change is through conformity to a pattern projected by the mind, through a reasonable, well studied plan, then it is still within the field of the mind; therefore whatever the mind calculates becomes the end, the vision for which we are willing to sacrifice ourselves and others. If you maintain that, then it follows that we as human beings are merely the creation of the mind, which implies conformity, compulsion, brutality, dictatorships, concentration camps—the whole business. When we worship the mind, all that is implied, is it not? If I realize this, if I see the futility of discipline, of control, if I see that the various forms of suppression only strengthen the 'me' and the 'mine', then what am I to do?

To consider this problem fully we must go into the question of what is consciousness. I wonder if you have thought about it for yourself or have merely quoted what authorities have said about consciousness? I do not know how you have understood from your own experience, from your own study of yourself, what this consciousness implies—not only the consciousness of everyday activity and pursuits but the consciousness that is hidden, deeper, richer and much more difficult to get at. If we are to discuss this question of a fundamental change in ourselves and therefore in the world, and in this change to awaken a certain vision, an enthusiasm, a zeal, a faith, a hope, a certainty which will give us the necessary impetus for action—if we are to understand that, isn't it necessary to go into this question of consciousness?

We can see what we mean by consciousness at the superficial level of the mind. Obviously it is the thinking process, thought. Thought is the result of memory, verbalization; it is the naming, recording and storing up of certain experiences, so as to be able to communicate; at this level there are also various inhibitions, controls, sanctions, disciplines. With all this we are quite familiar. When we go a little deeper there are all the accumulations of the race, the hidden motives, the collective and personal ambitions, prejudices, which are the result of perception, contact and desire. This total consciousness, the hidden as well as the open, is centred round the idea of the 'me', the self.

When we discuss how to bring about a change we generally mean a change at the superficial level, do we not? Through determination, conclusions, beliefs, controls, inhibitions, we struggle to reach a superficial end which we want, which we crave for, and we hope to arrive at that with the help of the unconscious, of the deeper layers of the mind; therefore we think it is necessary to uncover the depths of oneself. But there is everlasting conflict between the superficial levels and the so-called deeper levels—all psychologists, all those who have pursued self-knowledge are fully aware of that.

Will this inner conflict bring about a change? Is that not the most fundamental and important question in our daily life: how to bring about a radical change in ourselves? Will mere alteration at the superficial level bring it about? Will understanding the different layers of consciousness, of the 'me', uncovering the past, the various personal experiences from childhood up to now, examining in myself the collective experiences of my father, my mother, my ancestors, my race, the conditioning of the particular society in which I live—will the analysis of all that bring about a change which is not merely an adjustment?

I feel, and surely you also must feel, that a fundamental change in one's life is essential—a change which is not a mere reaction, which is not the outcome of the stress and strain of environmental demands. How is one to bring about such a change? My consciousness is the sum total of human experience, plus my particular contact with the present; can that bring about a change? Will the study of my own consciousness, of my activities, will the awareness of my thoughts and feelings, stilling the mind in order to observe without condemnation, will that process bring about a change? Can there be change through belief, through identification with a projected image called the ideal? Does not all this imply a certain conflict between what I am and what I should be? Will conflict bring about fundamental change? I am in constant battle within myself and with society, am I not? There is a ceaseless conflict going on between what I am and what I want to be; will this conflict, this struggle bring about a change? I see a change *is* essential; can I bring it about by examining the whole process of my consciousness, by struggling, by disciplining, by practising various forms of repression? I feel such a process cannot bring about a radical change. Of that one must be *completely* sure. And if that process cannot bring about a fundamental transformation, a deep inward revolution, then what will?

How are you to bring about true revolution? What is the power, the creative energy that brings about that revolution and how is it to be released? You have tried disciplines, you have tried the pursuit of ideals and various speculative theories: that you are God, and that if you can realize that Godhood or experience the *Atman*, the highest, or what you will, then that very realization will bring about a fundamental change. Will it? First you postulate that there is a reality of which you are a part and build up round it various theories, speculations, beliefs, doctrines, assumptions, according to which you live; by thinking and acting according to that pattern you hope to bring about a fundamental change. Will you?

Suppose you assume, as most so-called religious people do, that there is in you, fundamentally, deeply, the essence of

138

reality; and that if, through cultivating virtue, through various forms of discipline, control, suppression, denial, sacrifice, you can get into touch with that reality, then the required transformation will be brought about. Is not this assumption still part of thought? Is it not the outcome of a conditioned mind, a mind that has been brought up to think in a particular way, according to certain patterns? Having created the image, the idea, the theory, the belief, the hope, you then look to your creation to bring about this radical change.

One must first see the extraordinarily subtle activities of the 'me', of the mind, one must become aware of the ideas, beliefs, speculations and put them all aside, for they are really deceptions, are they not? Others may have experienced reality; but if *you* have not experienced it, what is the good of speculating about it or imagining that you are in essence something real, immortal, godly? That is still within the field of thought and anything that springs from thought is conditioned, is of time, of memory; therefore it is not real. If one actually realizes that—not speculatively, not imaginatively or foolishly, but actually sees the truth that any activity of the mind in its speculative search, in its philosophical groping, any assumption, any imagination or hope is only self-deception—then what is the power, the creative energy that brings about this fundamental transformation?

Perhaps, in coming to this point, we have used the conscious mind; we have followed the argument, we have opposed or accepted it, we have seen it clearly or dimly. To go further and experience more deeply requires a mind that is quiet and alert to find out, does it not? It is no longer pursuing ideas because, if you pursue an idea, there is the thinker following what is being said and so you immediately create duality. If you want to go further into this matter of fundamental change, is it not necessary for the active mind to be quiet? Surely it is only when the mind is quiet that it can understand the enormous difficulty, the complex implications of the thinker and the thought as two separate processes, the experiencer and the experienced, the observer and the observed. Revolution, this psychological, creative revolution in which the 'me' is not, comes only when the thinker and the thought are one, when there is no duality such as the thinker controlling thought; and I suggest it is this experience alone that releases the creative energy which in turn brings about a fundamental revolution, the breaking up of the psychological 'me'.

We know the way of power—power through domination, power through discipline, power through compulsion. Through political power we hope to change fundamentally; but such power only breeds further darkness, disintegration, evil, the strengthening of the 'me'. We are familiar with the various forms of acquisition, both individually and as groups, but we have never tried the way of love, and we don't even know what it means. Love is not possible so long as there is the thinker, the centre of the 'me'. Realizing all this, what is one to do?

Surely the only thing which can bring about a fundamental change, a creative, psychological release, is everyday watchfulness, being aware from moment to moment of our motives, the conscious as well as the unconscious. When we realize that disciplines, beliefs, ideals only strengthen the 'me' and are therefore utterly futile—when we are aware of that from day to day, see the truth of it, do we not come to the central point when the thinker is constantly separating himself from his thought, from his observations, from his experiences? So long as the thinker exists apart from his thought, which he is trying to dominate, there can be no fundamental transformation. So long as the 'me' is the observer, the one who gathers experience, strengthens himself through experience, there can be no radical change, no creative release. That creative release comes only when the thinker *is* the thought—but the gap cannot be bridged by any effort. When the mind realizes that any speculation, any verbalization, any form of thought only gives strength to the 'me', when it sees that as long as the thinker exists apart

140

from thought there must be limitation, the conflict of duality—when the mind realizes that, then it is watchful, everlastingly aware of how it is separating itself from experience, asserting itself, seeking power. In that awareness, if the mind pursues it ever more deeply and extensively without seeking an end, a goal, there comes a state in which the thinker and the thought are one. In that state there is no effort, there is no becoming, there is no desire to change; in that state the 'me' is not, for there is a transformation which is not of the mind.

It is only when the mind is empty that there is a possibility of creation; but I do not mean this superficial emptiness which most of us have. Most of us are superficially empty, and it shows itself through the desire for distraction. We want to be amused, so we turn to books, to the radio, we run to lectures, to authorities; the mind is everlastingly filling itself. I am not talking of that emptiness which is thoughtlessness. On the contrary, I am talking of the emptiness which comes through extraordinary thoughtfulness, when the mind sees its own power of creating illusion and goes beyond.

Creative emptiness is not possible so long as there is the thinker who is waiting, watching, observing in order to gather experience, in order to strengthen himself. Can the mind ever be empty of all symbols, of all words with their sensations, so that there is no experiencer who is accumulating? Is it possible for the mind to put aside *completely* all the reasonings, the experiences, the impositions, authorities, so that it is in a state of emptiness? You will not be able to answer this question, naturally; it is an impossible question for you to answer, because you do not know, you have never tried. But, if I may suggest, listen to it, let the question be put to you, let the seed be sown; and it will bear fruit if you *really* listen to it, if you do not resist it.

It is only the new that can transform, not the old. If you pursue the pattern of the old, any change is a modified continuity of the old; there is nothing new in that, there is nothing creative. The creative can come into being only when the mind itself is new; and the mind can renew itself only when it is capable of seeing all its own activities, not only at the superficial level, but deep down. When the mind sees its own activities, is aware of its own desires, demands, urges, pursuits, the creation of its own authorities, fears; when it sees in itself the resistance created by discipline, by control, and the hope which projects beliefs, ideals—when the mind sees through, is aware of this whole process, can it put aside all these things and be new, creatively empty? You will find out whether it can or cannot only if you experiment without having an opinion about it, without wanting to experience that creative state. If you *want* to experience it, you will; but what you experience is not creative emptiness, it is only a projection of desire. If you desire to experience the new, you are merely indulging in illusion; but if you begin to observe, to be aware of your own activities from day to day, from moment to moment, watching the whole process of yourself as in a mirror, then, as you go deeper and deeper, you will come to the ultimate question of this emptiness in which alone there can be the new.

Truth, God or what you will, is not something to be experienced, for the experiencer is the result of time, the result of memory, of the past, and so long as there is the experiencer there cannot be reality. There is reality only when the mind is completely free from the analyser, from the experiencer and the experienced. Then you will find the answer, then you will see that the change comes without your asking, that the state of creative emptiness is not a thing to be cultivated—it is there, it comes darkly, without any invitation; only in that state is there a possibility of renewal, newness, revolution.

QUESTIONS AND ANSWERS

1. ON THE PRESENT CRISIS

Question: You say the present crisis is without precedent. In what way is it exceptional?

Krishnamurti: Obviously the present crisis throughout the world is exceptional, without precedent. There have been crises of varying types at different periods throughout history, social, national, political. Crises come and go; economic recessions, depressions, come, get modified, and continue in a different form. We know that; we are familiar with that process. Surely the present crisis is different, is it not? It is different first because we are dealing not with money nor with tangible things but with ideas. The crisis is exceptional because it is in the field of ideation. We are quarrelling with ideas, we are justifying murder; everywhere in the world we are justifying murder as a means to a righteous end, which in itself is unprecedented. Before, evil was recognized to be evil, murder was recognized to be murder, but now murder is a means to achieve a noble result. Murder, whether of one person or of a group of people, is justified, because the murderer, or the group that the murderer represents, justifies it as a means of achieving a result which will be beneficial to man. That is we sacrifice the present for the future—and it does not matter what means we employ as long as our declared purpose is to produce a result which we say will be beneficial to man. Therefore, the implication is that a wrong means will produce a right end and you justify the wrong means through ideation. In the various crises that have taken place before, the issue has been the exploitation of things or of man; it is now the exploitation of ideas, which is much more pernicious, much more dangerous, because the exploitation of ideas is so devastating, so destructive. We have learned now the power of propaganda and that is one of the greatest calamities that can happen: to use ideas as a means to transform man. That is what is happening in the world to-day. Man is not important— systems, ideas, have become important. Man no longer has any significance. We can destroy millions of men as long as we produce a result and the result is justified by ideas. We have a magnificent structure of ideas to justify evil and surely that is unprecedented. Evil is evil; it cannot bring about good. War is not a means to peace. War may bring about secondary benefits, like more efficient aeroplanes, but it will not bring peace to man. War is intellectually justified as a means of bringing peace; when the intellect has the upper hand in human life, it brings about an unprecedented crisis.

There are other causes also which indicate an un- precedented crisis. One of them is the extraordinary im- portance man is giving to sensate values, to property, to name, to caste and country, to the particular label you wear. You are either a Mohammedan or a Hindu, a Christian or a Communist. Name and property, caste and country, have become predominantly important, which means that man is caught in sensate value, the value of things, whether made by the mind or by the hand. Things made by the hand or by the mind have become so important that we are killing, destroying, butchering, liquidating each other because of them. We are nearing the edge of a precipice; every action is leading us there, every political, every economic action is bringing us inevitably to the precipice, dragging us into this chaotic, confusing abyss. Therefore the crisis is un- precedented and it demands unprecedented action. To leave, to step out of that crisis, needs a timeless action, an action which is not based on idea, on system, because any action which is based on a system, on an idea, will inevitably lead to frustration. Such action merely brings us back to the abyss by a different route. As the crisis is unprecedented there must also be unprecedented action, which means that the regener- ation of the individual must be instantaneous, not a process of time. It must take place now, not to-morrow; for to-morrow is a process of disintegration. If I think of transforming myself to-morrow I invite confusion, I am still within the field of destruction. Is it possible to change now? Is it possible completely to transform oneself in the immediate, in the now? I say it is.

The point is that as the crisis is of an exceptional character to meet it there must be revolution in thinking; and this revolution cannot take place through another, through any book, through any organization. It must come through us, through each one of us. Only then can we create a new society, a new structure away from this horror, away from these extraordinarily destructive forces that are being accumulated, piled up; and that transformation comes into being only when you as an individual begin to be aware of yourself in every thought, action and feeling.

2. ON NATIONALISM

Question: What is it that comes when nationalism goes?

Krishnamurti: Obviously, intelligence. But I am afraid that is not the implication in this question. The implication is, what can be substituted for nationalism? Any substitution is an act which does not bring intelligence. If I leave one religion and join another, or leave one political party and later on join something else, this constant substitution indicates a state in which there is no intelligence.

How does nationalism go? Only by our understanding its full implications, by examining it, by being aware of its significance in outward and inward action. Outwardly it brings about divisions between people, classifications, wars and destruction, which is obvious to anyone who is observant. Inwardly, psychologically, this identification with the greater, with the country, with an idea, is obviously a form of self-expansion. Living in a little village or a big town or whatever it may be, I am nobody; but if I identify myself with the larger, with the country, if I call myself a Hindu, it flatters my vanity, it gives me gratification, prestige, a sense of well-being; and that identification with the larger, which is a psychological necessity for those who feel that self-expansion is essential, also creates conflict, strife, between people. Thus nationalism not only creates outward conflict but inward frustrations; when one understands nationalism, the whole process of nationalism, it falls away. The understanding of nationalism comes through intelligence, by carefully observing, by probing into the whole process of nationalism, patriotism. Out of that examination comes intelligence and then there is no substitution of something else for nationalism. The moment you substitute religion for nationalism, religion becomes another means of self-expansion, another source of psychological anxiety, a means of feeding oneself through a belief. Therefore any form of substitution, however noble, is a form of ignorance. It is like a man substituting chewing-gum or betel-nut or whatever it is for smoking, whereas if one really understands the whole problem of smoking, of habits, sensations, psychological demands and all the rest of it, then smoking drops away. You can understand only when there is a development of intelligence, when intelligence is functioning, and intelligence is not functioning when there is substitution. Substitution is merely a form of self-bribery, to tempt you not to do this but to do that. Nationalism, with its poison, with its misery and world strife, can disappear only when there is intelligence, and intelligence does not come merely by passing examinations and studying books. Intelligence comes into being when we understand problems as they arise. When there is understanding of the problem at its different levels, not only of the outward part but of its inward, psychological implications, then, in that process, intelligence comes into being. So when there is intelligence there is no substitution; and when there is intelligence, then nationalism, patriotism, which is a form of stupidity, disappears.

3. WHY SPIRITUAL TEACHERS?

Question: You say that *gurus* are unnecessary, but how can I find truth without the wise help and guidance which only a *guru* can give?

Krishnamurti: The question is whether a *guru* is necessary or not. Can truth be found through another? Some say it can and some say it cannot. We want to know the truth of this, not my opinion as against the opinion of another. I have no *opinion* in this matter. Either it is so or it is not. Whether it is essential that you should or should not have a *guru* is not a question of opinion. The truth of the matter is not dependent on opinion, however profound, erudite, popular, universal. The truth of the matter is to be found out, in fact.

First of all, why do we want a *guru*? We say we need a *guru* because we are confused and the *guru* is helpful; he will point out what truth is, he will help us to understand, he knows much more about life than we do, he will act as a father, as a teacher to instruct us in life; he has vast experience and we have but little; he will help us through his greater experience and so on and on. That is, basically, you go to a teacher because you are confused. If you were clear, you would not go near a *guru*. Obviously if you were profoundly happy, if there were no problems, if you understood life completely, you would not go to any *guru*. I hope you see the significance of this. Because you are confused, you seek out a teacher. You go to him to give you a way of life, to clarify your own confusion, to find truth. You choose your *guru* because you are confused and you hope he will give you what you ask. That is you choose a *guru* who will satisfy your demand; you choose according to the gratification he will give you and your choice is dependent on your gratification.

150

You do not choose a *guru* who says, "Depend on yourself"; you choose him according to your prejudices. So since you choose your *guru* according to the gratification he gives you, you are not seeking truth but a way out of confusion; and the way out of confusion is mistakenly called truth.

Let us examine first this idea that a *guru* can clear up our confusion. Can anyone clear up our confusion?—confusion being the product of our responses. We have created it. Do you think someone *else* has created it—this misery, this battle at all levels of existence, within and without? It is the result of our own lack of knowledge of ourselves. It is because we do not understand ourselves, our conflicts, our responses, our miseries, that we go to a *guru* whom we think will help us to be free of that confusion. We can understand ourselves only in relationship to the present; and that relationship itself is the *guru*, not someone outside. If I do not understand that relationship, whatever a *guru* may say is useless, because if I do not understand relationship, my relationship to property, to people, to ideas, who can resolve the conflict within me? To resolve that conflict, I must understand it myself, which means I must be aware of myself in relationship. To be aware, no *guru* is necessary. If I do not know myself, of what use is a *guru*? As a political leader is chosen by those who are in confusion and whose choice therefore is also confused, so I choose a *guru*. I can choose him only according to my confusion; hence he, like the political leader, is confused.

What is important is not who is right—whether I am right or whether those are right who say a *guru* is necessary; to find out why you need a *guru* is important. *Gurus* exist for exploitation of various kinds, but that is irrelevant. It gives you satisfaction if someone tells you how you are progressing, but to find out why you *need* a *guru*—there lies the key. Another can point out the way but *you* have to do all the work, even if you have a *guru*. Because you do not want to face that, you shift the responsibility to the *guru*. The *guru* becomes useless when there is a particle of self-knowledge. No *guru*, no book or scripture, can give you self-knowledge:

it comes when you are aware of yourself in relationship. To be, is to be related; not to understand relationship is misery, strife. Not to be aware of your relationship to property is one of the causes of confusion. If you do not know your right relationship to property there is bound to be conflict, which increases the conflict in society. If you do not understand the relationship between yourself and your wife, between yourself and your child, how can another resolve the conflict arising out of that relationship? Similarly with ideas, beliefs and so on. Being confused in your relationship with people, with property, with ideas, you seek a *guru*. If he is a real *guru*, he will tell you to understand yourself. *You* are the source of all misunderstanding and confusion; and you can resolve that conflict only when you understand yourself in relationship.

You cannot find truth through anybody else. How can you? Truth is not something static; it has no fixed abode; it is not an end, a goal. On the contrary, it is living, dynamic, alert, alive. How can it be an end? If truth is a fixed point it is no longer truth; it is then a mere opinion. Truth is the unknown, and a mind that is seeking truth will never find it, for mind is made up of the known, it is the result of the past, the outcome of time—which you can observe for yourself. Mind is the instrument of the known, hence it cannot find the unknown; it can only move from the known to the known. When the mind seeks truth, the truth it has read about in books, that 'truth' is self-projected; for then the mind is merely in pursuit of the known, a more satisfactory known than the previous one. When the mind *seeks* truth, it is seeking its own self-projection, not truth. After all, an ideal is self-projected; it is fictitious, unreal. What is real is what *is*, not the opposite. But a mind that is seeking reality, seeking God, is seeking the known. When you think of God, your God is the projection of your own thought, the result of social influences. You can think only of the known; you cannot think of the unknown, you cannot concentrate on truth. The moment you think of the unknown, it is merely the self-projected known. God or truth cannot be thought about. If you think about it, it is not truth. Truth cannot be sought: it comes to you. You can go only after what is known. When the mind is not tortured by the known, by the effects of the known, then only can truth reveal itself. Truth is in every leaf, in every tear; it is to be known from moment to moment. No one can lead you to truth; and if anyone leads you, it can only be to the known.

Truth can only come to the mind that is empty of the known. It comes in a state in which the known is absent, not functioning. The mind is the warehouse of the known, the residue of the known; for the mind to be in that state in which the unknown comes into being, it must be aware of itself, of its previous experiences, the conscious as well as the unconscious, of its responses, reactions, and structure. When there is complete self-knowledge, then there is the ending of the known, then the mind is completely empty of the known. It is only then that truth can come to you uninvited. Truth does not belong to you or to me. You cannot worship it. The moment it is known, it is unreal. The symbol is not real, the image is not real; but when there is the understanding of self, the cessation of self, then eternity comes into being.

4. ON KNOWLEDGE

Question: I gather definitely from you that learning and knowledge are impediments. To *what* are they impediments?

Krishnamurti: Obviously knowledge and learning are an impediment to the understanding of the new, the timeless, the eternal. Developing a perfect technique does not make you creative. You may know how to paint marvellously, you may have the technique; but you may not be a creative painter. You may know how to write poems, technically most perfect; but you may not be a poet. To be a poet implies, does it not?, being capable of receiving the new; to be sensitive enough to respond to something new, fresh. With most of us knowledge or learning has become an addiction and we think that through *knowing* we shall be creative. A mind that is crowded, encased in facts, in knowledge—is it capable of receiving something new, sudden, spontaneous? If your mind is crowded with the known, is there any space in it to receive something that is of the unknown? Surely knowledge is always of the known; and with the known we are trying to understand the unknown, something which is beyond measure.

Take, for example, a very ordinary thing that happens to most of us: those who are religious—whatever that word may mean for the moment—try to imagine what God is or try to think about what God is. They have read innumerable books, they have read about the experiences of the various saints, the Masters, the *Mahatmas* and all the rest, and they try to imagine or try to feel what the experience of another is; that is with the known you try to approach the unknown. Can you do it? Can you think of something that is not knowable? You can only think of something that

154

you know. But there is this extraordinary perversion taking place in the world at the present time: we think we shall understand if we have more information, more books, more facts, more printed matter.

To be aware of something that is not the projection of the known, there must be the elimination, through the understanding, of the process of the known. Why is it that the mind clings always to the known? Is it not because the mind is constantly seeking certainty, security? Its very nature is fixed in the known, in time; how can such a mind, whose very foundation is based on the past, on time, experience the timeless? It may conceive, formulate, picture the unknown, but that is all absurd. The unknown can come into being only when the known is understood, dissolved, put aside. That is extremely difficult, because the moment you have an experience of anything, the mind translates it into the terms of the known and reduces it to the past. I do not know if you have noticed that every experience is immediately translated into the known, given a name, tabulated and recorded. So the movement of the known is knowledge, and obviously such knowledge, learning, *is* a hindrance.

Suppose you had never read a book, religious or psychological, and you had to find the meaning, the significance of life. How would you set about it? Suppose there were no Masters, no religious organizations, no Buddha, no Christ, and you had to begin from the beginning. How would you set about it? First, you would have to understand your process of thinking, would you not?—and not project yourself, your thoughts, into the future and create a God which pleases you; that would be too childish. So first you would have to understand the process of your thinking. That is the only way to discover anything new, is it not?

When we say that learning or knowledge is an impediment, a hindrance, we are not including technical knowledge—how to drive a car, how to run machinery—or the efficiency which such knowledge brings. We have in mind quite a different thing: that sense of creative happiness which no amount of knowledge or learning will bring. To be creative in the truest sense of that word is to be free of the past from moment to moment, because it is the past that is continually shadowing the present. Merely to cling to information, to the experiences of others, to what someone has said, however great, and try to approximate your action to that—all that is knowledge, is it not? But to discover anything new you must start on your own; you must start on a journey completely denuded, especially of knowledge, because it is very easy, through knowledge and belief, to have experiences; but those experiences are merely the products of self-projection and therefore utterly unreal, false. If you are to discover for yourself what is the new, it is no good carrying the burden of the old, especially knowledge—the knowledge of another, however great. You use knowledge as a means of self-protection, security, and you want to be quite sure that you have the same experiences as the Buddha or the Christ or X. But a man who is protecting himself constantly through knowledge is obviously not a truth-seeker.

For the discovery of truth there is no path. You must enter the uncharted sea—which is not depressing, which is not being adventurous. When you want to find something new, when you are experimenting with anything, your mind has to be very quiet, has it not? If your mind is crowded, filled with facts, knowledge, they act as an impediment to the new; the difficulty is for most of us that the mind has become so important, so predominantly significant, that it interferes constantly with anything that may be new, with anything that may exist simultaneously with the known. Thus knowledge and learning are impediments for those who would seek, for those who would try to understand that which is timeless.

5. ON DISCIPLINE

Question: All religions have insisted on some kind of self-discipline to moderate the instincts of the brute in man. Through self-discipline the saints and mystics have asserted that they have attained godhood. Now you seem to imply that such disciplines are a hindrance to the realization of God. I am confused. Who is right in this matter?

Krishnamurti: It is not a question of who is right in this matter. What is important is to find out the truth of the matter for ourselves—not according to a particular saint or to a person who comes from India or from some other place, the more exotic the better.

You are caught between these two: someone says discipline, another says no discipline. Generally what happens is that you choose what is more convenient, what is more satisfying: you like the man, his looks, his personal idiosyncrasies, his personal favouritism and all the rest of it. Putting all that aside, let us examine this question directly and find out the truth of the matter for ourselves. In this question a great deal is implied and we have to approach it very cautiously and tentatively.

Most of us want someone in authority to tell us what to do. We look for a direction in conduct, because our instinct is to be safe, not to suffer more. Someone is said to have realized happiness, bliss or what you will and we hope that he will tell us what to do to arrive there. That is what we want: we want that same happiness, that same inward quietness, joy; and in this mad world of confusion we want someone to tell us what to do. That is really the basic instinct with most of us and, according to that instinct, we

157

pattern our action. Is God, is that highest thing, unnameable and not to be measured by words—is that come by through discipline, through following a particular pattern of action? We want to arrive at a particular goal, particular end, and we think that by practice, by discipline, by suppressing or releasing, sublimating or substituting, we shall be able to find that which we are seeking.

What is implied in discipline? Why do we discipline our-selves, if we do? Can discipline and intelligence go together? Most people feel that we must, through some kind of dis-cipline, subjugate or control the brute, the ugly thing in us. Is that brute, that ugly thing, controllable through dis-cipline? What do we mean by discipline? A course of action which promises a reward, a course of action which, if pur-sued, will give us what we want—it may be positive or negative; a pattern of conduct which, if practised diligently, sedulously, very, very ardently, will give me in the end what I want. It may be painful but I am willing to go through it to get that. The self, which is aggressive, selfish, hypocritical, anxious, fearful—you know, all of it—that self, which is the cause of the brute in us, we want to transform, subjugate, destroy. How is this to be done? Is it to be done through discipline, or through an intelligent understanding of the past of the self, what the self is, how it comes into being, and so on? Shall we destroy the brute in man through com-pulsion or through intelligence? Is intelligence a matter of discipline? Let us for the time being forget what the saints and all the rest of the people have said; let us go into the matter for ourselves, as though we were for the first time looking at this problem; then we may have something creative at the end of it, not just quotations of what other people have said, which is all so vain and useless.

We first say that in us there is conflict, the black against the white, greed against non-greed and so on. I am greedy, which creates pain; to be rid of that greed, I must discipline myself. That is I must resist any form of conflict which gives

158

me pain, which in this case I call greed. I then say it is anti-social, it is unethical, it is not saintly and so on and so on—the various social-religious reasons we give for resisting it. Is greed destroyed or put away from us through compulsion? First, let us examine the process involved in suppression, in compulsion, in putting it away, resisting. What happens when you do that, when you resist greed? What is the thing that is resisting greed? That is the first question, isn't it? Why do you resist greed and who is the entity that says, "I must be free of greed"? The entity that says, "I must be free" is also greed, is he not? Up to now, greed has paid him, but now it is painful; therefore he says, "I must get rid of it". The motive to get rid of it is still a process of greed, because he is wanting to be something which he is not. Non-greed is now profitable, so I am pursuing non-greed; but the motive, the intention, is still to *be* something, to be non-greedy—which is still greed, surely; which is again a negative form of the emphasis on the 'me'.

We find that being greedy is painful, for various reasons which are obvious. So long as we enjoy it, so long as it pays us to be greedy, there is no problem. Society encourages us in different ways to be greedy; so do religions encourage us in different ways. So long as it is profitable, so long as it is not painful, we pursue it but the moment it becomes painful we want to resist it. That resistance is what we call discipline against greed; but are we free from greed through resistance, through sublimation, through suppression? Any act on the part of the 'me' who wants to be free from greed is still greed. Therefore any action, any response on my part with regard to greed, is obviously not the solution.

First of all there must be a quiet mind, an undisturbed mind, to understand anything, especially something which I do not know, something which my mind cannot fathom—which, this questioner says, is God. To understand anything, any intricate problem—of life or relationship, in fact any problem—there must be a certain quiet depth to the mind.

Is that quiet depth come by through any form of compulsion? The superficial mind may compel itself, make itself quiet; but surely such quietness is the quietness of decay, death. It is not capable of adaptability, pliability, sensitivity. So resistance is not the way.

Now to see that requires intelligence, doesn't it? To see that the mind is made dull by compulsion is already the beginning of intelligence, isn't it?—to see that discipline is merely conformity to a pattern of action through fear. That is what is implied in disciplining ourselves: we are afraid of not getting what we want. What happens when you discipline the mind, when you discipline your being? It becomes very hard, doesn't it?; unpliable, not quick, not adjustable. Don't you know people who have disciplined themselves —if there are such people? The result is obviously a process of decay. There is an inward conflict which is put away, hidden away; but it is there, burning.

Thus we see that discipline, which is resistance, merely creates a habit and habit obviously cannot be productive of intelligence: habit never is, practice never is. You may become very clever with your fingers by practising the piano all day, making something with your hands; but intelligence is demanded to direct the hands and we are now inquiring into that intelligence.

You see somebody whom you consider happy or as having realized, and he does certain things; you, wanting that happiness, imitate him. This imitation is called discipline, isn't it? We imitate in order to receive what another has; we copy in order to be happy, which you think he is. Is happiness found through discipline? By practising a certain rule, by practising a certain discipline, a mode of conduct, are you ever free? Surely there must be freedom for discovery, must there not? If you would discover anything, you must be free inwardly, which is obvious. Are you free by shaping your mind in a particular way which you call discipline? Obviously you are not. You are merely a repetitive machine, resisting according to a certain conclusion, according to a certain mode of conduct. Freedom cannot come through discipline. Freedom can only come into being with intelligence; and that intelligence is awakened, or you have that intelligence, the moment you see that any form of compulsion denies freedom, inwardly or outwardly.

The first requirement, not as a discipline, is obviously freedom; only virtue gives that freedom. Greed is confusion; anger is confusion; bitterness is confusion. When you *see* that, obviously you are free of them; you do not resist them but you see that only in freedom can you discover and that any form of compulsion is not freedom, and therefore there is no discovery. What virtue does is to give you freedom. The unvirtuous person is a confused person; in confusion, how can you discover anything? How can you? Thus virtue is not the end-product of a discipline, but virtue is freedom and freedom cannot come through any action which is not virtuous, which is not true in itself. Our difficulty is that most of us have read so much, most of us have superficially followed so many disciplines—getting up every morning at a certain hour, sitting in a certain posture, trying to hold our minds in a certain way—you know, practise, practise, discipline, because you have been told that if you do these things for a number of years you will have God at the end of it. I may put it crudely, but that is the basis of our thinking. Surely God doesn't come so easily as all that? God is not a mere marketable thing: I do this and you give me that.

Most of us are so conditioned by external influences, by religious doctrines, beliefs, and by our own inward demand to arrive at something, to gain something, that it is very difficult for us to think of this problem anew without thinking in terms of discipline. First we must see very clearly the implications of discipline, how it narrows down the mind, limits the mind, compels the mind to a particular action, through our desire, through influence and all the rest of it; a conditioned mind, however 'virtuous' that conditioning, cannot possibly be free and therefore cannot understand reality. God, reality or what you will—the name doesn't matter—can come into being only when there is freedom, and there is no freedom where there is compulsion, positive or negative, through fear. There is no freedom if you are seeking an end, for you are tied to that end. You may be free from the past but the future holds you, and that is not freedom. It is only in freedom that one can discover anything: a new idea, a new feeling, a new perception. Any form of discipline which is based on compulsion denies that freedom, whether political or religious; and since discipline, which is conformity to an action with an end in view, is binding, the mind can never be free. It can function only within that groove, like a gramophone record.

Thus, through practice, through habit, through cultivation of a pattern, the mind only achieves what it has in view. Therefore it is not free; therefore it cannot realize that which is immeasurable. To be aware of that whole process—why you are constantly disciplining yourself to public opinion; to certain saints; the whole business of conforming to opinion, whether of a saint or of a neighbour, it is all the same—to be aware of this whole conformity through practice, through subtle ways of submitting yourself, of denying, asserting, suppressing, sublimating, all implying conformity to a pattern: this is already the beginning of freedom, from which there is a virtue. Virtue surely is not the cultivation of a particular idea. Non-greed, for instance, if pursued as an end is no longer virtue, is it? That is if you are conscious that you are non-greedy, are you virtuous? That is what we are doing through discipline.

Discipline, conformity, practice, only give emphasis to self-consciousness as *being* something. The mind practises non-greed and therefore it is not free from its own consciousness as being non-greedy; therefore, it is not really non-greedy. It has merely taken on a new cloak which it calls non-greed. We can see the total process of all this: the motivation, the desire for an end, the conformity to a pattern, the desire to be secure in pursuing a pattern—all this is merely the moving from the known to the known, always within the limits of the mind's own self-enclosing process. To see all this, to be aware of it, is the beginning of intelligence, and intelligence is neither virtuous nor non-virtuous, it cannot be fitted into a pattern as virtue or non-virtue. Intelligence brings freedom, which is not licentiousness, not disorder. Without this intelligence there can be no virtue; virtue gives freedom and in freedom there comes into being reality. If you see the whole process totally, in its entirety, then you will find there is no conflict. It is because we are in conflict and because we want to escape from that conflict that we resort to various forms of disciplines, denials and adjustments. When we see what is the process of conflict there is no question of discipline, because then we understand from moment to moment the ways of conflict. That requires great alertness, watching yourself all the time; the curious part of it is that although you may not be watchful all the time there is a recording process going on inwardly, once the intention is there—the sensitivity, the inner sensitivity, is taking the picture all the time, so that the inner will project that picture the moment you are quiet.

Therefore, it is not a question of discipline. Sensitivity can never come into being through compulsion. You may compel a child to do something, put him in a corner, and he may be quiet; but inwardly he is probably seething, looking out of the window, doing something to get away. That is what we are still doing. So the question of discipline and of who is right and who is wrong can be solved only by yourself.

Also, you see, we are afraid to go wrong because we want to be a success. Fear is at the bottom of the desire to be disciplined, but the unknown cannot be caught in the net of discipline. On the contrary, the unknown must have freedom and not the pattern of your mind. That is why the tranquillity of the mind is essential. When the mind is conscious that it is tranquil, it is no longer tranquil; when the mind is conscious that it is non-greedy, free from greed, it recognizes itself in the new robe of non-greed but that is not tranquillity. That is why one must also understand the problem in this question of the person who controls and that which is controlled. They are not separate phenomena but a joint phenomenon: the controller and the controlled are one.

6. ON LONELINESS

Question: I am beginning to realize that I am very lonely. What am I to do?

Krishnamurti: The questioner wants to know why he feels loneliness? Do you know what loneliness means and are you aware of it? I doubt it very much, because we have smothered ourselves in activities, in books, in relationships, in ideas which really prevent us from being aware of loneliness. What do we mean by loneliness? It is a sense of being empty, of having nothing, of being extraordinarily uncertain, with no anchorage anywhere. It is not despair, nor hopelessness. but a sense of void, a sense of emptiness and a sense of frustration. I am sure we have all felt it, the happy and the unhappy, the very, very active and those who are addicted to knowledge. They all know this. It is the sense of real inexhaustible pain, a pain that cannot be covered up, though we do try to cover it up.

Let us approach this problem again to see what is actually taking place, to see what you do when you feel lonely. You try to escape from your feeling of loneliness, you try to get on with a book, you follow some leader, or you go to a cinema, or you become socially very, very active, or you go and worship and pray, or you paint, or you write a poem about loneliness. That is what is actually taking place. Becoming aware of loneliness, the pain of it, the extraordinary and fathomless fear of it, you seek an escape and that escape becomes more important and therefore your activities, your knowledge, your gods, your radios all become important, don't they? When you give importance to secondary values, they lead you to misery and chaos; the secondary values are inevitably the sensate values; and modern civilization based on these gives you this escape—escape through your job, your family, your name, your studies, through painting etc.; all our culture is based on that escape. Our civilization is founded on it and that is a fact.

Have you ever tried to be alone? When you do try, you will feel how extraordinarily difficult it is and how extraordinarily intelligent we must be to be alone, because the mind will not let us be alone. The mind becomes restless, it busies itself with escapes, so what are we doing? We are trying to fill this extraordinary void with the known. We discover how to be active, how to be social; we know how to study, how to turn on the radio. We are filling that thing which we do not know with the things we know. We try to fill that emptiness with various kinds of knowledge, relationship or things. Is that not so? That is our process, that is our existence. Now when you realize what you are doing, do you still think you can fill that void? You have tried every means of filling this void of loneliness. Have you succeeded in filling it? You have tried cinemas and you did not succeed and therefore you go after your *gurus* and your books or you become very active socially. Have you succeeded in filling it or have you merely covered it up? If you have merely covered it up, it is still there; therefore it will come back. If you are able to escape altogether then you are locked up in an asylum or you become very, very dull. That is what is happening in the world.

Can this emptiness, this void, be filled? If not, can we run away from it, escape from it? If we have experienced and found one escape to be of no value, are not all other escapes therefore of no value? It does not matter whether you fill the emptiness with this or with that. So-called meditation is also an escape. It does not matter much that you change your way of escape.

How then will you find what to do about this loneliness? You can only find what to do when you have stopped escaping. Is that not so? When you are willing to face what *is*—which means you must not turn on the radio, which means you must turn your back to civilization—then that loneliness comes to an end, because it is completely transformed. It is no longer loneliness. If you understand what *is* then what *is* is the real. Because the mind is continuously avoiding, escaping, refusing to see what *is*, it creates its own hindrances. Because we have so many hindrances that are preventing us from seeing, we do not understand what *is* and therefore we are getting away from reality; all these hindrances have been created by the mind in order not to see what *is*. To see what *is* not only requires a great deal of capacity and awareness of action but it also means turning your back on everything that you have built up, your bank account, your name and everything that we call civilization. When you see what *is*, you will find how loneliness is transformed.

7. ON SUFFERING

Question: What is the significance of pain and suffering?

Krishnamurti: When you suffer, when you have pain, what is the significance of it? Physical pain has one significance but probably we mean psychological pain and suffering, which has quite a different significance at different levels. What is the significance of suffering? Why do you want to find the *significance* of suffering? Not that it has no significance—we are going to find out. But why do you *want* to find it? Why do you want to find out why you suffer? When you put that question to yourself, "Why do I suffer?", and are looking for the cause of suffering, are you not escaping from suffering? When I seek the significance of suffering, am I not avoiding, evading it, running away from it? The fact is, I am suffering; but the moment I bring the mind to operate upon it and say, "Now, why?", I have already diluted the intensity of suffering. In other words, we want suffering to be diluted, alleviated, put away, explained away. Surely that doesn't give an understanding of suffering. If I am free from that desire to run away from it, then I begin to understand what is the *content* of suffering.

What is suffering? A disturbance, isn't it?, at different levels—at the physical and at the different levels of the subconscious. It is an acute form of disturbance which I don't like. My son is dead. I have built round him all my hopes—or round my daughter, my husband, what you will. I have enshrined him with all the things I wanted him to be and I have kept him as my companion—you know, all that sort of thing. Suddenly he is gone. So there is a disturbance, isn't there? That disturbance I call suffering.

If I don't like that suffering, then I say, "Why am I

suffering?", "I loved him so much", "He was this", "I had that". I try to escape in words, in labels, in beliefs, as most of us do. They act as a narcotic. If I do not do that, what happens? I am simply aware of suffering. I don't condemn it, I don't justify it—I am suffering. Then I can follow its movement, can't I? Then I can follow the whole content of what it means—'I follow' in the sense of trying to understand something.

What does it mean? What is it that is suffering? Not *why* there is suffering, not what is the *cause* of suffering, but what is actually happening? I do not know if you see the difference. Then I am simply aware of suffering, not as apart from me, not as an observer watching suffering—it is part of me, that is the whole of me is suffering. Then I am able to follow its movement, see where it leads. Surely if I do that it opens up, does it not? Then I see that I have laid emphasis on the 'me'—not on the person whom I love. He only acted to cover me from my misery, from my loneliness, from my misfortune. As *I* am not something, I hoped *he* would be that. That has gone; I am left, I am lost, I am lonely. Without him, I am nothing. So I cry. It is not that *he* is gone but that I am left. I am alone. To come to that point is very difficult, isn't it? It is difficult really to recognize it and not merely say, "I am alone and how am I to get rid of that loneliness?", which is another form of escape, but to be *conscious* of it, to *remain* with it, to see its movement. I am only taking this as an example. Gradually, if I allow it to unfold, to open up, I see that I am suffering because I am lost; I am being called to give my attention to something which I am not willing to look at; something is being forced upon me which I am reluctant to see and to understand. There are innumerable people to help me to escape— thousands of so-called religious people, with their beliefs and dogmas, hopes and fantasies—"it is *karma*, it is God's will"—you know, all giving me a way out. But if I can stay with it and not put it away from me, not try to circumscribe or deny it, then what happens? What is the state of my mind when it is thus following the movement of suffering?

Is suffering merely a word, or an actuality? If it is an actuality and not just a word, then the word has no meaning now, so there is merely the feeling of intense pain. With regard to what? With regard to an image, to an experience, to something which you have or have not. If you have it, you call it pleasure; if you haven't it is pain. Therefore pain, sorrow, is in relationship *to* something. Is that something merely a verbalization, or an actuality? That is when sorrow exists, it exists only in relationship to something. It cannot exist by itself—even as fear cannot exist by itself but only in relationship *to* something: to an individual, to an incident, to a feeling. Now, you are fully aware of the suffering. Is that suffering apart from you and therefore you are merely the observer who perceives the suffering, or is that suffering *you*?

When there is no *observer* who is suffering, is the suffering different from you? You *are* the suffering, are you not? You are not apart from the pain—you *are* the pain. What happens? There is no labelling, there is no giving it a name and thereby brushing it aside—you are merely that pain, that feeling, that sense of agony. When you are that, what happens? When you do not name it, when there is no fear with regard to it, is the centre related to it? If the centre is related to it, then it is afraid of it. Then it must act and do something about it. But if the centre *is* that, then what do you do? There is nothing to be done, is there? If you *are* that and you are not accepting it, not labelling it, not pushing it aside—if you *are* that thing, what happens? Do you say you suffer then? Surely, a fundamental transformation has taken place. Then there is no longer "I suffer", because there is no centre to suffer and the centre suffers because we have never examined what the centre is. We just live from word to word, from reaction to reaction. We never say, "Let me see what that thing is that suffers". You cannot see by enforcement, by discipline. You must look with interest, with spontaneous comprehension. Then

170

you will see that the thing we call suffering, pain, the thing that we avoid, and the discipline, have all gone. As long as I have no relationship to the thing as outside me, the problem is not; the moment I establish a relationship with it outside me, the problem is. As long as I treat suffering as something outside—I suffer because I lost my brother, because I have no money, because of this or that—I establish a relationship to it and that relationship is fictitious. But if I *am* that thing, if I see the fact, then the whole thing is transformed, it all has a different meaning. Then there is *full* attention, *integrated* attention and that which is completely regarded is understood and dissolved, and so there is no fear and therefore the word 'sorrow' is non-existent.

8. ON AWARENESS

Question: What is the difference between awareness and introspection? And who is aware in awareness?

Krishnamurti: Let us first examine what we mean by introspection. We mean by introspection looking within oneself, examining oneself. Why does one examine oneself? In order to improve, in order to change, in order to modify. You introspect in order to become something, otherwise you would not indulge in introspection. You would not examine yourself if there were not the desire to modify, change, to become something other than what you are. That is the obvious reason for introspection. I am angry and I introspect, examine myself, in order to get rid of anger or to modify or change anger. Where there is introspection, which is the desire to modify or change the responses, the reactions of the self, there is always an end in view; when that end is not achieved, there is moodiness, depression. Therefore introspection invariably goes with depression. I don't know if you have noticed that when you introspect, when you look into yourself in order to change yourself, there is always a wave of depression. There is always a moody wave which you have to battle against; you have to examine yourself again in order to overcome that mood and so on. Introspection is a process in which there is no release because it is a process of transforming what *is* into something which it is not. Obviously that is exactly what is taking place when we introspect, when we indulge in that peculiar action. In that action, there is always an accumulative process, the 'I' examining something in order to change it, so there is always a dualistic conflict and therefore a process

172

of frustration. There is never a release; and, realizing that frustration, there is depression.

Awareness is entirely different. Awareness is observation without condemnation. Awareness brings understanding, because there is no condemnation or identification but silent observation. If I want to understand something, I must observe, I must not criticize, I must not condemn, I must not pursue it as pleasure or avoid it as non-pleasure. There must merely be the silent observation of a fact. There is no end in view but awareness of everything as it arises. That observation and the understanding of that observation cease when there is condemnation, identification, or justification. Introspection is self-improvement and therefore introspection is self-centredness. Awareness is not self-improvement. On the contrary, it is the ending of the self, of the 'I', with all its peculiar idiosyncrasies, memories, demands and pursuits. In introspection there is identification and condemnation. In awareness there is no condemnation or identification; therefore there is no self-improvement. There is a vast difference between the two.

The man who wants to improve himself can never be aware, because improvement implies condemnation and the achievement of a result. Whereas in awareness there is observation without condemnation, without denial or acceptance. That awareness begins with outward things, being aware, being in contact with objects, with nature. First, there is awareness of things about one, being sensitive to objects, to nature, then to people, which means relationship; then there is awareness of ideas. This awareness, being sensitive to things, to nature, to people, to ideas, is not made up of separate processes, but is one unitary process. It is a constant observation of everything, of every thought and feeling and action as they arise within oneself. As awareness is not condemnatory, there is no accumulation. You condemn only when you have a standard, which means there is accumulation and therefore improvement of the self. Awareness is to understand the activities of the self, the 'I', in its

173

relationship with people, with ideas and with things. That awareness is from moment to moment and therefore it cannot be practised. When you practise a thing, it becomes a habit and awareness is not habit. A mind that is habitual is insensitive, a mind that is functioning within the groove of a particular action is dull, unpliable, whereas awareness demands constant pliability, alertness. This is not difficult. It is what you actually do when you are interested in something, when you are interested in watching your child, your wife, your plants, the trees, the birds. You observe without condemnation, without identification; therefore in that observation there is complete communion; the observer and the observed are completely in communion. This actually takes place when you are deeply, profoundly interested in something.

Thus there is a vast difference between awareness and the self-expansive improvement of introspection. Introspection leads to frustration, to further and greater conflict; whereas awareness is a process of release from the action of the self; it is to be aware of your daily movements, of your thoughts, of your actions and to be aware of another, to observe him. You can do that only when you love somebody, when you are deeply interested in something; when I want to know myself, my whole being, the whole content of myself and not just one or two layers, then there obviously must be no condemnation. Then I must be open to every thought, to every feeling, to all the moods, to all the suppressions; and as there is more and more expansive awareness, there is greater and greater freedom from all the hidden movement of thoughts, motives and pursuits. Awareness is freedom, it brings freedom, it yields freedom, whereas introspection cultivates conflict, the process of self-enclosure; therefore there is always frustration and fear in it.

The questioner also wants to know who is aware. When you have a profound experience of any kind, what is taking place? When there is such an experience, are you aware that you are experiencing? When you are angry, at the split second of anger or of jealousy or of joy, are you aware that you are joyous or that you are angry? It is only when the experience is over that there is the experiencer and the experienced. Then the experiencer observes the experienced, the object of experience. At the moment of experience, there is neither the observer nor the observed: there is only the experiencing. Most of us are not experiencing. We are always outside the state of experiencing and therefore we ask this question as to who is the observer, who is it that is aware? Surely such a question is a wrong question, is it not? The moment there is experiencing, there is neither the person who is aware nor the object of which he is aware. There is neither the observer nor the observed but only a state of experiencing. Most of us find it is extremely difficult to live in a state of experiencing, because that demands an extraordinary pliability, a quickness, a high degree of sensitivity; and that is denied when we are pursuing a result, when we want to succeed, when we have an end in view, when we are calculating—all of which brings frustration. A man who does not demand anything, who is not seeking an end, who is not searching out a result with all its implications, such a man is in a state of constant experiencing. Everything then has a movement, a meaning; nothing is old, nothing is charred, nothing is repetitive, because what *is* is never old. The challenge is always new. It is only the response to the challenge that is old; the old creates further residue, which is memory, the observer, who separates himself from the observed, from the challenge, from the experience.

You can experiment with this for yourself very simply and very easily. Next time you are angry or jealous or greedy or violent or whatever it may be, watch yourself. In that state, 'you' are not. There is only that state of being. The moment, the second afterwards, you term it, you name it, you call it jealousy, anger, greed; so you have created immediately the observer and the observed, the experiencer and the experienced. When there is the experiencer and the experienced, then the experiencer tries to modify the experience, change it, remember things about it and so on, and therefore maintains the division between himself and the experienced. If you don't name that feeling—which means you are not seeking a result, you are not condemning, you are merely silently aware of the feeling—then you will see that in that state of feeling, of experiencing, there is no observer and no observed, because the observer and the observed are a joint phenomenon and so there is only experiencing.

Therefore introspection and awareness are entirely different. Introspection leads to frustration, to further conflict, for in it is implied the desire for change and change is merely a modified continuity. Awareness is a state in which there is no condemnation, no justification or identification, and therefore there is understanding; in that state of passive, alert awareness there is neither the experiencer nor the experienced.

Introspection, which is a form of self-improvement, of self-expansion, can never lead to truth, because it is always a process of self-enclosure; whereas awareness is a state in which truth can come into being, the truth of what *is*, the simple truth of daily existence. It is only when we understand the truth of daily existence that we can go far. You must begin near to go far but most of us want to jump, to begin far without understanding what is close. As we understand the near, we shall find the distance between the near and the far is not. There is no distance—the beginning and the end are one.

9. ON RELATIONSHIP

Question: You have often talked of relationship. What does it mean to you?

Krishnamurti: First of all, there is no such thing as being isolated. To be is to be related and without relationship there is no existence. What do we mean by relationship? It is an interconnected challenge and response between two people, between you and me, the challenge which you throw out and which I accept or to which I respond; also the challenge I throw out to you. The relationship of two people creates society; society is not independent of you and me; the mass is not by itself a separate entity but you and I in our relationship to each other create the mass, the group, the society. Relationship is the awareness of interconnection between two people. What is that relationship generally based on? Is it not based on so-called interdependence, mutual assistance? At least, we say it is mutual help, mutual aid and so on, but actually, apart from words, apart from the emotional screen which we throw up against each other, what is it based upon? On mutual gratification, is it not? If I do not please you, you get rid of me; if I please you, you accept me either as your wife or as your neighbour or as your friend. That is the fact.

What is it that you call the family? Obviously it is a relationship of intimacy, of communion. In your family, in your relationship with your wife, with your husband, is there communion? Surely that is what we mean by relationship, do we not? Relationship means communion without fear, freedom to understand each other, to communicate directly. Obviously relationship means that—to be in communion

177

with another. Are you? Are you in communion with your wife? Perhaps you are physically but that is not relationship. You and your wife live on opposite sides of a wall of isolation, do you not? You have your own pursuits, your ambitions, and she has hers. You live behind the wall and occasionally look over the top—and that you call relationship. That is a fact, is it not? You may enlarge it, soften it, introduce a new set of words to describe it but that is the fact—that you and another live in isolation, and that life in isolation you call relationship.

If there is real relationship between two people, which means there is communion between them, then the implications are enormous. Then there is no isolation; there is love and not responsibility or duty. It is the people who are isolated behind their walls who talk about duty and responsibility. A man who loves does not talk about responsibility—he loves. Therefore he shares with another his joy, his sorrow, his money. Are your families such? Is there direct communion with your wife, with your children? Obviously not. Therefore the family is merely an excuse to continue your name or tradition, to give you what you want, sexually or psychologically, so the family becomes a means of self-perpetuation, of carrying on your name. That is one kind of immortality, one kind of permanency. The family is also used as a means of gratification. I exploit others ruthlessly in the business world, in the political or social world outside, and at home I try to be kind and generous. How absurd! Or the world is too much for me, I want peace and I go home. I suffer in the world and I go home and try to find comfort. So I use relationship as a means of gratification, which means I do not want to be disturbed by my relationship.

Thus relationship is sought where there is mutual satisfaction, gratification; when you do not find that satisfaction you change relationship; either you divorce or you remain together but seek gratification elsewhere or else you move from one relationship to another till you find what you seek

—which is satisfaction, gratification, and a sense of self-protection and comfort. After all, that is our relationship in the world, and it is thus in fact. Relationship is sought where there can be security, where you as an individual can live in a state of security, in a state of gratification, in a state of ignorance—all of which always creates conflict, does it not? If you do not satisfy me and I am seeking satisfaction, naturally there must be conflict, because we are both seeking security in each other; when that security becomes uncertain you become jealous, you become violent, you become possessive and so on. So relationship invariably results in possession, in condemnation, in self-assertive demands for security, for comfort and for gratification, and in that there is naturally no love.

We talk about love, we talk about responsibility, duty, but there is really no love; relationship is based on gratification, the effect of which we see in the present civilization. The way we treat our wives, children, neighbours, friends is an indication that in our relationship there is really no love at all. It is merely a mutual search for gratification. As this is so, what then is the purpose of relationship? What is its ultimate significance? If you observe yourself in relationship with others, do you not find that relationship is a process of self-revelation? Does not my contact with you reveal my own state of being if I am aware, if I am alert enough to be conscious of my own reaction in relationship? Relationship is really a process of self-revelation, which is a process of self-knowledge; in that revelation there are many unpleasant things, disquieting, uncomfortable thoughts, activities. Since I do not like what I discover, I run away from a relationship which is not pleasant to a relationship which is pleasant. Therefore, relationship has very little significance when we are merely seeking mutual gratification but becomes extraordinarily significant when it is a means of self-revelation and self-knowledge.

After all, there is no relationship in love, is there? It is only when you love something and expect a return of your love that there is a relationship. When you love, that is when you give yourself over to something entirely, wholly, then there is no relationship.

If you do love, if there is such a love, then it is a marvellous thing. In such love there is no friction, there is not the one and the other, there is complete unity. It is a state of integration, a complete being. There are such moments, such rare, happy, joyous moments, when there is complete love, complete communion. What generally happens is that love is not what is important but the other, the object of love becomes important; the one to whom love is given becomes important and not love itself. Then the object of love, for various reasons, either biological, verbal or because of a desire for gratification, for comfort and so on, becomes important and love recedes. Then possession, jealousy and demands create conflict and love recedes further and further; the further it recedes, the more the problem of relationship loses its significance, its worth and its meaning. Therefore, love is one of the most difficult things to comprehend. It cannot come through an intellectual urgency, it cannot be manufactured by various methods and means and disciplines. It is a state of being when the activities of the self have ceased; but they will not cease if you merely suppress them, shun them or discipline them. You must understand the activities of the self in all the different layers of consciousness. We have moments when we do love, when there is no thought, no motive, but those moments are very rare. Because they are rare we cling to them in memory and thus create a barrier between living reality and the action of our daily existence.

In order to understand relationship it is important to understand first of all what *is*, what is actually taking place in our lives, in all the different subtle forms; and also what relationship actually means. Relationship is self-revelation; it is because we do not want to be revealed to ourselves that we hide in comfort, and then relationship loses its extraordinary depth, significance and beauty. There can be true relationship only when there is love but love is not the search for gratification. Love exists only when there is self-forgetfulness, when there is complete communion, not between one or two, but communion with the highest; and that can only take place when the self is forgotten.

Question: How can we solve our present political chaos and the crisis in the world? Is there anything an individual can do to stop the impending war?

Krishnamurti: War is the spectacular and bloody projection of our everyday life, is it not? War is merely an outward expression of our inward state, an enlargement of our daily action. It is more spectacular, more bloody, more destructive, but it is the collective result of our individual activities. Therefore, you and I are responsible for war and what can we do to stop it? Obviously the ever-impending war cannot be stopped by you and me, because it is already in movement; it is already taking place, though at present chiefly on the psychological level. As it is already in movement, it cannot be stopped—the issues are too many, too great, and are already committed. But you and I, seeing that the house is on fire, can understand the causes of that fire, can go away from it and build in a new place with different materials that are not combustible, that will not produce other wars. That is all that we can do. You and I can see what creates wars, and if we are interested in stopping wars, then we can begin to transform ourselves, who are the causes of war.

An American lady came to see me a couple of years ago, during the war. She said she had lost her son in Italy and that she had another son aged sixteen whom she wanted to save; so we talked the thing over. I suggested to her that to save her son she had to cease to be an American; she had to cease to be greedy, cease piling up wealth, seeking power, domination, and be morally simple—not merely simple in clothes, in outward things, but simple in her thoughts and feelings, in her relationships. She said, "That is too much.

182

You are asking far too much. I cannot do it, because circumstances are too powerful for me to alter". Therefore she was responsible for the destruction of her son.

Circumstances can be controlled by us, because we have created the circumstances. Society is the product of relationship, of yours and mine together. If we change in our relationship, society changes; merely to rely on legislation, on compulsion, for the transformation of outward society, while remaining inwardly corrupt, while continuing inwardly to seek power, position, domination, is to destroy the outward, however carefully and scientifically built. That which is inward is always overcoming the outward.

What causes war—religious, political or economic? Obviously belief, either in nationalism, in an ideology, or in a particular dogma. If we had no belief but goodwill, love and consideration between us, then there would be no wars. But we are fed on beliefs, ideas and dogmas and therefore we breed discontent. The present crisis is of an exceptional nature and we as human beings must either pursue the path of constant conflict and continuous wars, which are the result of our everyday action, or else see the causes of war and turn our back upon them.

Obviously what causes war is the desire for power, position, prestige, money; also the disease called nationalism, the worship of a flag; and the disease of organized religion, the worship of a dogma. All these are the causes of war; if you as an individual belong to any of the organized religions, if you are greedy for power, if you are envious, you are bound to produce a society which will result in destruction. So again it depends upon you and not on the leaders—not on so-called statesmen and all the rest of them. It depends upon you and me but we do not seem to realize that. If once we really felt the responsibility of our own actions, how quickly we could bring to an end all these wars, this appalling misery! But you see, we are indifferent. We have three meals a day, we have our jobs, we have our bank accounts, big or little, and we say, "For God's sake, don't disturb us, leave us alone". The higher up we are, the more we want security, permanency, tranquillity, the more we want to be left alone, to maintain things fixed as they are; but they cannot be maintained as they are, because there is nothing to maintain. Everything is disintegrating. We do not want to face these things, we do not want to face the fact that you and I are responsible for wars. You and I may talk about peace, have conferences, sit round a table and discuss, but inwardly, psychologically, we want power, position, we are motivated by greed. We intrigue, we are nationalistic, we are bound by beliefs, by dogmas, for which we are willing to die and destroy each other. Do you think such men, you and I, can have peace in the world? To have peace, we must be peaceful; to live peacefully means not to create antagonism. Peace is not an ideal. To me, an ideal is merely an escape, an avoidance of what *is*, a contradiction of what *is*. An ideal prevents direct action upon what *is*. To have peace, we will have to love, we will have to begin not to live an ideal life but to see things as they are and act upon them, transform them. As long as each one of us is seeking psychological security, the physiological security we need—food, clothing and shelter—is destroyed. We are seeking psychological security, which does not exist; and we seek it, if we can, through power, through position, through titles, names—all of which is destroying physical security. This is an obvious fact, if you look at it.

To bring about peace in the world, to stop all wars, there must be a revolution in the individual, in you and me. Economic revolution without this inward revolution is meaningless, for hunger is the result of the maladjustment of economic conditions produced by our psychological states— greed, envy, ill-will and possessiveness. To put an end to sorrow, to hunger, to war, there must be a psychological revolution and few of us are willing to face that. We will discuss peace, plan legislation, create new leagues, the United Nations and so on and on; but we will not win peace because we will not give up our position, our authority, our

184

money, our properties, our stupid lives. To rely on others is utterly futile; others cannot bring us peace. No leader is going to give us peace, no government, no army, no country. What will bring peace is inward transformation which will lead to outward action. Inward transformation is not isolation, is not a withdrawal from outward action. On the contrary, there can be right action only when there is right thinking and there is no right thinking when there is no self-knowledge. Without knowing yourself, there is no peace.

To put an end to outward war, you must begin to put an end to war in yourself. Some of you will nod your heads and say, "I agree", and go outside and do exactly the same as you have been doing for the last ten or twenty years. Your agreement is merely verbal and has no significance, for the world's miseries and wars are not going to be stopped by your casual assent. They will be stopped only when you realize the danger, when you realize your responsibility, when you do not leave it to somebody else. If you realize the suffering, if you see the urgency of immediate action and do not postpone, then you will transform yourself; peace will come only when you yourself are peaceful, when you yourself are at peace with your neighbour.

Question: How am I to get rid of fear, which influences all my activities?

Krishnamurti: What do we mean by fear? Fear of what? There are various types of fear and we need not analyse every type. But we can see that fear comes into being when our comprehension of relationship is not complete. Relationship is not only between people but between ourselves and nature, between ourselves and property, between ourselves and ideas; as long as that relationship is not fully understood, there must be fear. Life is relationship. To be is to be related and without relationship there is no life. Nothing can exist in isolation; so long as the mind is seeking isolation, there must be fear. Fear is not an abstraction; it exists only in relation to something.

The question is, how to be rid of fear? First of all, anything that is overcome has to be conquered again and again. No problem can be finally overcome, conquered; it can be understood but not conquered. They are two completely different processes and the conquering process leads to further confusion, further fear. To resist, to dominate, to do battle with a problem or to build a defence against it is only to create further conflict, whereas if we can understand fear, go into it fully step by step, explore the whole content of it, then fear will never return in any form.

As I said, fear is not an abstraction; it exists only in relationship. What do we mean by fear? Ultimately we are afraid, are we not?, of not being, of not becoming. Now, when there is fear of not being, of not advancing, or fear of the unknown, of death, can that fear be overcome by determination, by a conclusion, by any choice? Obviously not. Mere suppression, sublimation, or substitution, creates further resistance, does it not? Therefore fear can never be overcome through any form of discipline, through any form of resistance. That fact must be clearly seen, felt and experienced: fear cannot be overcome through any form of defence or resistance nor can there be freedom from fear through the search for an answer or through mere intellectual or verbal explanation.

Now what are we afraid of? Are we afraid of a fact or of an idea *about* the fact? Are we afraid of the thing as it is, or are we afraid of what we *think* it is? Take death, for example. Are we afraid of the fact of death or of the idea of death? The fact is one thing and the idea about the fact is another. Am I afraid of the word 'death' or of the fact itself? Because I am afraid of the word, of the idea, I never understand the fact, I never look at the fact, I am never in direct relation with the fact. It is only when I am in complete communion with the fact that there is no fear. If I am not in communion with the fact, then there is fear, and there is no communion with the fact so long as I have an idea, an opinion, a theory, *about* the fact, so I have to be very clear whether I am afraid of the word, the idea or of the fact. If I am face to face with the fact, there is nothing to understand about it: the fact is there, and I can deal with it. If I am afraid of the word, then I must understand the word, go into the whole process of what the word, the term, implies.

For example, one is afraid of loneliness, afraid of the ache, the pain of loneliness. Surely that fear exists because one has never really looked at loneliness, one has never been in complete communion with it. The moment one is completely open to the fact of loneliness one can understand what it is, but one has an idea, an opinion about it, based on previous knowledge; it is this idea, opinion, this previous knowledge *about* the fact, that creates fear. Fear is obviously the outcome of naming, of terming, of projecting a symbol to represent the fact; that is fear is not independent of the word, of the term.

I have a reaction, say, to loneliness; that is I say I am afraid of being nothing. Am I afraid of the fact itself or is that fear awakened because I have previous knowledge of the fact, knowledge being the word, the symbol, the image? How can there be fear of a fact? When I am face to face with a fact, in direct communion with it, I can look at it, observe it; therefore there is no fear of the fact. What causes fear is my apprehension *about* the fact, what the fact might be or do.

It is my opinion, my idea, my experience, my knowledge about the fact, that creates fear. So long as there is verbalization of the fact, giving the fact a name and therefore identifying or condemning it, so long as thought is judging the fact as an observer, there must be fear. Thought is the product of the past, it can only exist through verbalization, through symbols, through images; so long as thought is regarding or translating the fact, there must be fear.

Thus it is the mind that creates fear, the mind being the process of thinking. Thinking is verbalization. You cannot think without words, without symbols, images; these images, which are the prejudices, the previous knowledge, the apprehensions of the mind, are projected upon the fact, and out of that there arises fear. There is freedom from fear only when the mind is capable of looking at the fact without translating it, without giving it a name, a label. This is quite difficult, because the feelings, the reactions, the anxieties that we have, are promptly identified by the mind and given a word. The feeling of jealousy is identified by that word. Is it possible not to identify a feeling, to look at that feeling without naming it? It is the naming of the feeling that gives it continuity, that gives it strength. The moment you give a name to that which you call fear, you strengthen it; but if you can look at that feeling without terming it, you will see that it withers away. Therefore if one would be completely free of fear it is essential to understand this whole process of terming, of projecting symbols, images, giving names to facts. There can be freedom from fear only when there is self-knowledge. Self-knowledge is the beginning of wisdom, which is the ending of fear.

12. ON BOREDOM AND INTEREST

Question: I am not interested in anything, but most people are busy with many interests. I don't have to work, so I don't. Should I undertake some useful work?

Krishnamurti: Become a social worker or a political worker or a religious worker—is that it? Because you have nothing else to do, therefore you become a reformer! If you have nothing to do, if you are bored, why not be bored? Why not *be* that? If you are in sorrow, *be* sorrowful. Don't try to find a way out of it, because your being bored has an immense significance, if you can understand it, live with it. If you say, "I am bored, therefore I will do something else", you are merely trying to escape from boredom, and, as most of our activities *are* escapes, you do much more harm socially and in every other way. The mischief is much greater when you escape than when you are what you are and remain with it. The difficulty is, how to remain with it and not run away; as most of our activities are a process of escape it is immensely difficult for you to stop escaping and face it. Therefore I am glad if you are really bored and I say, "Full stop, let's stay there, let's look at it. Why should you do anything?"

If you are bored, why are you bored? What is the thing called boredom? Why is it that you are not interested in anything? There must be reasons and causes which have made you dull: suffering, escapes, beliefs, incessant activity, have made the mind dull, the heart unpliable. If you could find out why you are bored, why there is no interest, then surely you would solve the problem, wouldn't you? Then the awakened interest will function. If you are not interested in why you are bored, you cannot force yourself to be interested in an activity, merely to be doing something—

like a squirrel going round in a cage. I know that this is the kind of activity most of us indulge in. But we can find out inwardly, psychologically, why we are in this state of utter boredom; we can see why most of us are in this state: we have exhausted ourselves emotionally and mentally; we have tried so many things, so many sensations, so many amusements, so many experiments, that we have become dull, weary. We join one group, do everything wanted of us and then leave it; we then go to something else and try that. If we fail with one psychologist, we go to somebody else or to the priest; if we fail there, we go to another teacher, and so on; we always keep going. This process of constantly stretching and letting go *is* exhausting, isn't it? Like all sensations, it soon dulls the mind.

We have done that, we have gone from sensation to sensation, from excitement to excitement, till we come to a point when we are really exhausted. Now, realizing that, don't proceed any further; take a rest. Be quiet. Let the mind gather strength by itself; don't force it. As the soil renews itself during the winter time, so, when the mind is allowed to be quiet, it renews itself. But it is very difficult to allow the mind to be quiet, to let it lie fallow after all this, for the mind wants to be doing something all the time. When you come to that point where you are really allowing yourself to be as you are—bored, ugly, hideous, or whatever it is—then there is a possibility of dealing with it.

What happens when you accept something, when you accept what you are? When you accept that you are what you are, where is the problem? There is a problem only when we do not accept a thing as it is and wish to transform it—which does not mean that I am advocating contentment; on the contrary. If we accept what we are, then we see that the thing which we dreaded, the thing which we called boredom, the thing which we called despair, the thing which we called fear, has undergone a complete change. There is a complete transformation of the thing of which we were afraid.

That is why it is important, as I said, to understand the process, the ways of our own thinking. Self-knowledge cannot be gathered through anybody, through any book, through any confession, psychology, or psycho-analyst. It has to be found by yourself, because it is *your* life; without the widening and deepening of that knowledge of the self, do what you will, alter any outward or inward circumstances, influences—it will ever be a breeding-ground of despair, pain, sorrow. To go beyond the self-enclosing activities of the mind, you must understand them; and to understand them is to be aware of action in relationship, relationship to things, to people and to ideas. In that relationship, which is the mirror, we begin to see ourselves, without any justification or condemnation; and from that wider and deeper knowledge of the ways of our own mind, it is possible to proceed further; it is possible for the mind to be quiet, to receive that which is real.

13. ON HATE

Question: If I am perfectly honest, I have to admit that I resent, and at times hate, almost everybody. It makes my life very unhappy and painful. I understand intellectually that I am this resentment, this hatred; but I cannot cope with it. Can you show me a way?

Krishnamurti: What do we mean by 'intellectually'? When we say that we understand something intellectually, what do we mean by that? Is there such a thing as intellectual understanding? Or is it that the mind merely understands the words, because that is our only way of communicating with each other? Can we, however, really understand anything merely verbally, mentally? That is the first thing we have to be clear about: whether so-called intellectual understanding is not an impediment to understanding. Surely understanding is integral, not divided, not partial? Either I understand something or I don't. To say to oneself, "I understand something intellectually", is surely a barrier to understanding. It is a partial process and therefore no understanding at all.

Now the question is this: "How am I, who am resentful, hateful, how am I to be free of, or cope with that problem?" How do we cope with a problem? What *is* a problem? Surely, a problem is something which is disturbing.

I am resentful, I am hateful; I hate people and it causes pain. And I am aware of it. What am I to do? It is a very disturbing factor in my life. What am I to do, how am I to be really free of it—not just momentarily slough it off but fundamentally be free of it? How am I to do it?

It is a problem to me because it disturbs me. If it were

not a disturbing thing, it would not be a problem to me, would it? Because it causes pain, disturbance, anxiety, because I think it is ugly, I want to get rid of it. Therefore the thing that I am objecting to is the disturbance, isn't it? I give it different names at different times, in different moods; one day I call it this and another something else but the desire is, basically, not to be disturbed. Isn't that it? Because pleasure is not disturbing, I accept it. I don't want to be free from pleasure, because there is no disturbance—at least, not for the time being, but hate, resentment, are very disturbing factors in my life and I want to get rid of them.

My concern is not to be disturbed and I am trying to find a way in which I shall never be disturbed. Why should I *not* be disturbed? I *must* be disturbed, to find out, must I not? I must go through tremendous upheavals, turmoil, anxiety, to find out, must I not? If I am not disturbed I shall remain asleep and perhaps that is what most of us do want—to be pacified, to be put to sleep, to get away from any disturbance, to find isolation, seclusion, security. If I do not mind being disturbed—really, not just superficially, if I don't mind being disturbed, because I want to find out—then my attitude towards hate, towards resentment, undergoes a change, doesn't it? If I do not mind being disturbed, then the name is not important, is it? The word 'hate' is not important, is it? Or 'resentment' against people is not important, is it? Because then I am directly experiencing the state which I call resentment without verbalizing that experience.

Anger is a very disturbing quality, as hate and resentment are; and very few of us experience anger directly without verbalizing it. If we do not verbalize it, if we do not call it anger, surely there is a different experience, is there not? Because we term it, we reduce a new experience or fix it in the terms of the old, whereas, if we do not name it, then there is an experience which is directly understood and this understanding brings about a transformation in that experiencing.

Take, for example, meanness. Most of us, if we are mean, are unaware of it—mean about money matters, mean about forgiving people, you know, just being mean. I am sure we are familiar with that. Now, being aware of it, how are we going to be free from that quality?—not to become generous, that is not the important point. To be free from meanness implies generosity, you haven't got to *become* generous. Obviously, one must be aware of it. You may be very generous in giving a large donation to your society, to your friends, but awfully mean about giving a bigger tip—you know what I mean by 'mean'. One is unconscious of it. When one becomes aware of it, what happens? We exert our will to be generous; we try to overcome it; we discipline ourselves to be generous and so on and so on. But, after all, the exertion of will to *be* something is still part of meanness in a larger circle, so if we do not do any of those things but are merely aware of the implications of meanness, without giving it a term, then we will see that there takes place a radical transformation.

Please experiment with this. First, one *must* be disturbed, and it is obvious that most of us do not like to be disturbed. We think we have found a pattern of life—the Master, the belief, whatever it is—and there we settle down. It is like having a good bureaucratic job and functioning there for the rest of one's life. With that same mentality we approach various qualities of which we want to be rid. We do not see the importance of being disturbed, of being inwardly insecure, of not being dependent. Surely it is only in insecurity that you discover, that you see, that you understand? We want to be like a man with plenty of money, at ease; he will not be disturbed; he doesn't *want* to be disturbed.

Disturbance is essential for understanding and any attempt to find security is a hindrance to understanding. When we want to get rid of something which is disturbing, it is surely a hindrance. If we can experience a feeling directly, without naming it, I think we shall find a great deal in it; then there is no longer a battle with it, because the experiencer and the thing experienced are one, and that is essential. So long as the experiencer verbalizes the feeling, the experience, he separates himself from it and acts upon it; such action is an artificial, illusory action. But if there is no verbalization, then the experiencer and the thing experienced are one. That integration is necessary and has to be radically faced.

14. ON GOSSIP

Question: Gossip has value in self-revelation, especially in revealing others to me. Seriously, why not use gossip as a means of discovering what is? I do not shiver at the word 'gossip' just because it has been condemned for ages.

Krishnamurti: I wonder why we gossip? Not because it reveals others to us. And why should others be revealed to us? Why do you want to know others? Why this extraordinary concern about others? First of all, why do we gossip? It is a form of restlessness, is it not? Like worry, it is an indication of a restless mind. Why this desire to interfere with others, to know what others are doing, saying? It is a very superficial mind that gossips, isn't it?—an inquisitive mind which is wrongly directed. The questioner seems to think that others are revealed to him by his being concerned with them—with their doings, with their thoughts, with their opinions. But do we know others if we don't know ourselves? Can we judge others, if we do not know the way of our own thinking, the way we act, the way we behave? Why this extraordinary concern over others? Is it not an escape, really, this desire to find out what others are thinking and feeling and gossiping about? Doesn't it offer an escape from ourselves? Is there not in it also the desire to interfere with others' lives? Isn't our own life sufficiently difficult, sufficiently complex, sufficiently painful, without dealing with others', interfering with others'? Is there time to think about others in that gossipy, cruel, ugly manner? Why do we do this? You know, everybody does it. Practically everybody gossips about somebody else. Why?

I think, first of all, we gossip about others because we are not sufficiently interested in the process of our own thinking and of our own action. We want to see what others are doing and perhaps, to put it kindly, to imitate others. Generally, when we gossip it is to condemn others, but, stretching it charitably, it is perhaps to imitate others. Why do we want to imitate others? Doesn't it all indicate an extraordinary shallowness on our own part? It is an extraordinarily dull mind that wants excitement, and goes outside itself to get it. In other words, gossip is a form of sensation, isn't it?, in which we indulge. It may be a different kind of sensation, but there is always this desire to find excitement, distraction. If one really goes into this question deeply, one comes back to oneself, which shows that one is really extraordinarily shallow and seeking excitement from outside by talking about others. Catch yourself the next time you are gossiping about somebody; if you are aware of it, it will indicate an awful lot to you about yourself. Don't cover it up by saying that you are merely inquisitive about others. It indicates restlessness, a sense of excitement, a shallowness, a lack of real, profound interest in people which has nothing to do with gossip.

The next problem is, how to stop gossip. That is the next question, isn't it? When you are aware that you are gossiping, how do you stop gossiping? If it has become a habit, an ugly thing that continues day after day, how do you stop it? Does that question arise? When you know you are gossiping, when you are aware that you are gossiping, aware of all its implications, do you then say to yourself, "How am I to stop it?" Does it not stop of its own accord, the moment you are aware that you are gossiping? The 'how' does not arise at all. The 'how' arises only when you are unaware; and gossip indicates a lack of awareness. Experiment with this for yourself the next time you are gossiping, and see how quickly, how immediately you stop gossiping when you are aware of what you are talking about, aware that your tongue is running away with you. It does not demand the action of will to stop it. All that is necessary is to be aware, to be conscious of what you are saying and to see the implications of it. You

198

don't have to condemn or justify gossip. Be aware of it and you will see how quickly you stop gossiping; because it reveals to oneself one's own ways of action, one's behaviour, thought-pattern; in that revelation, one discovers oneself, which is far more important than gossiping about others, about what they are doing, what they are thinking, how they behave.

Most of us who read daily newspapers are filled with gossip, global gossip. It is all an escape from ourselves, from our own pettiness, from our own ugliness. We think that through a superficial interest in world events we are becoming more and more wise, more capable of dealing with our own lives. All these, surely, are ways of escaping from ourselves, are they not? In ourselves we are so empty, shallow; we are so frightened of ourselves. We are so poor in ourselves that gossip acts as a form of rich entertainment, an escape from ourselves. We try to fill that emptiness in us with knowledge, with rituals, with gossip, with group meetings— with the innumerable ways of escape, so the escapes become all-important, and not the understanding of what *is*. The understanding of what *is* demands attention; to know that one is empty, that one is in pain, needs immense attention and not escapes, but most of us like these escapes, because they are much more pleasurable, more pleasant. Also, when we know ourselves as we are, it is very difficult to deal with ourselves; that is one of the problems with which we are faced. We don't know what to do. When I know that I am empty, that I am suffering, that I am in pain, I don't know what to do, how to deal with it. So one resorts to all kinds of escapes.

The question is, what to do? Obviously, of course, one cannot escape; for that is most absurd and childish. But when you are faced with yourself as you are, what are you to do? First, is it possible not to deny or justify it but just to remain with it, as you are?—which is extremely arduous, because the mind seeks explanation, condemnation, identification. If it does not do any of those things but remains with it, then it is like accepting something. If I accept that I am brown, that is the end of it; but if I am desirous of changing to a lighter colour, then the problem arises. To accept what *is* is most difficult; one can do that only when there is no escape and condemnation or justification is a form of escape. Therefore when one understands the whole process of why one gossips and when one realizes the absurdity of it, the cruelty and all the things involved in it, then one is left with what one is; and we approach it always either to destroy it, or to change it into something else. If we don't do either of those things but approach it with the intention of understanding it, being with it *completely*, then we will find that it is no longer the thing that we dreaded. Then there is a possibility of transforming that which is.

15. ON CRITICISM

Question: What place has criticism in relationship? What is the difference between destructive and constructive criticism?

Krishnamurti: First of all, why do we criticize? Is it in order to understand? Or is it merely a nagging process? If I criticize you, do I understand you? Does understanding come through judgement? If I want to comprehend, if I want to understand not superficially but deeply the whole significance of my relationship to you, do I begin to criticize you? Or am I aware of this relationship between you and me, silently observing it—not projecting my opinions, criticisms, judgements, identifications or condemnations, but silently observing what is happening? And if I do not criticize, what happens? One is apt to go to sleep, is one not? Which does not mean that we do not go to sleep if we are nagging. Perhaps that becomes a habit and we put ourselves to sleep through habit. Is there a deeper, wider understanding of relationship, through criticism? It doesn't matter whether criticism is constructive or destructive—that is irrelevant, surely. Therefore the question is: "What is the necessary state of mind and heart that will understand relationship?" What is the process of understanding? How do we understand something? How do you understand your child, if you are interested in your child? You observe, don't you? You watch him at play, you study him in his different moods; you don't project your opinion on to him. You don't say he should be this or that. You are alertly watchful, aren't you?, actively aware. Then, perhaps, you begin to understand the child. If you are constantly criticizing, constantly injecting your own particular personality, your idiosyncrasies, your opinions, deciding the way he should or should not be, and all the rest of it, obviously you create a barrier in that relationship. Unfortunately most of us criticize in order to shape, in order to interfere; it gives us a certain amount of pleasure, a certain gratification, to shape something—the relationship with a husband, child or whoever it may be. You feel a sense of power in it, you are the boss, and in that there is a tremendous gratification. Surely through all that process there is no understanding of relationship. There is mere imposition, the desire to mould another to the particular pattern of your idiosyncrasy, your desire, your wish. All these prevent, do they not?, the understanding of relationship.

Then there is self-criticism. To be critical of oneself, to criticize, condemn, or justify oneself—does that bring understanding of oneself? When I begin to criticize myself, do I not limit the process of understanding, of exploring? Does introspection, a form of self-criticism, unfold the self? What makes the unfoldment of the self possible? To be constantly analytical, fearful, critical—surely that does not help to unfold. What brings about the unfoldment of the self so that you begin to understand it is the constant awareness of it without any condemnation, without any identification. There must be a certain spontaneity; you cannot be constantly analysing it, disciplining it, shaping it. This spontaneity is essential to understanding. If I merely limit, control, condemn, then I put a stop to the movement of thought and feeling, do I not? It is in the movement of thought and feeling that I discover—not in mere control. When one discovers, then it is important to find out how to act about it. If I act according to an idea, according to a standard, according to an ideal, then I force the self into a particular pattern. In that there is no understanding, there is no transcending. If I can watch the self without any condemnation, without any identification, then it is possible to go beyond it. That is why this whole process of approximating oneself to an ideal is so utterly wrong. Ideals are

202

home-made gods and to conform to a self-projected image is surely not a release.

Thus there can be understanding only when the mind is silently aware, observing—which is arduous, because we take delight in being active, in being restless, critical, in condemning, justifying. That is our whole structure of being; and, through the screen of ideas, prejudices, points of view, experiences, memories, we try to understand. Is it possible to be free of all these screens and so understand directly? Surely we do that when the problem is very intense; we do not go through all these methods—we approach it directly. The understanding of relationship comes only when this process of self-criticism is understood and the mind is quiet. If you are listening to me and are trying to follow, with not too great an effort, what I wish to convey, then there is a possibility of our understanding each other. But if you are all the time criticizing, throwing up your opinions, what you have learned from books, what somebody else has told you and so on and so on, then you and I are not related, because this screen is between us. If we are both trying to find out the issues of the problem, which lie in the problem itself, if both of us are eager to go to the bottom of it, find the truth of it, discover what it is—then we are related. Then your mind is both alert and passive, watching to see what is true in this. Therefore your mind must be extraordinarily swift, not anchored to any idea or ideal, to any judgement, to any opinion that you have consolidated through your particular experiences. Understanding comes, surely, when there is the swift pliability of a mind which is passively aware. Then it is capable of reception, then it is sensitive. A mind is not sensitive when it is crowded with ideas, prejudices, opinions, either for or against.

To understand relationship, there must be a passive awareness—which does not destroy relationship. On the contrary, it makes relationship much more vital, much more significant. Then there is in that relationship a possibility of real affection; there is a warmth, a sense of nearness, which is not mere sentiment or sensation. If we can so approach or be in that relationship to everything, then our problems will be easily solved—the problems of property, the problems of possession, because we are that which we possess. The man who possesses money *is* the money. The man who identifies himself with property *is* the property or the house or the furniture. Similarly with ideas or with people; when there is possessiveness, there is no relationship. Most of us possess because we have nothing else if we do not possess. We are empty shells if we do not possess, if we do not fill our life with furniture, with music, with knowledge, with this or that. And that shell makes a lot of noise and that noise we call living; and with that we are satisfied. When there is a disruption, a breaking away of that, then there is sorrow, because then you suddenly discover yourself as you are—an empty shell, without much meaning. To be aware of the whole content of relationship is action, and from that action there is a possibility of true relationship, a possibility of discovering its great depth, its great significance and of knowing what love is.

16. ON BELIEF IN GOD

Question: Belief in God has been a powerful incentive to better living. Why do you deny God? Why do you not try to revive man's faith in the idea of God?

Krishnamurti: Let us look at the problem widely and intelligently. I am not denying God—it would be foolish to do so. Only the man who does not know reality indulges in meaningless words. The man who says he knows, does not know; the man who is experiencing reality from moment to moment has no means of communicating that reality.

Belief is a denial of truth, belief hinders truth; to believe in God is not to find God. Neither the believer nor the non-believer will find God; because reality is the unknown, and your belief or non-belief in the unknown is merely a self-projection and therefore not real. I know you believe and I know it has very little meaning in your life. There are many people who believe; millions believe in God and take consolation. First of all, why do you believe? You believe because it gives you satisfaction, consolation, hope, and you say it gives significance to life. Actually your belief has very little significance, because you believe and exploit, you believe and kill, you believe in a universal God and murder each other. The rich man also believes in God; he exploits ruthlessly, accumulates money, and then builds a temple or becomes a philanthropist.

The men who dropped the atomic bomb on Hiroshima said that God was with them; those who flew from England to destroy Germany said that God was their co-pilot. The dictators, the prime ministers, the generals, the presidents, all talk of God, they have immense faith in God. Are they doing service, making a better life for man? The people who say they believe in God have destroyed half the world and the world is in complete misery. Through religious intolerance there are divisions of people as believers and non-believers, leading to religious wars. It indicates how extraordinarily politically-minded you are.

Is belief in God "a powerful incentive to better living"? Why do you want an incentive to better living? Surely, your incentive must be your own desire to live cleanly and simply, must it not? If you look to an incentive, you are not interested in making life possible for all, you are merely interested in your incentive, which is different from mine—and we will quarrel over the incentive. If we live happily together not because we believe in God but because we are human beings, then we will share the entire means of production in order to produce things for all. Through lack of intelligence we accept the idea of a super-intelligence which we call 'God'; but this 'God', this super-intelligence, is not going to give us a better life. What leads to a better life is intelligence; and there cannot be intelligence if there is belief, if there are class divisions, if the means of production are in the hands of a few, if there are isolated nationalities and sovereign governments. All this obviously indicates lack of intelligence and it is the lack of intelligence that is preventing a better living, not non-belief in God.

You all believe in different ways, but your belief has no reality whatsoever. Reality is what you are, what you do, what you think, and your belief in God is merely an escape from your monotonous, stupid and cruel life. Furthermore, belief invariably divides people: there is the Hindu, the Buddhist, the Christian, the communist, the socialist, the capitalist and so on. Belief, idea, divides; it never brings people together. You may bring a few people together in a group but that group is opposed to another group. Ideas and beliefs are never unifying; on the contrary, they are separative, disintegrating and destructive. Therefore your belief in God is really spreading misery in the world; though it may have brought you momentary consolation, in actuality it has brought you more misery and destruction in the form of wars, famines, class-divisions and the ruthless action of separate individuals. So your belief has no validity at all. If you really believed in God, if it were a real experience to you, then your face would have a smile; you would not be destroying human beings.

Now, what is reality, what is God? God is not the word, the word is not the thing. To know that which is immeasurable, which is not of time, the mind must be free of time, which means the mind must be free from all thought, from all ideas about God. What do you know about God or truth? You do not really know anything about that reality. All that you know are words, the experiences of others or some moments of rather vague experience of your own. Surely that is not God, that is not reality, that is not beyond the field of time. To know that which is beyond time, the process of time must be understood, time being thought, the process of becoming, the accumulation of knowledge. That is the whole background of the mind; the mind itself is the background, both the conscious and the unconscious, the collective and the individual. So the mind must be free of the known, which means the mind must be completely silent, not *made* silent. The mind that achieves silence as a result, as the outcome of determined action, of practice, of discipline, is not a silent mind. The mind that is forced, controlled, shaped, put into a frame and kept quiet, is not a still mind. You may succeed for a period of time in forcing the mind to be superficially silent, but such a mind is not a still mind. Stillness comes only when you understand the whole process of thought, because to understand the process is to end it and the ending of the process of thought is the beginning of silence.

Only when the mind is completely silent not only on the upper level but fundamentally, right through, on both the superficial and the deeper levels of consciousness—only then can the unknown come into being. The unknown is not something to be experienced by the mind; silence alone can be experienced, nothing but silence. If the mind experiences anything but silence, it is merely projecting its own desires and such a mind is not silent; so long as the mind is not silent, so long as thought in any form, conscious or unconscious, is in movement, there can be no silence. Silence is freedom from the past, from knowledge, from both conscious and unconscious memory; when the mind is completely silent, not in use, when there is the silence which is not a product of effort, then only does the timeless, the eternal come into being. That state is not a state of remembering—there is no entity that remembers, that experiences.

Therefore God or truth or what you will is a thing that comes into being from moment to moment, and it happens only in a state of freedom and spontaneity, not when the mind is disciplined according to a pattern. God is not a thing of the mind, it does not come through self-projection, it comes only when there is virtue, which is freedom. Virtue is facing the fact of what *is* and the facing of the fact is a state of bliss. Only when the mind is blissful, quiet, without any movement of its own, without the projection of thought, conscious or unconscious—only then does the eternal come into being.

17. ON MEMORY

Question: Memory, you say, is incomplete experience. I have a memory and a vivid impression of your previous talks. In what sense is it an incomplete experience? Please explain this idea in all its details.

Krishnamurti: What do we mean by memory? You go to school and are full of facts, technical knowledge. If you are an engineer, you use the memory of technical knowledge to build a bridge. That is factual memory. There is also psychological memory. You have said something to me, pleasant or unpleasant, and I retain it; when I next meet you, I meet you with that memory, the memory of what you have said or have not said. There are two facets to memory, the psychological and the factual. They are always interrelated, therefore not clear cut. We know that factual memory is essential as a means of livelihood but is psychological memory essential? What is the factor which retains the psychological memory? What makes one psychologically remember insult or praise? Why does one retain certain memories and reject others? Obviously one retains memories which are pleasant and avoids memories which are unpleasant. If you observe, you will see that painful memories are put aside more quickly than the pleasurable ones. Mind is memory, at whatever level, by whatever name you call it; mind is the product of the past, it is founded on the past, which is memory, a conditioned state. Now with that memory we meet life, we meet a new challenge. The challenge is always new and our response is always old, because it is the outcome of the past. So experiencing without memory is one state and experiencing with memory is another. That is there is a challenge, which is always new. I meet it with the response, with the conditioning of the old. So what happens? I absorb the new,

I do not understand it; and the experiencing of the new is conditioned by the past. Therefore there is a partial understanding of the new, there is never complete understanding. It is only when there is complete understanding of anything that it does not leave the scar of memory.

When there is a challenge, which is ever new, you meet it with the response of the old. The old response conditions the new and therefore twists it, gives it a bias, therefore there is no complete understanding of the new so that the new is absorbed into the old and accordingly strengthens the old. This may seem abstract but it is not difficult if you go into it a little closely and carefully. The situation in the world at the present time demands a new approach, a new way of tackling the world problem, which is ever new. We are incapable of approaching it anew because we approach it with our conditioned minds, with national, local, family and religious prejudices. Our previous experiences are acting as a barrier to the understanding of the new challenge, so we go on cultivating and strengthening memory and therefore we never understand the new, we never meet the challenge fully, completely. It is only when one is able to meet the challenge anew, afresh, without the past, only then does it yield its fruits, its riches.

The questioner says, "I have a memory and a vivid impression of your previous talks. In what sense is it an incomplete experience?" Obviously, it is an incomplete experience if it is merely an impression, a memory. If you understand what has been said, see the truth of it, that truth is not a memory. Truth is not a memory, because truth is ever new, constantly transforming itself. You have a memory of the previous talk. Why? Because you are using the previous talk as a guide, you have not fully understood it. You want to go into it and unconsciously or consciously it is being maintained. If you understand something completely, that is see the truth of something wholly, you will find there is no memory whatsoever. Our education is the cultivation of memory, the strengthening of memory. Your religious practices and rituals, your reading and knowledge, are all the strengthening of memory. What do we mean by that? Why do we hold to memory? I do not know if you have noticed that, as one grows older, one looks back to the past, to its joys, to its pains, to its pleasures; if one is young, one looks to the future. Why are we doing this? Why has memory become so important? For the simple and obvious reason that we do not know how to live wholly, completely in the present. We are using the present as a means to the future and therefore the present has no significance. We cannot live in the present because we are using the present as a passage to the future. Because I am going to become something, there is never a complete understanding of myself, and to understand myself, what I am exactly now, does not require the cultivation of memory. On the contrary, memory is a hindrance to the understanding of what *is*. I do not know if you have noticed that a new thought, a new feeling, comes only when the mind is not caught in the net of memory. When there is an interval between two thoughts, between two memories, when that interval can be maintained, then out of that interval a new state of being comes which is no longer memory. We have memories, and we cultivate memory as a means of continuance. The 'me' and the 'mine' becomes very important so long as the cultivation of memory exists, and as most of us are made up of 'me' and 'mine', memory plays a very important part in our lives. If you had no memory, your property, your family, your ideas, would not be important as such; so to give strength to 'me' and 'mine', you cultivate memory. If you observe, you will see that there is an interval between two thoughts, between two emotions. In that interval, which is not the product of memory, there is an extraordinary freedom from the 'me' and the 'mine' and that interval is timeless.

Let us look at the problem differently. Surely memory is time, is it not? Memory creates yesterday, to-day and to-morrow. Memory of yesterday conditions to-day and therefore shapes to-morrow. That is the past through the present creates the future. There is a time process going on, which is the will to become. Memory is time, and through time we hope to achieve a result. I am a clerk to-day and, given time and opportunity, I will become the manager or the owner. Therefore I must have time, and with the same mentality we say, "I shall achieve reality, I shall approach God". Therefore I must have time to realize, which means I must cultivate memory, strengthen memory by practice, by discipline, to be something, to achieve, to gain, which means continuation in time. Through time we hope to achieve the timeless, through time we hope to gain the eternal. Can you do that? Can you catch the eternal in the net of time, through memory, which is of time? The timeless can be only when memory, which is the 'me' and the 'mine', ceases. If you see the truth of that—that through time the timeless cannot be understood or received—then we can go into the problem of memory. The memory of technical things is essential; but the psychological memory that maintains the self, the 'me' and the 'mine', that gives identification and self-continuance, is wholly detrimental to life and to reality. When one sees the truth of that, the false drops away; therefore there is no psychological retention of yesterday's experience.

You see a lovely sunset, a beautiful tree in a field and when you first look at it, you enjoy it completely, wholly; but you go back to it with the desire to enjoy it again. What happens when you go back with the desire to enjoy it? There is no enjoyment, because it is the memory of yesterday's sunset that is now making you return, that is pushing, urging you to enjoy. Yesterday there was no memory, only a spontaneous appreciation, a direct response; to-day you are desirous of recapturing the experience of yesterday. That is, memory is intervening between you and the sunset, therefore there is no enjoyment, there is no richness, fullness of beauty. Again, you have a friend, who said something to you yesterday, an insult or a compliment and you retain that memory; with that memory you meet your friend to-day. You do not really meet your friend—you carry with you the memory of yesterday, which intervenes. So we go on, surrounding ourselves and our actions with memory, and therefore there is no newness, no freshness. That is why memory makes life weary, dull and empty. We live in antagonism with each other because the 'me' and the 'mine' are strengthened through memory. Memory comes to life through action in the present; we give life to memory through the present but when we do not give life to memory, it fades away. Memory of facts, of technical things, is an obvious necessity, but memory as psychological retention is detrimental to the understanding of life, the communion with each other.

18. SURRENDER TO 'WHAT *IS*'

Question: What is the difference between surrendering to the will of God and what you are saying about the acceptance of what is?

Krishnamurti: Surely there is a vast difference, is there not? Surrendering to the will of God implies that you already know the will of God. You are not surrendering to something you do not know. If you know reality, you cannot surrender to it; you cease to exist; there is no surrendering to a higher will. If you are surrendering to a higher will, then that higher will is the projection of yourself, for the real cannot be known through the known. It comes into being only when the known ceases to be. The known is a creation of the mind, because thought is the result of the known, of the past, and thought can only create what it knows; therefore what it knows is not the eternal. That is why, when you surrender to the will of God, you are surrendering to your own projections; it may be gratifying, comforting but it is not the real.

To understand what *is* demands a different process—perhaps the word 'process' is not right but what I mean is this: to understand what *is* is much more difficult, it requires greater intelligence, greater awareness, than merely to accept or give yourself over to an idea. To understand what *is* does not demand effort; effort is a distraction. To understand something, to understand what *is* you cannot be distracted, can you? If I want to understand what you are saying I cannot listen to music, to the noise of people outside, I must give my whole attention to it. Thus it is extraordinarily difficult and arduous to be aware of what *is*, because our very thinking has become a distraction. We do

214

not want to understand what *is*. We look at what *is* through the spectacles of prejudice, of condemnation or of identification, and it is very arduous to remove these spectacles and to look at what *is*. Surely what *is* is a fact, is the truth, and all else is an escape, is not the truth. To understand what *is*, the conflict of duality must cease, because the negative response of becoming something other than what *is* is the denial of the understanding of what *is*. If I want to understand arrogance I must not go into the opposite, I must not be distracted by the effort of becoming or even by the effort of trying to understand what *is*. If I am arrogant, what happens? If I do not name arrogance, it ceases; which means that in the problem itself is the answer and not away from it.

It is not a question of accepting what *is*; you do not accept what *is*, you do not accept that you are brown or white, because it is a fact; only when you are trying to become something else do you have to accept. The moment you recognize a fact it ceases to have any significance; but a mind that is trained to think of the past or of the future, trained to run away in multifarious directions, such a mind is incapable of understanding what *is*. Without understanding what *is* you cannot find what is real and without that understanding life has no significance, life is a constant battle wherein pain and suffering continue. The real can only be understood by understanding what *is*. It cannot be understood if there is any condemnation or identification. The mind that is always condemning or identifying cannot understand; it can only understand that within which it is caught. The understanding of what *is*, being aware of what *is*, reveals extraordinary depths, in which is reality, happiness and joy.

Question: Is not the longing expressed in prayer a way to God?

Krishnamurti: First of all, we are going to examine the problems contained in this question. In it are implied prayer, concentration and meditation. Now what do we mean by prayer? First of all, in prayer there is petition, supplication to what you call God, reality. You, as an individual, are demanding, petitioning, begging, seeking guidance from something which you call God; therefore your approach is one of seeking a reward, seeking a gratification. You are in trouble, national or individual, and you pray for guidance; or you are confused and you beg for clarity, you look for help to what you call God. In this is implied that God, whatever God may be—we won't discuss that for the moment —is going to clear up the confusion which you and I have created. After all, it is we who have brought about the confusion, the misery, the chaos, the appalling tyranny, the lack of love, and we want what we call God to clear it up. In other words, we want our confusion, our misery, our sorrow, our conflict, to be cleared away by somebody else, we petition another to bring us light and happiness.

Now when you pray, when you beg, petition for something, it generally comes into being. When you ask, you receive; but what you receive will not create order, because what you receive does not bring clarity, understanding. It only satisfies, gives gratification but does not bring about understanding, because, when you demand, you receive that which you yourself project. How can reality, God, answer your particular demand? Can the immeasurable, the unutterable, be concerned with our petty little worries,

216

miseries, confusions, which we ourselves have created? Therefore what is it that answers? Obviously the immeasurable cannot answer the measured, the petty, the small. But what is it that answers? At the moment when we pray we are fairly silent, in a state of receptivity; then our own subconscious brings a momentary clarity. You want something, you are longing for it, and in that moment of longing, of obsequious begging, you are fairly receptive; your conscious, active mind is comparatively still, so the unconscious projects itself into that and you have an answer. It is surely not an answer from reality, from the immeasurable—it is your own unconscious responding. So don't let us be confused and think that when your prayer is answered you are in relationship with reality. Reality must come to you; you cannot go to it.

In this problem of prayer there is another factor involved: the response of that which we call the inner voice. As I said, when the mind is supplicating, petitioning, it is comparatively still; when you hear the inner voice, it is your own voice projecting itself into that comparatively still mind. Again, how can it be the voice of reality? A mind that is confused, ignorant, craving, demanding, petitioning, how can it understand reality? The mind can receive reality only when it is absolutely still, not demanding, not craving, not longing, not asking, whether for yourself, for the nation or for another. When the mind is absolutely still, when desire ceases, then only reality comes into being. A person who is demanding, petitioning, supplicating, longing for direction will find what he seeks but it will not be the truth. What he receives will be the response of the unconscious layers of his own mind which project themselves into the conscious; that still, small voice which directs him is not the real but only the response of the unconscious.

In this problem of prayer there is also the question of concentration. With most of us, concentration is a process of exclusion. Concentration is brought about through effort, compulsion, direction, imitation, and so concentration is a process of exclusion. I am interested in so-called meditation but my thoughts are distracted, so I fix my mind on a picture, an image, or an idea and exclude all other thoughts. This process of concentration, which is exclusion, is considered to be a means of meditating. That is what you do, is it not? When you sit down to meditate, you fix your mind on a word, on an image, or on a picture but the mind wanders all over the place. There is the constant interruption of other ideas, other thoughts, other emotions and you try to push them away; you spend your time battling with your thoughts. This process you call meditation. That is you are trying to concentrate on something in which you are not interested and your thoughts keep on multiplying, increasing, interrupting, so you spend your energy in exclusion, in warding off, pushing away; if you can concentrate on your chosen thought, on a particular object, you think you have at last succeeded in meditation. Surely that is not meditation, is it? Meditation is not an exclusive process—exclusive in the sense of warding off, building resistance against encroaching ideas. Prayer is not meditation and concentration as exclusion is not meditation.

What is meditation? Concentration is not meditation, because where there is interest it is comparatively easy to concentrate on something. A general who is planning war, butchery, is very concentrated. A business man making money is very concentrated—he may even be ruthless, putting aside every other feeling and concentrating completely on what he wants. A man who is interested in anything is naturally, spontaneously concentrated. Such concentration is not meditation, it is merely exclusion.

So what is meditation? Surely meditation is understanding—meditation of the heart is understanding. How can there be understanding if there is exclusion? How can there be understanding when there is petition, supplication? In understanding there is peace, there is freedom; that which you understand, from that you are liberated. Merely to concentrate or to pray does not bring understanding.

Understanding is the very basis, the fundamental process of meditation. You don't have to accept my word for it but if you examine prayer and concentration very carefully, deeply, you will find that neither of them leads to understanding. They merely lead to obstinacy, to a fixation, to illusion. Whereas meditation, in which there is understanding, brings about freedom, clarity and integration.

What, then, do we mean by understanding? Understanding means giving right significance, right valuation, to all things. To be ignorant is to give wrong values; the very nature of stupidity is the lack of comprehension of right values. Understanding comes into being when there are right values, when right values are established. And how is one to establish right values—the right value of property, the right value of relationship, the right value of ideas? For the right values to come into being, you must understand the thinker, must you not? If I don't understand the thinker, which is myself, what I choose has no meaning; that is if I don't know myself, then my action, my thought, has no foundation whatsoever. Therefore self-knowledge is the beginning of meditation—not the knowledge that you pick up from my books, from authorities, from *gurus*, but the knowledge that comes into being through self-inquiry, which is self-awareness. Meditation is the beginning of self-knowledge and without self-knowledge there is no meditation. If I don't understand the ways of my thoughts, of my feelings, if I don't understand my motives, my desires, my demands, my pursuit of patterns of action, which are ideas—if I do not know myself, there is no foundation for thinking; the thinker who merely asks, prays, or excludes, without understanding himself, must inevitably end in confusion, in illusion.

The beginning of meditation is self-knowledge, which means being aware of every movement of thought and feeling, knowing all the layers of my consciousness, not only the superficial layers but the hidden, the deeply concealed activities. To know the deeply concealed activities, the

219

hidden motives, responses, thoughts and feelings, there must be tranquillity in the conscious mind; that is the conscious mind must be still in order to receive the projection of the unconscious. The superficial, conscious mind is occupied with its daily activities, with earning a livelihood, deceiving others, exploiting others, running away from problems—all the daily activities of our existence. That superficial mind must understand the right significance of its own activities and thereby bring tranquillity to itself. It cannot bring about tranquillity, stillness, by mere regimentation, by compulsion, by discipline. It can bring about tranquillity, peace, stillness, only by understanding its own activities, by observing them, by being aware of them, by seeing its own ruthlessness, how it talks to the servant, to the wife, to the daughter, to the mother and so on. When the superficial, conscious mind is thus fully aware of all its activities, through that understanding it becomes spontaneously quiet, not drugged by compulsion or regimented by desire; then it is in a position to receive the intimation, the hints of the unconscious, of the many, many hidden layers of the mind—the racial instincts, the buried memories, the concealed pursuits, the deep wounds that are still unhealed. It is only when all these have projected themselves and are understood, when the whole consciousness is unburdened, unfettered by any wound, by any memory whatsoever, that it is in a position to receive the eternal.

Meditation is self-knowledge and without self-knowledge there is no meditation. If you are not aware of all your responses all the time, if you are not fully conscious, fully cognizant of your daily activities, merely to lock yourself in a room and sit down in front of a picture of your *guru*, of your Master, to meditate, is an escape, because without self-knowledge there is no right thinking and, without right thinking, what you do has no meaning, however noble your intentions are. Thus prayer has no significance without self-knowledge but when there is self-knowledge there is right thinking and hence right action. When there is right action, there is no confusion and therefore there is no supplication to someone else to lead you out of it. A man who is fully aware is meditating; he does not pray, because he does not want anything. Through prayer, through regimentation, through repetition and all the rest of it, you can bring about a certain stillness, but that is mere dullness, reducing the mind and the heart to a state of weariness. It is drugging the mind; and exclusion, which you call concentration, does not lead to reality—no exclusion ever can. What brings about understanding is self-knowledge, and it is not very difficult to be aware if there is right intention. If you are interested to discover the whole process of yourself—not merely the superficial part but the total process of your whole being—then it is comparatively easy. If you really want to know yourself, you will search out your heart and your mind to know their full content and when there is the intention to know, you will know. Then you can follow, without condemnation or justification, every movement of thought and feeling; by following every thought and every feeling as it arises you bring about tranquillity which is not compelled, not regimented, but which is the outcome of having no problem, no contradiction. It is like the pool that becomes peaceful, quiet, any evening when there is no wind; when the mind is still, then that which is immeasurable comes into being.

20. ON THE CONSCIOUS AND UNCONSCIOUS MIND

Question: The conscious mind is ignorant and afraid of the unconscious mind. You are addressing mainly the conscious mind and is that enough? Will your method bring about release of the unconscious? Please explain in detail how one can tackle the unconscious mind fully.

Krishnamurti: We are aware that there is the conscious and the unconscious mind but most of us function only on the conscious level, in the upper layer of the mind, and our whole life is practically limited to that. We live in the so-called conscious mind and we never pay attention to the deeper unconscious mind from which there is occasionally an intimation, a hint; that hint is disregarded, perverted or translated according to our particular conscious demands at the moment. Now the questioner asks, "You are addressing mainly the conscious mind and is that enough?" Let us see what we mean by the conscious mind. Is the conscious mind different from the unconscious mind? We have divided the conscious from the unconscious; is this justified? Is this true? Is there such a division between the conscious and the unconscious? Is there a definite barrier, a line where the conscious ends and the unconscious begins? We are aware that the upper layer, the conscious mind, is active but is that the only instrument that is active throughout the day? If I were addressing merely the upper layer of the mind, then surely what I am saying would be valueless, it would have no meaning. Yet most of us cling to what the conscious mind has accepted, because the conscious mind finds it convenient to adjust to certain obvious facts; but the unconscious may rebel, and often does, and so there is conflict between the so-called conscious and the unconscious.

Therefore, our problem is this, is it not? There is in fact only one state, not two states such as the conscious and the unconscious; there is only a state of being, which is consciousness, though you may divide it as the conscious and the unconscious. But that consciousness is always of the past, never of the present; you are conscious only of things that are over. You are conscious of what I am trying to convey the second afterwards, are you not?; you understand it a moment later. You are never conscious or aware of the now. Watch your own hearts and minds and you will see that consciousness is functioning between the past and the future and that the present is merely a passage of the past to the future. Consciousness is therefore a movement of the past to the future.

If you watch your own mind at work, you will see that the movement to the past and to the future is a process in which the present is not. Either the past is a means of escape from the present, which may be unpleasant, or the future is a hope away from the present. So the mind is occupied with the past or with the future and sloughs off the present. That is the mind is conditioned by the past, conditioned as an Indian, a Brahmin or a non-Brahmin, a Christian, a Buddhist and so on, and that conditioned mind projects itself into the future; therefore it is never capable of looking directly and impartially at any fact. It either condemns and rejects the fact or accepts and identifies itself with the fact. Such a mind is obviously not capable of seeing any fact as a fact. That is our state of consciousness which is conditioned by the past and our thought is the conditioned response to the challenge of a fact; the more you respond according to the conditioning of belief, of the past, the more there is the strengthening of the past. That strengthening of the past is obviously the continuity of itself, which it calls the future. So that is the state of our mind, of our consciousness—a pendulum swinging backwards and forwards between the past and the future. That is our consciousness, which is made up not only of the upper layers of the mind but of the deeper layers as well. Such consciousness obviously cannot function at a different level, because it only knows those two movements of backwards and forwards.

If you watch very carefully you will see that it is not a constant movement but that there is an interval between two thoughts; though it may be but an infinitesimal fraction of a second, there is an interval that has significance in the swinging backwards and forwards of the pendulum. We see the fact that our thinking is conditioned by the past which is projected into the future; the moment you admit the past, you must also admit the future, because there are not two such states as the past and the future but one state which includes both the conscious and the unconscious, both the collective past and the individual past. The collective and the individual past, in response to the present, give out certain responses which create the individual consciousness; therefore consciousness is of the past and that is the whole background of our existence. The moment you have the past, you inevitably have the future, because the future is merely the continuity of the modified past but it is still the past, so our problem is how to bring about a transformation in this process of the past without creating another conditioning, another past.

To put it differently, the problem is this: Most of us reject one particular form of conditioning and find another form, a wider, more significant or more pleasant conditioning. You give up one religion and take on another, reject one form of belief and accept another. Such substitution is obviously not understanding life, life being relationship. Our problem is how to be free from all conditioning. Either you say it is impossible, that no human mind can ever be free from conditioning, or you begin to experiment, to inquire, to discover. If you assert that it is impossible, obviously you are out of the running. Your assertion may be based on limited or wide experience or on the mere acceptance of a belief but such assertion is the denial of search, of research, of inquiry, of discovery. To find out if it is possible for the mind to be completely free from all conditioning, you must be free to inquire and to discover.

Now I say it is definitely possible for the mind to be free from all conditioning—not that you should accept my authority. If you accept it on authority, you will never discover, it will be another substitution and that will have no significance. When I say it is possible, I say it because for me it is a fact and I can show it to you verbally, but if you are to find the truth of it for yourself, you must experiment with it and follow it swiftly.

The understanding of the whole process of conditioning does not come to you through analysis or introspection, because the moment you have the analyser that very analyser himself is part of the background and therefore his analysis is of no significance. That is a fact and you must put it aside. The analyser who examines, who analyses the thing which he is looking at, is himself part of the conditioned state and therefore whatever his interpretation, his understanding, his analysis may be, it is still part of the background. So that way there is no escape and to break the background is essential, because to meet the challenge of the new, the mind must be new; to discover God, truth, or what you will, the mind must be fresh, uncontaminated by the past. To analyse the past, to arrive at conclusions through a series of experiments, to make assertions and denials and all the rest of it, implies, in its very essence, the continuance of the background in different forms; when you see the truth of that fact you will discover that the analyser has come to an end. Then there is no entity apart from the background: there is only thought as the background, thought being the response of memory, both conscious and unconscious, individual and collective.

The mind is the result of the past, which is the process of conditioning. How is it possible for the mind to be free? To be free, the mind must not only see and understand its pendulum-like swing between the past and the future but also be aware of the interval between thoughts. That interval is spontaneous, it is not brought about through any causation, through any wish, through any compulsion.

If you watch very carefully, you will see that though the response, the movement of thought, seems so swift, there are gaps, there are intervals between thoughts. Between two thoughts there is a period of silence which is not related to the thought process. If you observe you will see that that period of silence, that interval, is not of time and the discovery of that interval, the full experiencing of that interval, liberates you from conditioning—or rather it does not liberate 'you' but there is liberation from conditioning. So the understanding of the process of thinking is meditation. We are now not only discussing the structure and the process of thought, which is the background of memory, of experience, of knowledge, but we are also trying to find out if the mind can liberate itself from the background. It is only when the mind is not giving continuity to thought, when it is still with a stillness that is not induced, that is without any causation—it is only then that there can be freedom from the background.

21. ON SEX

Question: We know sex as an inescapable physical and psychological necessity and it seems to be a root-cause of chaos in the personal life of our generation. How can we deal with this problem?

Krishnamurti: Why is it that whatever we touch we turn into a problem? We have made God a problem, we have made love a problem, we have made relationship, living a problem, and we have made sex a problem. Why? Why is everything we do a problem, a horror? Why are we suffering? Why has sex become a problem? Why do we submit to living with problems, why do we not put an end to them? Why do we not die to our problems instead of carrying them day after day, year after year? Sex is certainly a relevant question but there is the primary question, why do we make life into a problem? Working, sex, earning money, thinking, feeling, experiencing—you know, the whole business of living—why is it a problem? Is it not essentially because we always think from a particular point of view, from a fixed point of view? We are always thinking from a centre towards the periphery but the periphery is the centre for most of us and so anything we touch is superficial. But life is not superficial; it demands living completely and because we are living only superficially we know only superficial reaction. Whatever we do on the periphery must inevitably create a problem, and that is our life: we live in the superficial and we are content to live there with all the problems of the superficial. Problems exist so long as we live in the superficial, on the periphery, the periphery being the 'me' and its sensations, which can be externalized or made subjective, which can be identified with the universe, with the country or with some other thing made up by the mind.

So long as we live within the field of the mind there must be complications, there must be problems; that is all we know. Mind is sensation, mind is the result of accumulated sensations and reactions and anything it touches is bound to create misery, confusion, an endless problem. The mind is the real cause of our problems, the mind that is working mechanically night and day, consciously and unconsciously. The mind is a most superficial thing and we have spent generations, we spend our whole lives, cultivating the mind, making it more and more clever, more and more subtle, more and more cunning, more and more dishonest and crooked, all of which is apparent in every activity of our life. The very nature of our mind is to be dishonest, crooked, incapable of facing facts, and that is the thing which creates problems; that is the thing which is the problem itself.

What do we mean by the problem of sex? Is it the act, or is it a thought about the act? Surely it is not the act. The sexual act is no problem to you, any more than eating is a problem to you, but if you *think* about eating or anything else all day long because you have nothing else to think about, it becomes a problem to you. Is the sexual act the problem or is it the thought about the act? Why do you think about it? Why do you build it up, which you are obviously doing? The cinemas, the magazines, the stories, the way women dress, everything is building up your thought of sex. Why does the mind build it up, why does the mind think about sex at all? Why? Why has it become a central issue in your life? When there are so many things calling, demanding your attention, you give complete attention to the thought of sex. What happens, why are your minds so occupied with it? Because that is a way of ultimate escape, is it not? It is a way of complete self-forgetfulness. For the time being, at least for that moment, you can forget yourself—and there is no other way of forgetting yourself. Everything else you do in life gives emphasis to the 'me',

228

to the self. Your business, your religion, your gods, your leaders, your political and economic actions, your escapes, your social activities, your joining one party and rejecting another—all that is emphasizing and giving strength to the 'me'. That is there is only one act in which there is no emphasis on the 'me', so it becomes a problem, does it not? When there is only one thing in your life which is an avenue to ultimate escape, to complete forgetfulness of yourself if only for a few seconds, you cling to it because that is the only moment in which you are happy. Every other issue you touch becomes a nightmare, a source of suffering and pain, so you cling to the one thing which gives complete self-forgetfulness, which you call happiness. But when you cling to it, it too becomes a nightmare, because then you want to be free from it, you do not want to be a slave to it. So you invent, again from the mind, the idea of chastity, of celibacy, and you try to be celibate, to be chaste, through suppression, all of which are operations of the mind to cut itself off from the fact. This again gives particular emphasis to the 'me' who is trying to become something, so again you are caught in travail, in trouble, in effort, in pain.

Sex becomes an extraordinarily difficult and complex problem so long as you do not understand the mind which thinks about the problem. The act itself can never be a problem but the thought about the act creates the problem. The act you safeguard; you live loosely, or indulge yourself in marriage, thereby making your wife into a prostitute which is all apparently very respectable, and you are satisfied to leave it at that. Surely the problem can be solved only when you understand the whole process and structure of the 'me' and the 'mine': my wife, my child, my property, my car, my achievement, my success; until you understand and resolve all that, sex as a problem will remain. So long as you are ambitious, politically, religiously or in any way, so long as you are emphasizing the self, the thinker, the experiencer, by feeding him on ambition whether in the name of yourself as an individual or in the name of the country, of the party or of an idea which you call religion—so long as there is this activity of self-expansion, you will have a sexual problem. You are creating, feeding, expanding yourself on the one hand, and on the other you are trying to forget yourself, to lose yourself if only for a moment. How can the two exist together? Your life is a contradiction; emphasis on the 'me' and forgetting the 'me'. Sex is not a problem; the problem is this contradiction in your life; and the contradiction cannot be bridged over by the mind, because the mind itself is a contradiction. The contradiction can be understood only when you understand fully the whole process of your daily existence. Going to the cinemas and watching women on the screen, reading books which stimulate the thought, the magazines with their half-naked pictures, your way of looking at women, the surreptitious eyes that catch yours—all these things are encouraging the mind through devious ways to emphasize the self and at the same time you try to be kind, loving, tender. The two cannot go together. The man who is ambitious, spiritually or otherwise, can never be without a problem, because problems cease only when the self is forgotten, when the 'me' is non-existent, and that state of the non-existence of the self is not an act of will, it is not a mere reaction. Sex becomes a reaction; when the mind tries to solve the problem, it only makes the problem more confused, more troublesome, more painful. The act is not the problem but the mind is the problem, the mind which says it must be chaste. Chastity is not of the mind. The mind can only suppress its own activities and suppression is not chastity. Chastity is not a virtue, chastity cannot be cultivated. The man who is cultivating humility is surely not a humble man; he may call his pride humility, but he is a proud man, and that is why he seeks to become humble. Pride can never become humble and chastity is not a thing of the mind—you cannot become chaste. You will know chastity only when there is love, and love is not of the mind nor a thing of the mind.

Therefore the problem of sex which tortures so many people all over the world cannot be resolved till the mind is understood. We cannot put an end to thinking but thought comes to an end when the thinker ceases and the thinker ceases only when there is an understanding of the whole process. Fear comes into being when there is division between the thinker and his thought; when there is no thinker, then only is there no conflict in thought. What is implicit needs no effort to understand. The thinker comes into being through thought; then the thinker exerts himself to shape, to control his thoughts or to put an end to them. The thinker is a fictitious entity, an illusion of the mind. When there is a realization of thought as a fact, then there is no need to think about the fact. If there is simple, choiceless awareness, then that which is implicit in the fact begins to reveal itself. Therefore thought as fact ends. Then you will see that the problems which are eating at our hearts and minds, the problems of our social structure, can be resolved. Then sex is no longer a problem, it has its proper place, it is neither an impure thing nor a pure thing. Sex has its place; but when the mind gives it the predominant place, then it becomes a problem. The mind gives sex a predominant place because it cannot live without some happiness and so sex becomes a problem; when the mind understands its whole process and so comes to an end, that is when thinking ceases, then there is creation and it is that creation which makes us happy. To be in that state of creation is bliss, because it is self-forgetfulness in which there is no reaction as from the self. This is not an abstract answer to the daily problem of sex—it is the only answer. The mind denies love and without love there is no chastity; it is because there is no love that you make sex into a problem.

Question: What do you mean by love?

Krishnamurti: We are going to discover by understanding what love is not, because, as love is the unknown, we must come to it by discarding the known. The unknown cannot be discovered by a mind that is full of the known. What we are going to do is to find out the values of the known, look at the known, and when that is looked at purely, without condemnation, the mind becomes free from the known; then we shall know what love is. So, we must approach love negatively, not positively.

What is love with most of us? When we say we love somebody, what do we mean? We mean we possess that person. From that possession arises jealousy, because if I lose him or her what happens? I feel empty, lost; therefore I legalize possession; I hold him or her. From holding, possessing that person, there is jealousy, there is fear and all the innumerable conflicts that arise from possession. Surely such possession is not love, is it?

Obviously love is not sentiment. To be sentimental, to be emotional, is not love, because sentimentality and emotion are mere sensations. A religious person who weeps about Jesus or Krishna, about his *guru* or somebody else, is merely sentimental, emotional. He is indulging in sensation, which is a process of thought, and thought is not love. Thought is the result of sensation, so the person who is sentimental, who is emotional, cannot possibly know love. Again, aren't we emotional and sentimental? Sentimentality, emotionalism, is merely a form of self-expansion. To be full of emotion is obviously not love, because a sentimental person can be cruel when his sentiments are not responded to, when his feelings have no outlet. An emotional person can be stirred

232

to hatred, to war, to butchery. A man who is sentimental, full of tears for his religion, surely has no love.

Is forgiveness love? What is implied in forgiveness? You insult me and I resent it, remember it; then, either through compulsion or through repentance, I say, "I forgive you". First I retain and then I reject. Which means what? I am still the central figure. I am still important, it is I who am forgiving somebody. As long as there is the attitude of forgiving it is I who am important, not the man who is supposed to have insulted me. So when I accumulate resentment and then deny that resentment, which you call forgiveness, it is not love. A man who loves obviously has no enmity and to all these things he is indifferent. Sympathy, forgiveness, the relationship of possessiveness, jealousy and fear—all these things are not love. They are all of the mind, are they not? As long as the mind is the arbiter, there is no love, for the mind arbitrates only through possessiveness and its arbitration is merely possessiveness in different forms. The mind can only corrupt love, it cannot give birth to love, it cannot give beauty. You can write a poem about love, but that is not love.

Obviously there is no love when there is no real respect, when you don't respect another, whether he is your servant or your friend. Have you not noticed that you are not respectful, kindly, generous, to your servants, to people who are so-called 'below' you? You have respect for those above, for your boss, for the millionaire, for the man with a large house and a title, for the man who can give you a better position, a better job, from whom you can get something. But you kick those below you, you have a special language for them. Therefore where there is no respect, there is no love; where there is no mercy, no pity, no forgiveness, there is no love. And as most of us are in this state we have no love. We are neither respectful nor merciful nor generous. We are possessive, full of sentiment and emotion which can be turned either way: to kill, to butcher or to unify over some foolish, ignorant intention. So how can there be love?

You can know love only when all these things have stopped, come to an end, only when you don't possess, when you are not merely emotional with devotion to an object. Such devotion is a supplication, seeking something in a different form. A man who prays does not know love. Since you are possessive, since you seek an end, a result, through devotion, through prayer, which makes you sentimental, emotional, naturally there is no love; obviously there is no love when there is no respect. You may say that you have respect but your respect is for the superior, it is merely the respect that comes from wanting something, the respect of fear. If you really felt respect, you would be respectful to the lowest as well as to the so-called highest; since you haven't that, there is no love. How few of us are generous, forgiving, merciful! You are generous when it pays you, you are merciful when you can see something in return. When these things disappear, when these things don't occupy your mind and when the things of the mind don't fill your heart, then there is love; and love alone can transform the present madness and insanity in the world—not systems, not theories, either of the left or of the right. You really love only when you do not possess, when you are not envious, not greedy, when you are respectful, when you have mercy and compassion, when you have consideration for your wife, your children, your neighbour, your unfortunate servants.

Love cannot be thought about, love cannot be cultivated, love cannot be practised. The practice of love, the practice of brotherhood, is still within the field of the mind, therefore it is not love. When all this has stopped, then love comes into being, then you will know what it is to love. Then love is not quantitative but qualitative. You do not say, "I love the whole world" but when you know how to love one, you know how to love the whole. Because we do not know how to love one, our love of humanity is fictitious. When you love, there is neither one nor many: there is only love. It is only when there is love that all our problems can be solved and then we shall know its bliss and its happiness.

23. ON DEATH

Question: What relation has death to life?

Krishnamurti: Is there a division between life and death? Why do we regard death as something apart from life? Why are we afraid of death? And why have so many books been written about death? Why is there this line of demarcation between life and death? And is that separation real, or merely arbitrary, a thing of the mind?

When we talk about life, we mean living as a process of continuity in which there is identification. Me and my house, me and my wife, me and my bank account, me and my past experiences—that is what we mean by life, is it not? Living is a process of continuity in memory, conscious as well as unconscious, with its various struggles, quarrels, incidents, experiences and so on. All that is what we call life; in opposition to that there is death, which is putting an end to all that. Having created the opposite, which is death, and being afraid of it, we proceed to look for the relationship between life and death; if we can bridge the gap with some explanation, with belief in continuity, in the hereafter, we are satisfied. We believe in reincarnation or in some other form of continuity of thought and then we try to establish a relationship between the known and the unknown. We try to bridge the known and the unknown and thereby try to find the relationship between the past and the future. That is what we are doing, is it not?, when we inquire if there is any relationship between life and death. We want to know how to bridge the living and the ending—that is our fundamental desire.

Now, can the end, which is death, be known while living? If we can know what death is while we are living, then we

235

shall have no problem. It is because we cannot experience the unknown while we are living that we are afraid of it. Our struggle is to establish a relationship between ourselves, which is the result of the known, and the unknown which we call death. Can there be a relationship between the past and something which the mind cannot conceive, which we call death? Why do we separate the two? Is it not because our mind can function only within the field of the known, within the field of the continuous? One only knows oneself as a thinker, as an actor with certain memories of misery, of pleasure, of love, affection, of various kinds of experience; one only knows oneself as being continuous—otherwise one would have no recollection of oneself as being something. Now when that something comes to the end, which we call death, there is fear of the unknown; so we want to draw the unknown into the known and our whole effort is to give continuity to the unknown. That is, we do not want to know life, which includes death, but we want to know how to continue and not come to an end. We do not want to know life and death, we only want to know how to continue without ending.

That which continues has no renewal. There can be nothing new, there can be nothing creative, in that which has continuance—which is fairly obvious. It is only when continuity ends that there is a possibility of that which is ever new. But it is this ending that we dread and we don't see that only in ending can there be renewal, the creative, the unknown—not in carrying over from day to day our experiences, our memories and misfortunes. It is only when we die each day to all that is old that there can be the new. The new cannot be where there is continuity—the new being the creative, the unknown, the eternal, God or what you will. The person, the continuous entity, who seeks the unknown, the real, the eternal, will never find it, because he can find only that which he projects out of himself and that which he projects is not the real. Only in ending, in dying, can the new be known; and the man who seeks to find a relationship between life and death, to bridge the continuous with that which he thinks is beyond, is living in a fictitious, unreal world, which is a projection of himself.

Now is it possible, while living, to die—which means coming to an end, being as nothing? Is it possible, while living in this world where everything is becoming more and more or becoming less and less, where everything is a process of climbing, achieving, succeeding, is it possible, in such a world, to know death? Is it possible to end all memories—not the memory of facts, the way to your house and so on, but the inward attachment through memory to psychological security, the memories that one has accumulated, stored up, and in which one seeks security, happiness? Is it possible to put an end to all that—which means dying every day so that there may be a renewal to-morrow? It is only then that one knows death while living. Only in that dying, in that coming to an end, putting an end to continuity, is there renewal, that creation which is eternal.

24. ON TIME

Question: Can the past dissolve all at once, or does it invariably need time?

Krishnamurti: We are the result of the past. Our thought is founded upon yesterday and many thousand yesterdays. We are the result of time, and our responses, our present attitudes, are the cumulative effect of many thousand moments, incidents and experiences. So the past is, for the majority of us, the present, which is a fact which cannot be denied. You, your thoughts, your actions, your responses, are the result of the past. Now the questioner wants to know if that past can be wiped out immediately, which means not in time but immediately wiped out; or does this cumulative past require time for the mind to be freed in the present? It is important to understand the question, which is this: As each one of us is the result of the past, with a background of innumerable influences, constantly varying, constantly changing, is it possible to wipe out that background without going through the process of time?

What is the past? What do we mean by the past? Surely we do not mean the chronological past. We mean, surely, the accumulated experiences, the accumulated responses, memories, traditions, knowledge, the sub-conscious storehouse of innumerable thoughts, feelings, influences and responses. With that background, it is not possible to understand reality, because reality must be of no time: it is timeless. So one cannot understand the timeless with a mind which is the outcome of time. The questioner wants to know if it is possible to free the mind, or for the mind, which is the result of time, to cease to be immediately; or must one go through a long series of examinations and analyses and so free the mind from its background.

238

The mind *is* the background; the mind *is* the result of time; the mind *is* the past, the mind is not the future. It can project itself into the future and the mind uses the present as a passage into the future, so it is still—whatever it does, whatever its activity, its future activity, its present activity, its past activity—in the net of time. Is it possible for the mind to cease completely, for the thought process to come to an end? Now there are obviously many layers to the mind; what we call consciousness has many layers, each layer inter-related with the other layer, each layer dependent on the other, interacting; our whole consciousness is not only experiencing but also naming or terming and storing up as memory. That is the whole process of consciousness, is it not?

When we talk about consciousness, do we not mean the experiencing, the naming or the terming of that experience and thereby storing up that experience in memory? All this, at different levels, is consciousness. Can the mind, which is the result of time, go through the process of analysis, step by step, in order to free itself from the background or is it possible to be free entirely from time and look at reality directly?

To be free of the background, many of the analysts say that you must examine every response, every complex, every hindrance, every blockage, which obviously implies a process of time. This means the analyser must understand what he is analysing and he must not misinterpret what he analyses. If he mistranslates what he analyses it will lead him to wrong conclusions and therefore establish another background. The analyser must be capable of analysing his thoughts and feelings without the slightest deviation; and he must not miss one step in his analysis, because to take a wrong step, to draw a wrong conclusion, is to re-establish a background along a different line, on a different level. This problem also arises: Is the analyser different from what he analyses? Are not the analyser and the thing that is analysed a joint phenomenon?

Surely the experiencer and the experience are a joint

239

phenomenon; they are not two separate processes, so first of all let us see the difficulty of analysing. It is almost impossible to analyse the whole content of our consciousness and thereby be free through that process. After all, who is the analyser? The analyser is not different, though he may think he is different, from that which he is analysing. He may separate himself from that which he analyses but the analyser is part of that which he analyses. I have a thought, I have a feeling—say, for example, I am angry. The person who analyses anger is still part of anger and therefore the analyser as well as the analysed are a joint phenomenon, they are not two separate forces or processes. So the difficulty of analysing ourselves, unfolding, looking at ourselves page after page, watching every reaction, every response, is incalculably difficult and long. Therefore that is not the way to free ourselves from the background, is it? There must be a much simpler, a more direct way, and that is what you and I are going to find out. In order to find out we must discard that which is false and not hold on to it. So analysis is not the way, and we must be free of the process of analysis.

Then what have you left? You are only used to analysis, are you not? The observer observing—the observer and the observed being a joint phenomenon—the observer trying to analyse that which he observes will not free him from his background. If that is so, and it is, you abandon that process, do you not? If you see that it is a false way, if you realize not merely verbally but actually that it is a false process, then what happens to your analysis? You stop analysing, do you not? Then what have you left? Watch it, follow it, and you will see how rapidly and swiftly one can be free from the background. If that is not the way, what else have you left? What is the state of the mind which is accustomed to analysis, to probing, looking into, dissecting, drawing conclusions and so on? If that process has stopped, what is the state of your mind?

You say that the mind is blank. Proceed further into that blank mind. In other words, when you discard what is
240

known as being false, what has happened to your mind? After all, what have you discarded? You have discarded the false process which is the outcome of a background. Is that not so? With one blow, as it were, you have discarded the whole thing. Therefore your mind, when you discard the analytical process with all its implications and see it as false, is freed from yesterday and therefore is capable of looking directly, without going through the process of time, and thereby discarding the background immediately.

To put the whole question differently, thought is the result of time, is it not? Thought is the result of environment, of social and religious influences, which is all part of time. Now, can thought be free of time? That is, thought which is the result of time, can it stop and be free from the process of time? Thought can be controlled, shaped; but the control of thought is still within the field of time and so our difficulty is: How can a mind that is the result of time, of many thousand yesterdays, be instantaneously free of this complex background? You can be free of it, not to-morrow but in the present, in the now. That can be done only when you realize that which is false; and the false is obviously the analytical process and that is the only thing we have. When the analytical process completely stops, not through enforcement but through understanding the inevitable false-ness of that process, then you will find that your mind is completely dissociated from the past—which does not mean that you do not recognize the past but that your mind has no direct communion with the past. So it can free itself from the past immediately, now, and this dissociation from the past, this complete freedom from yesterday, not chrono-logically but psychologically, is possible; and that is the only way to understand reality.

To put it very simply, when you want to understand something, what is the state of your mind? When you want to understand your child, when you want to understand somebody, something that someone is saying, what is the state of your mind? You are not analysing, criticizing, judging what the other is saying; you are listening, are you not? Your mind is in a state where the thought process is not active but is very alert. That alertness is not of time, is it? You are merely being alert, passively receptive and yet fully aware; and it is only in this state that there is understanding. When the mind is agitated, questioning, worrying, dissecting, analysing, there is no understanding. When there is the intensity to understand, the mind is obviously tranquil. This, of course, you have to experiment with, not take my word for it, but you can see that the more and more you analyse, the less and less you understand. You may understand certain events, certain experiences, but the whole content of consciousness cannot be emptied through the analytical process. It can be emptied only when you see the falseness of the approach through analysis. When you see the false as the false, then you begin to see what is true; and it is truth that is going to liberate you from the background.

25. ON ACTION WITHOUT IDEA

Question: For Truth to come, you advocate action without idea. Is it possible to act at all times without idea, that is, without a purpose in view?

Krishnamurti: What is our action at present? What do we mean by action? Our action—what we want to do or to be— is based on idea, is it not? That is all we know; we have ideas, ideals, promises, various formulas as to what we are and what we are not. The basis of our action is reward in the future or fear of punishment. We know that, don't we? Such activity is isolating, self-enclosing. You have an idea of virtue and according to that idea you live, you act, in relationship. To you, relationship, collective or individual, is action which is towards the ideal, towards virtue, towards achievement and so on.

When my action is based on an ideal which is an idea— such as "I must be brave", "I must follow the example", "I must be charitable", "I must be socially conscious" and so on—that idea shapes my action, guides my action. We all say, "There is an example of virtue which I must follow"; which means, "I must live according to that". So action is based on that idea. Between action and idea, there is a gulf, a division, there is a time process. That is so, is it not? In other words, I am not charitable, I am not loving, there is no forgiveness in my heart but I feel I must be charitable. So there is a gap, between what I am and what I should be; we are all the time trying to bridge that gap. That is our activity, is it not?

Now what would happen if the idea did not exist? At one stroke, you would have removed the gap, would you not? You would *be* what you *are*. You say "I am ugly, I must become beautiful; what am I to do?"—which is action based on idea. You say "I am not compassionate, I must become compassionate". So you introduce idea separate from action. Therefore there is never true action of what you are but always action based on the ideal of what you will be. The stupid man always says he is going to become clever. He sits working, struggling to become; he never stops, he never says "I am stupid". So his action, which is based on idea, is not action at all.

Action means doing, moving. But when you have idea, it is merely ideation going on, thought-process going on in relation to action. If there is no idea, what would happen? You are what you are. You are uncharitable, you are unforgiving, you are cruel, stupid, thoughtless. Can you remain with that? If you do, then see what happens. When I recognize I am uncharitable, stupid, what happens when I am aware it *is* so? Is there not charity, is there not intelligence? When I recognize uncharitableness completely, not verbally, not artificially, when I realize I am uncharitable and unloving, in that very seeing of what *is* is there not love? Don't I immediately become charitable? If I see the necessity of being clean, it is very simple; I go and wash. But if it is an ideal that I should be clean, then what happens? Cleanliness is then postponed or is superficial.

Action based on idea is very superficial, is not true action at all, is only ideation, which is merely the thought-process going on.

Action which transforms us as human beings, which brings regeneration, redemption, transformation—call it what you will—such action is not based on idea. It is action irrespective of the sequence of reward or punishment. Such action is timeless, because mind, which is the time process, the calculating process, the dividing, isolating process, does not enter into it.

This question is not so easily solved. Most of you put questions and expect an answer "yes" or "no". It is easy to ask questions like "What do you mean?" and then sit back and let me explain but it is much more arduous to find out the answer for yourselves, go into the problem so profoundly, so clearly and without any corruption that the problem ceases to be. That can only happen when the mind is really silent in the face of the problem. The problem, if you love it, is as beautiful as the sunset. If you are antagonistic to the problem, you will never understand. Most of us are antagonistic because we are frightened of the result, of what may happen if we proceed, so we lose the significance and the purview of the problem.

26. ON THE OLD AND THE NEW

Question: When I listen to you, all seems clear and new. At home, the old, dull restlessness asserts itself. What is wrong with me?

Krishnamurti: What is actually taking place in our lives? There is constant challenge and response. That is existence, that is life, is it not?—a constant challenge and response. The challenge is always new and the response is always old. I met you yesterday and you come to me to-day. You are different, you are modified, you have changed, you are new; but I have the picture of you as you were yesterday. Therefore I absorb the new into the old. I do not meet you anew but I have yesterday's picture of you, so my response to the challenge is always conditioned. Here, for the moment, you cease to be a Brahmin, a Christian, high-caste or whatever it is—you forget everything. You are just listening, absorbed, trying to find out. When you resume your daily life, you become your old self—you are back in your job, your caste, your system, your family. In other words, the new is always being absorbed by the old, into the old habits, customs, ideas, traditions, memories. There is never the new, for you are always meeting the new with the old. The challenge is new but you meet it with the old. The problem in this question is how to free thought from the old so as to be new all the time. When you see a flower, when you see a face, when you see the sky, a tree, a smile, how are you to meet it anew? Why is it that we do not meet it anew? Why is it that the old absorbs the new and modifies it; why does the new cease when you go home?

The old response arises from the thinker. Is not the thinker always the old? Because your thought is founded on the past, when you meet the new it is the thinker who is meeting it; the experience of yesterday is meeting it. The thinker is always the old. So we come back to the same problem in a different way: How to free the mind from itself as the thinker? How to eradicate memory, not factual memory but psychological memory, which is the accumulation of experience? Without freedom from the residue of experience, there can be no reception of the new. To free thought, to be free of the thought process and so to meet the new is arduous, is it not?, because all our beliefs, all our traditions, all our methods in education are a process of imitation, copying, memorizing, building up the reservoir of memory. That memory is constantly responding to the new; the response of that memory we call thinking and that thinking meets the new. So how can there be the new? Only when there is no residue of memory can there be newness and there is residue when experience is not finished, concluded, ended; that is when the understanding of experience is incomplete. When experience is complete, there is no residue—that is the beauty of life. Love is not residue, love is not experience, it is a state of being. Love is eternally new. Therefore our problem is: Can one meet the new constantly, even at home? Surely one can. To do that, one must bring about a revolution in thought, in feeling; you can be free only when every incident is thought out from moment to moment, when every response is fully understood, not merely casually looked at and thrown aside. There is freedom from accumulating memory only when every thought, every feeling is completed, thought out to the end. In other words, when each thought and feeling is thought out, concluded, there is an ending and there is a space between that ending and the next thought. In that space of silence, there is renewal, the new creativeness takes place.

This is not theoretical, this is not impractical. If you try to think out every thought and every feeling, you will discover that it is extraordinarily practical in your daily life, for then you are new and what is new is eternally enduring. To be new is creative and to be creative is to be happy; a happy man is not concerned whether he is rich or poor, he does not care to what level of society he belongs, to what caste or to what country. He has no leaders, no gods, no temples, no churches and therefore no quarrels, no enmity.

Surely that is the most practical way of solving our difficulties in this present world of chaos? It is because we are not creative, in the sense in which I am using that word, that we are so anti-social at all the different levels of our consciousness. To be very practical and effective in our social relationships, in our relationship with everything, one must be happy; there cannot be happiness if there is no ending, there cannot be happiness if there is a constant process of becoming. In ending, there is renewal, rebirth, a newness, a freshness, a joy.

The new is absorbed into the old and the old destroys the new, so long as there is background, so long as the mind, the thinker, is conditioned by his thought. To be free from the background, from the conditioning influences, from memory, there must be freedom from continuity. There is continuity so long as thought and feelings are not ended completely. You complete a thought when you pursue the thought to its end and thereby bring an end to every thought, to every feeling. Love is not habit, memory; love is always new. There can be a meeting of the new only when the mind is fresh; and the mind is not fresh so long as there is the residue of memory. Memory is factual, as well as psychological. I am not talking of factual memory but of psychological memory. So long as experience is not completely understood, there is residue, which is the old, which is of yesterday, the thing that is past; the past is always absorbing the new and therefore destroying the new. It is only when the mind is free from the old that it meets everything anew, and in that there is joy.

27. ON NAMING

Question: How can one be aware of an emotion without naming or labelling it? If I am aware of a feeling, I seem to know what that feeling is almost immediately after it arises. Or do you mean something different when you say, 'Do not name'?

Krishnamurti: Why do we name anything? Why do we give a label to a flower, to a person, to a feeling? Either to communicate one's feelings, to describe the flower and so on and so on; or to identify oneself with that feeling. Is not that so? I name something, a feeling, to communicate it. 'I am angry.' Or I identify myself with that feeling in order to strengthen it or to dissolve it or to do something about it. We give a name to something, to a rose, to communicate it to others or, by giving it a name, we think we have understood it. We say, "That is a rose", rapidly look at it and go on. By giving it a name, we think we have understood it; we have classified it and think that thereby we have understood the whole content and beauty of that flower.

By giving a name to something, we have merely put it into a category and we think we have understood it; we don't look at it more closely. If we do not give it a name, however, we are *forced* to look at it. That is we approach the flower or whatever it is with a newness, with a new quality of examination; we look at it as though we had never looked at it before. Naming is a very convenient way of disposing of things and of people—by saying that they are Germans, Japanese, Americans, Hindus, you can give them a label and destroy the label. If you do not give a label to people you are forced to look at them and then it is much more difficult to kill somebody. You can destroy the label with a bomb and

249

feel righteous, but if you do not give a label and must therefore look at the individual thing—whether it is a man or a flower or an incident or an emotion—then you are forced to consider your relationship with it, and with the action following. So terming or giving a label is a very convenient way of disposing of anything, of denying, condemning or justifying it. That is one side of the question.

What is the core from which you name, what is the centre which is always naming, choosing, labelling? We all feel there is a centre, a core, do we not?, from which we are acting, from which we are judging, from which we are naming. What *is* that centre, that core? Some would like to think it is a spiritual essence, God, or what you will. So let us find out what is that core, that centre, which is naming, terming, judging. Surely that core is memory, isn't it? A series of sensations, identified and enclosed—the past, given life through the present. That core, that centre, feeds on the present through naming, labelling, remembering.

We will see presently, as we unfold it, that so long as this centre, this core, exists, there can be no understanding. It is only with the dissipation of this core that there is understanding, because, after all, that core is memory; memory of various experiences which have been given names, labels, identifications. With those named and labelled experiences, from that centre, there is acceptance and rejection, determination to be or not to be, according to the sensations, pleasures and pains of the memory of experience. So that centre *is* the word. If you do not name that centre, is there a centre? That is if you do not think in terms of words, if you do not use words, can you think? Thinking comes into being through verbalization; or verbalization begins to respond to thinking. The centre, the core is the memory of innumerable experiences of pleasure and pain, verbalized. Watch it in yourself, please, and you will see that words have become much more important, labels have become much more important, than the substance; and we live on words.

For us, words like truth, God, have become very important
250

—or the feeling which those words represent. When we say the word 'American', 'Christian', 'Hindu' or the word 'anger'—we *are* the word representing the feeling. But we don't know what that feeling is, because the *word* has become important. When you call yourself a Buddhist, a Christian, what does the word mean, what is the meaning behind that word, which you have never examined? Our centre, the core *is* the word, the label. If the label does not matter, if what matters is that which is *behind* the label, then you are able to inquire but if you are identified with the label and stuck with it, you cannot proceed. And we *are* identified with the label: the house, the form, the name, the furniture, the bank account, our opinions, our stimulants and so on and so on. We are all those things—those things being represented by a name. The *things* have become important, the names, the labels; and therefore the centre, the core, *is* the word.

If there is no word, no label, there is no centre, is there? There is a dissolution, there is an emptiness—not the emptiness of fear, which is quite a different thing. There is a sense of being as nothing; because you have removed all the labels or rather because you have understood why you give labels to feelings and ideas you are completely new, are you not? There is no centre from which you are acting. The centre, which is the word, has been dissolved. The label has been taken away and where are you as the centre? You are there but there has been a transformation. That transformation is a little bit frightening; therefore, you do not proceed with what is still involved in it; you are already beginning to judge it, to decide whether you like it or don't like it. You don't proceed with the understanding of what is coming but you are already judging, which means that you have a centre from which you are acting. Therefore you stay fixed the moment you judge; the words 'like' and 'dislike' become important. But what happens when you do not name? You look at an emotion, at a sensation, more directly and therefore have quite a different relationship to it, just

251

as you have to a flower when you do not name it. You are *forced* to look at it anew. When you do not name a group of people, you are compelled to look at each individual face and not treat them all as the mass. Therefore you are much more alert, much more observing, more understanding; you have a deeper sense of pity, love; but if you treat them all as the mass, it is over.

If you do not label, you have to regard every feeling as it arises. When you label, is the feeling different from the label? Or does the label awaken the feeling? Please think it over. When we label, most of us intensify the feeling. The feeling and the naming are instantaneous. If there were a gap between naming and feeling, then you could find out if the feeling is different from the naming and then you would be able to deal with the feeling without naming it.

The problem is this, is it not?, how to be free from a feeling which we name, such as anger? Not how to subjugate it, sublimate it, suppress it, which are all idiotic and immature, but how to be really free from it? To be really free from it, we have to discover whether the word is more important than the feeling. The word 'anger' has more significance than the feeling itself. Really to find that out there must be a gap between the feeling and the naming. That is one part.

If I do not name a feeling, that is to say if thought is not functioning merely because of words or if I do not think in terms of words, images or symbols, which most of us do—then what happens? Surely the mind then is not merely the observer. When the mind is not thinking in terms of words, symbols, images, there is no thinker separate from the thought, which is the word. Then the mind is quiet, is it not? —not *made* quiet, it *is* quiet. When the mind is really quiet, then the feelings which arise can be dealt with immediately. It is only when we give names to feelings and thereby strengthen them that the feelings have continuity; they are stored up in the centre, from which we give further labels, either to strengthen or to communicate them.

When the mind is no longer the centre, as the thinker made up of words, of past experiences—which are all memories, labels, stored up and put in categories, in pigeonholes—when it is not doing any of those things, then, obviously the mind is quiet. It is no longer bound, it has no longer a centre as the me—my house, my achievement, my work—which are still words, giving impetus to feeling and thereby strengthening memory. When none of these things is happening, the mind is very quiet. That state is not negation. On the contrary, to come to that point, you have to go through all this, which is an enormous undertaking; it is not merely learning a few sets of words and repeating them like a school-boy—'not to name', 'not to name'. To follow through all its implications, to experience it, to see how the mind works and thereby come to that point when you are no longer naming, which means that there is no longer a centre apart from thought—surely this whole process is real meditation.

When the mind is really tranquil, then it is possible for that which is immeasurable to come into being. Any other process, any other search for reality, is merely self-projected, home-made and therefore unreal. But this process is arduous and it means that the mind has to be constantly aware of everything that is inwardly happening to it. To come to this point, there can be no judgement or justification from the beginning to the end—not that this is an end. There is no end, because there is something extraordinary still going on. This is no promise. It is for you to experiment, to go into yourself deeper and deeper and deeper, so that all the many layers of the centre are dissolved and you can do it rapidly or lazily. It is extraordinarily interesting to watch the process of the mind, how it depends on words, how the words stimulate memory or resuscitate the dead experience and give life to it. In that process the mind is living either in the future or in the past. Therefore words have an enormous significance, neurologically as well as psychologically. And please do not learn all this from me or from a book. You cannot learn it

253

from another or find it in a book. What you learn or find in a book will not be the real. But you can experience it, you can watch yourself in action, watch yourself thinking, see how you think, how rapidly you are naming the feeling as it arises—and watching the whole process frees the mind from its centre. Then the mind, being quiet, can receive that which is eternal.

28. ON THE KNOWN AND THE UNKNOWN

Question: Our mind knows only the known. What is it in us that drives us to find the unknown, reality, God?

Krishnamurti: Does your mind urge toward the unknown? Is there an urge in us for the unknown, for reality, for God? Please think it out seriously. This is not a rhetorical question but let us actually find out. Is there an inward urge in each one of us to find the unknown? Is there? How can you find the unknown? If you do not know it, how can you find it? Is there an urge for reality, or is it merely a desire for the known, expanded? Do you understand what I mean? I have known many things; they have not given me happiness, satisfaction, joy. So now I am wanting something *else* that will give me greater joy, greater happiness, greater vitality —what you will. Can the known, which is my mind—because my mind *is* known, the result of the past,—can that mind seek the unknown? If I do not know reality, the unknown, how can I search for it? Surely it must come, I cannot go after it. If I go after it, I am going after something which is the known, projected by me.

Our problem is not what it is in us that drives us to find the unknown—that is clear enough. It is our own desire to be more secure, more permanent, more established, more happy, to escape from turmoil, from pain, confusion. That is our obvious drive. When there is that drive, that urge, you will find a marvellous escape, a marvellous refuge—in the Buddha, in the Christ or in political slogans and all the rest of it. That is not reality; that is not the unknowable, the unknown. Therefore the urge for the unknown must come to an end, the search for the unknown must stop; which means there must be understanding of the cumulative known, which is the mind. The mind must understand itself *as* the known,

255

because that is all it knows. You cannot think about something that you do not know. You can only think about something that you know.

Our difficulty is for the mind not to proceed *in* the known; that can only happen when the mind understands itself and how all its movement is from the past, projecting itself through the present, to the future. It is one continuous movement of the known; can that movement come to an end? It can come to an end only when the mechanism of its own process is understood, only when the mind understands itself and its workings, its ways, its purposes, its pursuits, its demands—not only the superficial demands but the deep inward urges and motives. This is quite an arduous task. It isn't just in a meeting or at a lecture or by reading a book, that you are going to find out. On the contrary, it needs constant watchfulness, constant awareness of every movement of thought—not only when you are waking but also when you are asleep. It must be a total process, not a sporadic, partial process.

Also, the *intention* must be right. That is there must be a cessation of the superstition that inwardly we all want the unknown. It is an illusion to think that we are all seeking God—we are not. We don't have to *search* for light. There will be light when there is no darkness and through darkness we cannot find the light. All that we can do is to remove those barriers that create darkness and the removal depends on the *intention*. If you are removing them *in order* to see light, then you are not removing anything, you are only substituting the word light for darkness. Even to look beyond the darkness is an escape from darkness.

We have to consider not what it is that is driving us but why there is in us such confusion, such turmoil, such strife and antagonism—all the stupid things of our existence. When these are not, then there *is* light, we don't have to look for it. When stupidity is gone, there is intelligence. But the man who is stupid and tries to become intelligent is still stupid. Stupidity can never be made wisdom; only when stupidity ceases is there wisdom, intelligence. The man who is stupid and tries to *become* intelligent, wise, obviously can never be so. To know what is stupidity, one must go into it, not superficially, but fully, completely, deeply, profoundly; one must go into all the different layers of stupidity and when there is the cessation of that stupidity, there is wisdom.

Therefore it is important to find out not if there is something more, something greater than the known, which is urging us to the unknown, but to see what it is in us that is creating confusion, wars, class differences, snobbishness, the pursuit of the famous, the accumulation of knowledge, the escape through music, through art, through so many ways. It is important, surely, to see them as they are and to come back to ourselves as we are. From there we can proceed. Then the throwing off of the known is comparatively easy. When the mind is silent, when it is no longer projecting itself into the future, wishing for something; when the mind is really quiet, profoundly peaceful, the unknown comes into being. You don't have to search for it. You cannot invite it. That which you can invite is only that which you know. You cannot invite an unknown guest. You can only invite one you know. But you do not know the unknown, God, reality, or what you will. It must come. It can come only when the field is right, when the soil is tilled, but if you till *in order* for it to come, then you will not have it.

Our problem is not how to seek the unknowable, but to understand the accumulative processes of the mind, which is ever the known. That is an arduous task: that demands constant attention, a constant awareness in which there is no sense of distraction, of identification, of condemnation; it is *being with what is*. Then only can the mind be still. No amount of meditation, discipline, can make the mind still, in the real sense of the word. Only when the breezes stop does the lake become quiet. You cannot *make* the lake quiet. Our job is not to pursue the unknowable but to understand the confusion, the turmoil, the misery, in ourselves; and then that thing darkly comes into being, in which there is joy.

29. TRUTH AND LIE

Question: How does truth, as you have said, when repeated, become a lie? What really is a lie? Why is it wrong to lie? Is not this a profound and subtle problem on all the levels of our existence?

Krishnamurti: There are two questions in this, so let us examine the first, which is: When a truth is repeated, how does it become a lie? What is it that we repeat? Can you repeat an understanding? I understand something. Can I repeat it? I can verbalize it, I can communicate it but the experience is not what is repeated, surely? We get caught in the word and miss the significance of the experience. If you have had an experience, can you repeat it? You may *want* to repeat it, you may have the desire for its repetition, for its sensation, but once you have had an experience, it is over, it *cannot* be repeated. What can be repeated is the sensation and the corresponding word that gives life to that sensation. As, unfortunately, most of us are propagandists, we are caught in the repetition of the word. So we live on words, and the truth is denied.

Take, for example, the feeling of love. Can you repeat it? When you hear the words 'Love your neighbour', is that a truth to you? It is truth only when you do love your neighbour; and that love cannot be repeated but only the word. Yet most of us are happy, content, with the repetition, 'Love your neighbour' or 'Don't be greedy'. So the truth of another, or an actual experience which you have had, merely through repetition, does not become a reality. On the contrary, repetition prevents reality. Merely repeating certain ideas is not reality.

The difficulty in this is to understand the question without thinking in terms of the opposite. A lie is not something opposed to truth. One can see the truth of what is being said, not in opposition or in contrast, as a lie or a truth; but just see that most of us repeat without understanding. For instance, we have been discussing naming and not naming a feeling and so on. Many of you will repeat it, I am sure, thinking that it is the 'truth'. You will never repeat an experience if it is a direct experience. You may communicate it but when it is a *real* experience the sensations behind it are gone, the emotional content behind the words is entirely dissipated.

Take, for example, the idea that the thinker and the thought are one. It may be a truth to you, because you have directly experienced it. If I repeated it, it would not be true, would it?—true, not as opposed to the false, please. It would not be actual, it would be merely repetitive and therefore would have no significance. You see, by repetition we create a dogma, we build a church and in that we take refuge. The word and not truth, becomes the 'truth'. The word is not the thing. To us, the thing is the *word* and that is why one has to be so extremely careful not to repeat something which one does not really understand. If you understand something, you can communicate it, but the words and the memory have lost their emotional significance. Therefore if one understands that, in ordinary conversation, one's outlook, one's vocabulary, changes.

As we are seeking truth through self-knowledge and are not mere propagandists, it is important to understand this. Through repetition one mesmerizes oneself by words or by sensations. One gets caught in illusions. To be free of that, it is imperative to experience directly and to experience directly one must be aware of oneself in the process of repetition, of habits, or words, of sensations. That awareness gives one an extraordinary freedom, so that there can be a renewal, a constant experiencing, a newness.

The other question is: "What really is a lie? Why is it wrong to lie? Is this not a profound and subtle problem on all the levels of our existence?"

What is a lie? A contradiction, isn't it?, a self-contradiction. One can consciously contradict or unconsciously; it can either be deliberate or unconscious; the contradiction can be either very, very subtle or obvious. When the cleavage in contradiction is very great, then either one becomes unbalanced or one realizes the cleavage and sets about to mend it.

To understand this problem, what is a lie and why we lie, one has to go into it without thinking in terms of an opposite. Can we look at this problem of contradiction in ourselves without trying not to be contradictory? Our difficulty in examining this question is, is it not?, that we so readily condemn a lie but, to understand it, can we think of it not in terms of truth and falsehood but of what is *contradiction*? Why do we contradict? Why is there contradiction in ourselves? Is there not an attempt to live up to a standard, up to a pattern—a constant approximation of ourselves to a pattern, a constant effort to *be* something, either in the eyes of another or in our own eyes? There is a desire, is there not? to conform to a pattern; when one is not living up to that pattern, there is contradiction.

Now why do we have a pattern, a standard, an approximation, an idea which we are trying to live up to? Why? Obviously to be secure, to be safe, to be popular, to have a good opinion of ourselves and so on. *There* is the seed of contradiction. As long as we are approximating ourselves to something, trying to *be* something, there *must* be contradiction; therefore there must be this cleavage between the false and the true. I think this is important, if you will quietly go into it. Not that there is not the false and the true; but why the contradiction in ourselves? Is it not because we are attempting to *be* something—to be noble, to be good, to be virtuous, to be creative, to be happy and so on? In the very desire to *be* something, there is a contradiction—not to be something else. It is this contradiction that is so destructive. If one is capable of complete identification with something, with this or with that, then contradiction ceases;

when we do identify ourselves completely with something, there is self-enclosure, there is a resistance, which brings about unbalance—which is an obvious thing.

Why is there contradiction in ourselves? I have done something and I do not want it to be discovered; I have thought something which does not come up to the mark, which puts me in a state of contradiction, and I do not like it. Where there is approximation, there must be fear and it is this fear that contradicts. Whereas if there is no becoming, no attempting to be something, then there is no sense of fear; there is no contradiction; there is no lie in us at any level, consciously or unconsciously—something to be suppressed, something to be shown up. As most of our lives are a matter of moods and poses, depending on our moods, we pose— which is contradiction. When the mood disappears, we are what we are. It is this contradiction that is really important, not whether you tell a polite white lie or not. So long as this contradiction exists, there must be a superficial existence and therefore superficial fears which have to be guarded— and then white lies—, you know, all the rest of it follows. Let us look at this question, not asking what is a lie and what is truth but, without these opposites, go into the problem of contradiction in ourselves—which is extremely difficult, because as we depend so much on sensations, most of our lives are contradictory. We depend on memories, on opinions; we have so many fears which we want to cover up—all these create contradiction in ourselves; when that contradiction becomes unbearable, one goes off one's head. One wants peace and everything that one does creates war, not only in the family but outside. Instead of understanding what creates conflict, we only try to become more and more one thing or the other, the opposite, thereby creating greater cleavage.

Is it possible to understand why there is contradiction in ourselves—not only superficially but much more deeply, psychologically? First of all, is one aware that one lives a contradictory life? We want peace and we are nationalists;

we want to avoid social misery and yet each one of us is individualistic, limited, self-enclosed. We are constantly living in contradiction. Why? Is it not because we are slaves to sensation? This is neither to be denied nor accepted. It requires a great deal of understanding of the implications of sensation, which are desires. We want so many things, all in contradiction with one another. We are so many conflicting masks; we take on a mask when it suits us and deny it when something else is more profitable, more pleasurable. It is this state of contradiction which creates the lie. In opposition to that, we create 'truth'. But surely truth is not the opposite of a lie. That which has an opposite is not truth. The opposite contains its own opposite, therefore it is not truth and to understand this problem very profoundly, one must be aware of all the contradictions in which we live. When I say, 'I love you', with it goes jealousy, envy, anxiety, fear—which is contradiction. It is this contradiction which must be understood and one can understand it only when one is aware of it, aware without any condemnation or justification —merely looking at it. To look at it passively, one has to understand all the processes of justification and condemnation.

It is not an easy thing, to look passively at something; but in understanding that, one begins to understand the whole process of the ways of one's feeling and thinking. When one is aware of the full significance of contradiction in oneself, it brings an extraordinary change: you are yourself, then, not something you are *trying* to be. You are no longer following an ideal, seeking happiness. You are what you are and from there you can proceed. Then there is no possibility of contradiction.

30. ON GOD

Question: You have realized reality. Can you tell us what God is?

Krishnamurti: How do you know I have realized? To know that I have realized, you also must have realized. This is not just a clever answer. To know something you must be of it. You must yourself have had the experience also and therefore your saying that I have realized has apparently no meaning. What does it matter if I have realized or have not realized? Is not what I am saying the truth? Even if I am the most perfect human being, if what I say is not the truth why would you even listen to me? Surely my realization has nothing whatever to do with what I am saying and the man who worships another because that other has realized is really worshipping authority and therefore he can never find the truth. To understand what has been realized and to know him who has realized is not at all important, is it?

I know the whole tradition says, "Be with a man who has realized." How can you know that he has realized? All that you can do is to keep company with him and even that is extremely difficult nowadays. There are very few good people, in the real sense of the word—people who are not seeking something, who are not after something. Those who are seeking something or are after something are exploiters and therefore it is very difficult for anyone to find a companion to love.

We idealize those who have realized and hope that they will give us something, which is a false relationship. How can the man who has realized communicate if there is no love? That is our difficulty. In all our discussions we do not really love each other; we are suspicious. You want something from me, knowledge, realization, or you want to keep company with me, all of which indicates that you do not love. You want something and therefore you are out to exploit. If we really love each other then there will be instantaneous communication. Then it does not matter if you have realized and I have not or if you are the high or the low. Since our hearts have withered, God has become awfully important. That is, you want to know God because you have lost the song in your heart and you pursue the singer and ask him whether he can teach you how to sing. He can teach you the technique but the technique will not lead you to creation. You cannot be a musician by merely knowing how to sing. You may know all the steps of a dance but if you have not creation in your heart, you are only functioning as a machine. You cannot love if your object is merely to achieve a result. There is no such thing as an ideal, because that is merely an achievement. Beauty is not an achievement, it is reality, now, not to-morrow. If there is love you will understand the unknown, you will know what God is and nobody need tell you—and that is the beauty of love. It is eternity in itself. Because there is no love, we want someone else, or God, to give it to us. If we really loved, do you know what a different world this would be? We should be really happy people. Therefore we should not invest our happiness in things, in family, in ideals. We should be happy and therefore things, people and ideals would not dominate our lives. They are all secondary things. Because we do not love and because we are not happy we invest in things, thinking they will give us happiness, and one of the things in which we invest is God.

You want me to tell you what reality is. Can the indescribable be put into words? Can you measure something immeasurable? Can you catch the wind in your fist? If you do, is that the wind? If you measure that which is immeasurable, is that the real? If you formulate it, is it the real? Surely not, for the moment you describe something which is indescribable, it ceases to be the real. The moment you translate the unknowable into the known, it ceases to be the unknowable. Yet that is what we are hankering after. All the time we want to *know*, because then we shall be able to continue, then we shall be able, we think, to capture ultimate happiness, permanency. We want to know because we are not happy, because we are striving miserably, because we are worn out, degraded. Yet instead of realizing the simple fact—that we *are* degraded, that we are dull, weary, in turmoil—we want to move away from what is the known into the unknown, which again becomes the known and therefore we can never find the real.

Therefore instead of asking who has realized or what God is why not give your whole attention and awareness to what *is*? Then you will find the unknown, or rather it will come to you. If you understand what is the known, you will experience that extraordinary silence which is not induced, not enforced, that creative emptiness in which alone reality can enter. It cannot come to that which is *becoming*, which is striving; it can only come to that which is *being*, which understands what *is*. Then you will see that reality is not in the distance; the unknown is not far off; it is in what *is*. As the answer to a problem is in the problem, so reality is in what *is*; if we can understand it, then we shall know truth.

It is extremely difficult to be aware of dullness, to be aware of greed, to be aware of ill-will, ambition and so on. The very fact of being aware of what *is* is truth. It is truth that liberates, not your striving to be free. Thus reality is not far but we place it far away because we try to use it as a means of self-continuity. It is here, now, in the immediate. The eternal or the timeless is now and the now cannot be understood by a man who is caught in the net of time. To free thought from time demands action, but the mind is lazy, it is slothful, and therefore ever creates other hindrances. It is only possible by right meditation, which means complete action, not a continuous action, and complete action can only be understood when the mind comprehends the process of continuity, which is memory—not the factual but the psychological memory. As long as memory functions, the mind cannot understand what *is*. But one's mind, one's whole being, becomes extraordinarily creative, passively alert, when one understands the significance of ending, because in ending there is renewal, while in continuity there is death, there is decay.

31. ON IMMEDIATE REALIZATION

Question: Can we realize on the spot the truth you are speaking of, without any previous preparation?

Krishnamurti: What do you mean by truth? Do not let us use a word of which we do not know the meaning; we can use a simpler word, a more direct word. Can you understand, can you comprehend a problem directly? That is what is implied, is it not? Can you understand what *is*, immediately, now? In understanding what *is*, you will understand the significance of truth; but to say that one must understand truth has very little meaning. Can you understand a problem directly, fully, and be free of it? That is what is implied in this question, is it not? Can you understand a crisis, a challenge, immediately, see its whole significance and be free of it? What you understand leaves no mark; therefore understanding or truth is the liberator. Can you be liberated now from a problem, from a challenge? Life is, is it not?, a series of challenges and responses and if your response to a challenge is conditioned, limited, incomplete, then that challenge leaves its mark, its residue, which is further strengthened by another new challenge. So there is a constant residual memory, accumulations, scars, and with all these scars you try to meet the new and therefore you never meet the new. Therefore you never understand, there is never a liberation from any challenge.

The problem, the question is, whether I can understand a challenge completely, directly; sense all its significance, all its perfume, its depth, its beauty and its ugliness and so be free of it. A challenge is always new, is it not? The problem is always new, is it not? A problem which you had yesterday, for example, has undergone such modification that when you meet it to-day, it is already new. But you meet it with the old, because you meet it without transforming, merely modifying your own thoughts.

Let me put it in a different way. I met you yesterday. In the meantime you have changed. You have undergone a modification but I still have yesterday's picture of you. I meet you to-day with my picture of you and therefore I do not understand you—I understand only the picture of you which I acquired yesterday. If I want to understand you, who are modified, changed, I must remove, I must be free of the picture of yesterday. In other words to understand a challenge, which is always new, I must also meet it anew, there must be no residue of yesterday; so I must say adieu to yesterday.

After all, what is life? It is something new all the time, is it not? It is something which is ever undergoing change, creating a new feeling. To-day is never the same as yesterday and that is the beauty of life. Can you and I meet every problem anew? Can you, when you go home, meet your wife and your child anew, meet the challenge anew? You will not be able to do it if you are burdened with the memories of yesterday. Therefore, to understand the truth of a problem, of a relationship, you must come to it afresh—not with an 'open mind', for that has no meaning. You must come to it without the scars of yesterday's memories—which means, as each challenge arises, be aware of all the responses of yesterday and by being aware of yesterday's residue, memories, you will find that they drop away without struggle and therefore your mind is fresh.

Can one realize truth immediately, without preparation? I say yes—not out of some fancy of mine, not out of some illusion; but psychologically experiment with it and you will see. Take any challenge, any small incident—don't wait for some great crisis—and see how you respond to it. Be aware of it, of your responses, of your intentions, of your attitudes and you will understand them, you will understand your

268

background. I assure you, you can do it immediately if you give your whole attention to it. If you are seeking the full meaning of your background, it yields its significance and then you discover in one stroke the truth, the understanding of the problem. Understanding comes into being from the now, the present, which is always timeless. Though it may be to-morrow, it is still now; merely to postpone, to prepare to receive that which is to-morrow, is to prevent yourself from understanding what is *now*. Surely you can understand directly what *is* now, can't you? To understand what *is*, you have to be undisturbed, undistracted, you have to give your mind and heart to it. It must be your sole interest at that moment, completely. Then what *is* gives you its full depth, its full meaning, and thereby you are free of that problem.

If you want to know the truth, the psychological significance of property, for instance, if you really want to understand it directly, now, how do you approach it? Surely you must feel akin to the problem, you must not be afraid of it, you must not have any creed, any answer, between yourself and the problem. Only when you are directly in relationship with the problem will you find the answer. If you introduce an answer, if you judge, have a psychological disinclination, then you will postpone, you will prepare to understand to-morrow what can only be understood in the 'now'. Therefore you will never understand. To perceive truth needs no preparation; preparation implies time and time is not the means of understanding truth. Time is continuity and truth is timeless, non-continuous. Understanding is non-continuous, it is from moment to moment, unresidual.

I am afraid I am making it all sound very difficult, am I not? But it is easy, simple to understand, if you will only *experiment* with it. If you go off into a dream, meditate over it, it becomes very difficult. When there is no barrier between you and me, I understand you. If I am open to you, I understand you directly—and to be open is not a matter of time.

Will time make me open? Will preparation, system, discipline, make me open to you? No. What will make me open to you is my intention to understand. I want to be open because I have nothing to hide, I am not afraid; therefore I am open and there is immediate communion, there is truth. To receive truth, to know its beauty, to know its joy, there must be instant receptivity, unclouded by theories, fears and answers.

32. ON SIMPLICITY

Question: What is simplicity? Does it imply seeing very clearly the essentials and discarding everything else?

Krishnamurti: Let us see what simplicity is not. Don't say —"That is negation" or "Tell us something positive". That is immature, thoughtless reaction. Those people who offer you the 'positive' are exploiters; they have something to give you which you want and through which they exploit you. We are doing nothing of that kind. We are trying to find out the truth of simplicity. Therefore you must discard, put ideas behind and observe anew. The man who has much is afraid of revolution, inwardly and outwardly.

Let us find out what is *not* simplicity. A complicated mind is not simple, is it? A clever mind is not simple; a mind that has an end in view for which it is working, a reward, a fear, is not a simple mind, is it? A mind that is burdened with knowledge is not a simple mind; a mind that is crippled with beliefs is not a simple mind, is it? A mind that has identified itself with something greater and is striving to keep that identity, is not a simple mind, is it? We think it is simple to have only one or two loin-cloths, we want the outward show of simplicity and we are easily deceived by that. That is why the man who is very rich worships the man who has renounced.

What is simplicity? Can simplicity be the discarding of non-essentials and the pursuing of essentials—which means a process of choice? Does it not mean choice—choosing essentials and discarding non-essentials? What is this process of choosing? What is the entity that chooses? Mind, is it not? It does not matter what you call it. You say, 'I will choose this, which is the essential'. How do you know what is the essential? Either you have a pattern of what other people have said or your own experience says that something is the essential. Can you rely on your experience? When you choose, your choice is based on desire, is it not? What you call 'the essential' is that which gives you satisfaction. So you are back again in the same process, are you not? Can a confused mind choose? If it does, the choice must also be confused.

Therefore the choice between the essential and the non-essential is not simplicity. It is a conflict. A mind in conflict, in confusion, can never be simple. When you discard, when you really observe and see all these false things, the tricks of the mind, when you look at it and are aware of it, then you will know for yourself what simplicity is. A mind which is bound by belief is never a simple mind. A mind that is crippled with knowledge is not simple. A mind that is distracted by God, by women, by music, is not a simple mind. A mind caught in the routine of the office, of rituals, of prayers, such a mind is not simple. Simplicity is action, without idea. But that is a very rare thing; that means creativeness. So long as there is not creation, we are centres of mischief, misery and destruction. Simplicity is not a thing which you can pursue and experience. Simplicity comes, as a flower opens at the right moment, when each one understands the whole process of existence and relationship. Because we have never thought about it, observed it, we are not aware of it; we value all the outer forms of few possessions but those are not simplicity. Simplicity is not to be found; it does not lie as a choice between the essential and the non-essential. It comes into being only when the self is not; when the mind is not caught in speculations, conclusions, beliefs, ideations. Such a free mind only can find truth. Such a mind alone can receive that which is immeasurable, which is unnameable; and that is simplicity.

33. ON SUPERFICIALITY

Question: How is one who is superficial to become serious?

Krishnamurti: First of all, we must be aware that we are superficial, must we not? What does it mean to be superficial? Essentially, to be dependent, does it not? To depend on stimulation, to depend on challenge, to depend on another, to depend psychologically on certain values, certain experiences, certain memories—does not all that make for superficiality? When I depend on going to church every morning or every week in order to be uplifted, in order to be helped, does that not make me superficial? If I have to perform certain rituals to maintain my sense of integrity or to regain a feeling which I may once have had, does that not make me superficial? Does it not make me superficial when I give myself over to a country, to a plan or to a particular political group? Surely this whole process of dependence is an evasion of myself; this identification with the greater is the denial of what I am. But I cannot deny what I am; I must understand what I am and not try to identify myself with the universe, with God, with a particular political party or what you will. All this leads to shallow thinking and from shallow thinking there is activity which is everlastingly mischievous, whether on a world-wide scale, or on the individual scale.

First of all, do we recognize that we are doing these things? We do not; we justify them. We say, "What shall I do if I don't do these things? I'll be worse off; my mind will go to pieces. Now, at least, I am struggling towards something better." The more we struggle the more superficial we are. I have to see that first, have I not? That is one of the most difficult things; to see what I am, to acknowledge that I am

273

stupid, that I am shallow, that I am narrow, that I am jealous. If I see what I am, if I recognize it, then with that I can start. Surely, a shallow mind is a mind that escapes from what is; not to escape requires arduous investigation, the denial of inertia. The moment I know I am shallow, there is already a process of deepening—if I don't do anything about the shallowness. If the mind says, "I am petty, and I am going to go into it, I am going to understand the whole of this pettiness, this narrowing influence", then there is a possibility of transformation; but a petty mind, acknowledging that it is petty and trying to be non-petty by reading, by meeting people, by travelling, by being incessantly active like a monkey, is still a petty mind.

Again, you see, there is a real revolution only if we approach this problem rightly. The right approach to the problem gives an extraordinary confidence which I assure you moves mountains—the mountains of one's own prejudices, conditionings. Being aware of a shallow mind, do not try to become deep. A shallow mind can never know great depths. It can have plenty of knowledge, information, it can repeat words—you know the whole paraphernalia of a superficial mind that is active. But if you know that you are superficial, shallow, if you are aware of the shallowness and observe all its activities without judging, without condemnation, then you will soon see that the shallow thing has disappeared entirely, without your action upon it. That requires patience, watchfulness, not an eager desire for a result, for achievement. It is only a shallow mind that wants an achievement, a result.

The more you are aware of this whole process, the more you will discover the activities of the mind but you must observe them without trying to put an end to them, because the moment you seek an end, you are again caught in the duality of the 'me' and the 'not-me'—which continues the problem.

34. ON TRIVIALITY

Question: With what should the mind be occupied?

Krishnamurti: Here is a very good example of how conflict is brought into being: the conflict between what *should* be and what *is*. First we establish what *should* be, the ideal, and then try to live according to that pattern. We say that the mind should be occupied with noble things, with unselfishness, with generosity, with kindliness, with love; that is the pattern, the belief, the *should* be, the must, and we try to live accordingly. So there is a conflict set going, between the projection of what *should* be and the actuality, the what *is*, and through that conflict we hope to be transformed. So long as we are struggling with the *should* be, we feel virtuous, we feel good, but which is important: the *should* be or what *is*? With what are our minds occupied—actually, not ideologically? With trivialities, are they not? With how one looks, with ambition, with greed, with envy, with gossip, with cruelty. The mind lives in a world of trivialities and a trivial mind creating a noble pattern is still trivial, is it not? The question is not with what should the mind be occupied but can the mind free itself from trivialities? If we are at all aware, if we are at all inquiring, we know our own particular trivialities: incessant talk, the everlasting chattering of the mind, worry over this and that, curiosity as to what people are doing or not doing, trying to achieve a result, groping after one's own aggrandizement and so on. With that we are occupied and we know it very well. Can that be transformed? *That* is the problem, is it not? To ask with what the mind should be occupied is mere immaturity.

Now, being aware that my mind is trivial and occupied with trivialities, can it free itself from this condition? Is not the mind, by its very nature, trivial? What is the mind but the result of memory? Memory of what? Of how to survive, not only physically but also psychologically through the development of certain qualities, virtues, the storing up of experiences, the establishing of itself in its own activities. Is that not trivial? The mind, being the result of memory, of time, is trivial in itself; what can it do to free itself from its own triviality? Can it do anything? Please see the importance of this. Can the mind, which is self-centred activity, free itself from that activity? Obviously, it cannot; whatever it does, it is still trivial. It can speculate about God, it can devise political systems, it can invent beliefs; but it is still within the field of time, its change is still from memory to memory, it is still bound by its own limitation. Can the mind break down that limitation? Or does that limitation break down when the mind is quiet, when it is not active, when it recognizes its own trivialities, however great it may have imagined them to be? When the mind, having seen its trivialities, is fully aware of them and so becomes really quiet—only then is there a possibility of these trivialities dropping away. So long as you are inquiring with what the mind should be occupied, it will be occupied with trivialities, whether it builds a church, whether it prays or whether it goes to a shrine. The mind itself is petty, small, and by merely saying it is petty you haven't dissolved its pettiness. You have to understand it, the mind has to recognize its own activities, and in the process of that recognition, in the awareness of the trivialities which it has consciously and unconsciously built, the mind becomes quiet. In that quietness there is a creative state and *this* is the factor which brings about a transformation.

35. ON THE STILLNESS OF THE MIND

Question: Why do you speak of the stillness of the mind, and what is this stillness?

Krishnamurti: Is it not necessary, if we would understand anything, that the mind should be still? If we have a problem, we worry over it, don't we? We go into it, we analyse it, we tear it to pieces, in the hope of understanding it. Now, do we understand through effort, through analysis, through comparison, through any form of mental struggle? Surely, understanding comes only when the mind is very quiet. We say that the more we struggle with the question of starvation, of war, or any other human problem, the more we come into conflict with it, the better we shall understand it. Now, is that true? Wars have been going on for centuries, the conflict between individuals, between societies; war, inward and outward, is constantly there. Do we resolve that war, that conflict, by further conflict, by further struggle, by cunning endeavour? Or do we understand the problem only when we are directly in front of it, when we are faced with the fact? We can face the fact only when there is no interfering agitation between the mind and the fact, so is it not important, if we are to understand, that the mind be quiet?

You will inevitably ask, "How can the mind be made still?" That is the immediate response, is it not? You say, "My mind is agitated and how can I keep it quiet?" Can any system make the mind quiet? Can a formula, a discipline, make the mind still? It can; but when the mind is *made* still, is that quietness, is that stillness? Or is the mind only enclosed within an idea, within a formula, within a phrase? Such a mind is a dead mind, is it not? That is why most

277

people who try to be spiritual, so-called spiritual, are dead—because they have trained their minds to be quiet, they have enclosed themselves within a formula for being quiet. Obviously, such a mind is never quiet; it is only suppressed, held down.

The mind is quiet when it sees the truth that understanding comes only when it is quiet; that if I would understand you, I must be quiet, I cannot have reactions against you, I must not be prejudiced, I must put away all my conclusions, my experiences and meet you face to face. Only then, when the mind is free from my conditioning, do I understand. When I see the truth of that, then the mind is quiet—and then there is no question of how to *make* the mind quiet. Only the truth can liberate the mind from its own ideation; to see the truth, the mind must realize the fact that so long as it is agitated it can have no understanding. Quietness of mind, tranquillity of mind, is not a thing to be produced by will-power, by any action of desire; if it is, then such a mind is enclosed, isolated, it is a dead mind and therefore incapable of adaptability, of pliability, of swiftness. Such a mind is not creative.

Our question, then, is not how to make the mind still but to see the truth of every problem as it presents itself to us. It is like the pool that becomes quiet when the wind stops. Our mind is agitated because we have problems; and to avoid the problems, we make the mind still. Now the mind has projected these problems and there are no problems apart from the mind; and so long as the mind projects any conception of sensitivity, practises any form of stillness, it can never be still. When the mind realizes that only by being still is there understanding—then it becomes very quiet. That quietness is not imposed, not disciplined, it is a quietness that cannot be understood by an agitated mind.

Many who seek quietness of mind withdraw from active life to a village, to a monastery, to the mountains, or they withdraw into ideas, enclose themselves in a belief or avoid people who give them trouble. Such isolation is not stillness of mind. The enclosure of the mind in an idea or the avoidance of people who make life complicated does not bring about stillness of mind. Stillness of mind comes only when there is no process of isolation through accumulation but complete understanding of the whole process of relationship. Accumulation makes the mind old; only when the mind is new, when the mind is fresh, without the process of accumulation—only then is there a possibility of having tranquillity of mind. Such a mind is not dead, it is most active. The still mind is the most active mind but if you will experiment with it, go into it deeply, you will see that in stillness there is no projection of thought. Thought, at all levels, is obviously the reaction of memory and thought can never be in a state of creation. It may express creativeness but thought in itself can never be creative. When there is silence, that tranquillity of mind which is not a result, then we shall see that in that quietness there is extraordinary activity, an extraordinary action which a mind agitated by thought can never know. In that stillness, there is no formulation, there is no idea, there is no memory; that stillness is a state of creation that can be experienced only when there is complete understanding of the whole process of the 'me'. Otherwise, stillness has no meaning. Only in that stillness, which is not a result, is the eternal discovered, which is beyond time.

36. ON THE MEANING OF LIFE

Question: We live but we do not know why. To so many of us, life seems to have no meaning. Can you tell us the meaning and purpose of our living?

Krishnamurti: Now why do you ask this question? Why are you asking me to tell you the meaning of life, the purpose of life? What do we mean by life? Does life have a meaning, a purpose? Is not living in itself its own purpose, its own meaning? Why do we want more? Because we are so dissatisfied with our life, our life is so empty, so tawdry, so monotonous, doing the same thing over and over again, we want something more, something beyond that which we are doing. Since our everyday life is so empty, so dull, so meaningless, so boring, so intolerably stupid, we say life must have a fuller meaning and that is why you ask this question. Surely a man who is living richly, a man who sees things as they are and is content with what he has, is not confused; he is clear, therefore he does not ask what is the purpose of life. For him the very living is the beginning and the end. Our difficulty is that, since our life is empty, we want to find a purpose to life and strive for it. Such a purpose of life can only be mere intellection, without any reality; when the purpose of life is pursued by a stupid, dull mind, by an empty heart, that purpose will also be empty. Therefore our purpose is how to make our life rich, not with money and all the rest of it but inwardly rich—which is not something cryptic. When you say that the purpose of life is to be happy, the purpose of life is to find God, surely that desire to find God is an escape from life and your God is merely a thing that is known. You can only make your way towards an object which you know; if you build a staircase to the thing that you call God, surely that is not God. Reality can be understood only in living, not in escape. When you seek a purpose of life, you are really escaping and not understanding what life is. Life is relationship, life is action in relationship; when I do not understand relationship, or when relationship is confused, then I seek a fuller meaning. Why are our lives so empty? Why are we so lonely, frustrated? Because we have never looked into ourselves and understood ourselves. We never admit to ourselves that this life is all we know and that it should therefore be understood fully and completely. We prefer to run away from ourselves and that is why we seek the purpose of life away from relationship. If we begin to understand action, which is our relationship with people, with property, with beliefs and ideas, then we will find that relationship itself brings its own reward. You do not have to seek. It is like seeking love. Can you find love by seeking it? Love cannot be cultivated. You will find love only in relationship, not outside relationship, and it is because we have no love that we want a purpose of life. When there is love, which is its own eternity, then there is no search for God, because love is God.

It is because our minds are full of technicalities and superstitious mutterings that our lives are so empty and that is why we seek a purpose beyond ourselves. To find life's purpose we must go through the door of ourselves; consciously or unconsciously we avoid facing things as they are in themselves and so we want God to open for us a door which is beyond. This question about the purpose of life is put only by those who do not love. Love can be found only in action, which is relationship.

37. ON THE CONFUSION OF THE MIND

Question: I have listened to all your talks and I have read all your books. Most earnestly I ask you, what can be the purpose of my life if, as you say, all thought has to cease, all knowledge to be suppressed, all memory lost? How do you relate that state of being, whatever it may be according to you, to the world in which we live? What relation has such a being to our sad and painful existence?

Krishnamurti: We want to know what this state is which can only be when all knowledge, when the recognizer, is not; we want to know what relationship this state has to our world of daily activity, daily pursuits. We know what our life is now—sad, painful, constantly fearful, nothing permanent; we know that very well. We want to know what relationship this other state has to that—and if we put aside knowledge, become free from our memories and so on, what is the purpose of existence.

What is the purpose of existence as we know it now?— not theoretically but actually? What is the purpose of our everyday existence? Just to survive, isn't it?—with all its misery, with all its sorrow and confusion, wars, destruction and so on. We can invent theories, we can say: "This should not be, but something else should be." But those are all theories, they are not facts. What we know is confusion, pain, suffering, endless antagonisms. We know also, if we are at all aware, how these come about. The purpose of life, from moment to moment, every day, is to destroy each other, to exploit each other, either as individuals or as collective human beings. In our loneliness, in our misery, we try to use others, we try to escape from ourselves—through amusements, through gods, through knowledge, through every form of belief, through identification. That is our purpose, conscious or unconscious, as we now live. Is there a deeper, wider purpose beyond, a purpose that is not of confusion, of acquisition? Has that effortless state any relation to our daily life?

Certainly that has no relation at all to our life. How can it have? If my mind is confused, agonized, lonely, how can that be related to something which is not of itself? How can truth be related to falsehood, to illusion? We do not want to admit that, because our hope, our confusion, makes us believe in something greater, nobler, which we say is related to us. In our despair we seek truth, hoping that in the discovery of it our despair will disappear.

So we can see that a confused mind, a mind ridden with sorrow, a mind that is aware of its own emptiness, loneliness, can never find that which is beyond itself. That which is beyond the mind can only come into being when the causes of confusion, misery, are dispelled or understood. All that I have been saying, talking about, is how to understand ourselves, for without self-knowledge the other is not, the other is only an illusion. If we can understand the total process of ourselves, from moment to moment, then we shall see that in clearing up our own confusion, the other comes into being. Then experiencing that will have a relation to this. But this will never have a relation to that. Being this side of the curtain, being in darkness, how can one have experience of light, of freedom? But when once there is the experience of truth, then you can relate it to this world in which we live.

If we have never known what love is, but only constant wrangles, misery, conflicts, how can we experience that love which is not of all this? But when once we have experienced that, then we do not have to bother to find out the relationship. Then love, intelligence, functions. But to experience that state, all knowledge, accumulated memories, self-identified activities, must cease, so that the mind is incapable of any projected sensations. Then, experiencing that, there is action in this world.

Surely that is the purpose of existence—to go beyond the self-centred activity of the mind. Having experienced that state, which is not measurable by the mind, then the very experiencing of that brings about an inward revolution. Then, if there is love, there is no social problem. There is no problem of any kind when there is love. Because we do not know how to love we have social problems and systems of philosophy on how to deal with our problems. I say these problems can never be solved by any system, either of the left or of the right or of the middle. They can be solved— our confusion, our misery, our self-destruction—only when we can experience that state which is not self-projected.

38. ON TRANSFORMATION

Question: What do you mean by transformation?

Krishnamurti: Obviously, there must be a radical revolution. The world crisis demands it. Our lives demand it. Our everyday incidents, pursuits, anxieties, demand it. Our problems demand it. There must be a fundamental, radical revolution, because everything about us has collapsed. Though seemingly there is order, in fact there is slow decay, destruction: the wave of destruction is constantly overtaking the wave of life.

So there must be a revolution—but not a revolution based on an idea. Such a revolution is merely the continuation of the idea, not a radical transformation. A revolution based on an idea brings bloodshed, disruption, chaos. Out of chaos you cannot create order; you cannot deliberately bring about chaos and hope to create order out of that chaos. You are not the God-chosen who are to create order out of confusion That is such a false way of thinking on the part of those people who wish to create more and more confusion in order to bring about order. Because for the moment they have power, they assume they know all the ways of producing order. Seeing the whole of this catastrophe—the constant repetition of wars, the ceaseless conflict between classes, between peoples, the awful economic and social inequality, the inequality of capacity and gifts, the gulf between those who are extraordinarily happy, unruffled, and those who are caught in hate, conflict, and misery—seeing all this, there must be a revolution, there must be complete transformation, must there not?

Is this transformation, is this radical revolution, an

ultimate thing or is it from moment to moment? I know we should *like* it to be the ultimate thing, because it is so much easier to think in terms of far away. Ultimately we shall be transformed, ultimately we shall be happy, ultimately we shall find truth; in the meantime, let us carry on. Surely such a mind, thinking in terms of the future, is incapable of acting in the present; therefore such a mind is not seeking transformation, it is merely avoiding transformation. What do we mean by transformation?

Transformation is not in the future, can never be in the future. It can only be *now*, from moment to moment. So what do we mean by transformation? Surely it is very simple: seeing the false as the false and the true as the true. Seeing the truth in the false and seeing the false in that which has been accepted as the truth. Seeing the false as the false and the true as the true is transformation, because when you see something very clearly as the truth, that truth liberates. When you see that something is false, that false thing drops away. When you see that ceremonies are mere vain repetitions, when you see the truth of it and do not justify it, there is transformation, is there not?, because another bondage is gone. When you see that class distinction is false, that it creates conflict, creates misery, division between people— when you see the truth of it, that very truth liberates. The very perception of that truth is transformation, is it not? As we are surrounded by so much that is false, perceiving the falseness from moment to moment is transformation. Truth is not cumulative. It is from moment to moment. That which is cumulative, accumulated, is memory, and through memory you can never find truth, for memory is of time— time being the past, the present and the future. Time, which is continuity, can never find that which is eternal; eternity is not continuity. That which endures is not eternal. Eternity is in the moment. Eternity is in the now. The now is not the reflection of the past nor the continuance of the past through the present to the future.

A mind which is desirous of a future transformation or

looks to transformation as an ultimate end, can never find truth, for truth is a thing that must come from moment to moment, must be discovered anew; there can be no discovery through accumulation. How can you discover the new if you have the burden of the old? It is only with the cessation of that burden that you discover the new. To discover the new, the eternal, in the present, from moment to moment, one needs an extraordinarily alert mind, a mind that is not seeking a result, a mind that is not becoming. A mind that is becoming can never know the full bliss of contentment; not the contentment of smug satisfaction; not the contentment of an achieved result, but the contentment that comes when the mind sees the truth in what *is* and the false in what *is*. The perception of that truth is from moment to moment; and that perception is delayed through verbalization of the moment.

Transformation is not an end, a result. Transformation is not a result. Result implies residue, a cause and an effect. Where there is causation, there is bound to be effect. The effect is merely the result of your desire to be transformed. When you desire to be transformed, you are still thinking in terms of becoming; that which is becoming can never know that which is being. Truth is *being* from moment to moment and happiness that continues is not happiness. Happiness is that state of being which is timeless. That timeless state can come only when there is a tremendous discontent— not the discontent that has found a channel through which it escapes but the discontent that has no outlet, that has no escape, that is no longer seeking fulfilment. Only then, in that state of supreme discontent, can reality come into being. That reality is not to be bought, to be sold, to be repeated; it cannot be caught in books. It has to be found from moment to moment, in the smile, in the tear, under the dead leaf, in the vagrant thoughts, in the fullness of love.

Love is not different from truth. Love is that state in which the thought process, as time, has completely ceased.

287

Where love is, there is transformation. Without love, revolution has no meaning, for then revolution is merely destruction, decay, a greater and greater ever-mounting misery. Where there is love, there is revolution, because love is transformation from moment to moment.